PRAISE FOR MANAGING GLOBAL ACCOUNTS

"Managing global customers is becoming a critical issue for corporations around the world. Customers are dramatically evolving their procurement practices and an effective global account management approach will be an increasingly important competitive advantage for the customer-focused firm. Capon and his coauthors lay out a roadmap for a superior global account management. This book is a must-read if you want to be world class in global account management."

> Jean-Claude Larréché,
> The Alfred H. Heineken Chaired Professor of Marketing,
> INSEAD, Fontainebleau, France

"Successful global account management can be the most difficult sales and marketing initiative undertaken by any firm. The authors of this book truly understand the complexities involved and they provide a thorough overview of the required critical success factors."

> Tom VanHootegem,
> Vice President, Strategic Segment Sales, OfficeMax Contract

"Managing world-spanning accounts is central to every global firm's success. Yet the task forces organizations into new molds, making it a daunting effort. This important book embraces every facet of the undertaking, weaving them all into one coherent framework—a rare accomplishment for any business text. That, plus its conversational style will make *Managing Global Accounts* an important and readily usable tool for years to come."

> Jordan D. Lewis,
> Author,
> *Trusted Partners: How Companies Build Mutual Trust and Win Together*

"If you are looking to start or revitalize your global account program, this book is a must-read. Generally there is a lack of understanding in the senior ranks of large organizations when starting a global account program that often leads to costly false starts and client upset. This book takes away the mystery and sets forth valid concepts and steps that will make these programs viable. It provides an experienced path to follow that will support any company developing their global account program. You will discover ideas and thoughts that usually come to a sales executive well into the development of such a program. The authors approach the subject from experience and leave the theory to others. These authors deserve a standing ovation from sales leaders charged with developing global account programs."

> James J. Brown,
> Executive Director,
> Russ Berrie Institute for Professional Sales, Christos Cotsakis
> College of Business,
> William Paterson University of New Jersey

"The authors have done an excellent job of integrating the technical and social aspects of the global account management process. In a very accessible book they look at the essential aspects that a global account manager needs to master."

> Fons Tropenaars,
> THT Consulting, Amsterdam

"As a VP managing global account managers in a global Fortune 300 company, I learned more from reading this book's first few chapters than I have in my last five business books. The authors have done a great job pulling together all the logistics from starting, hiring, training, supporting, and sustaining a successful program. If anyone ever wanted a book on how to correctly build a global account program using best practices, this is it!

"Three cheers to Capon, Schindler, and Potter for a great narrative of technical training and business savvy all in one tight package. I am confident that the careful reading, comprehension, and implementation of this book's tenets will save many firms tens of thousands of dollars in consultant fees. This is the real McCoy!"

> Chris Morrison,
> Divisional Vice President, Nalco Global Accounts

"This well-organized book is a very useful source of practical ideas for companies that want to unlock the full value of global supplier–customer collaboration. It belongs in any manager's bookshelf who wants to get their future approach towards global account management right."

> Christoph Senn,
> Sr Lecturer, University of St Gallen (HSG), Switzerland

"*Managing Global Accounts* addresses this important sales management topic thoroughly and insightfully. There is exceptional treatment of many issues that global account executives wrestle with . . . from understanding the forces that drive the need for effective global coverage, to aligning programs and power structures that enable global account program success. It is great reading for those interested in assessing their on-going global account coverage efforts. It is equally compelling for those who are in the process of building a global account organization."

> Gary S. Tubridy,
> Sr Vice President, The Alexander Group, Inc.

"Finally a book which can help corporations transform the art of selling into the science of growth. Companies now have the chance to impact their customer assets in the same way they have optimized their supply chains. It is all here and the winners will know how to use it."

> David Macaulay,
> Sr Vice President, Siemens AG

"Nearly every company today is forced to confront the challenge of supporting customer requirements in a global business environment. However, the task of leveraging the firm's position and information capital around the world as one unit is enormous, even for a sophisticated multinational company. Strategic Account Management Association (SAMA) knows that organizational commitment—management support as well as resource—is mandatory for success. Unfortunately, too many firms fail to make a strong business case for change, or worse yet, get buy-in for the wrong set of expectations. If only *Managing Global Accounts* had come along sooner! This book offers firms what they have been clamoring for—a framework for asking the right questions, performing the right analytics, and making the translation to an action plan that fits their unique circumstances. Firms that have already implemented global account management can effectively reassess and recalibrate based on the authors' practical, real-world experience. And for those whose firms have yet to fully embrace the concepts, *Managing Global Accounts* will become your guide and ally in convincing your most important stakeholders that Global Customer Management—and all that requires—is not an option for firms that intend to be competitive."

> Lisa Napolitano, CEO,
> Strategic Account Management Association (SAMA)

Also by Noel Capon

Corporate Strategic Planning
With John U. Farley and James M. Hulbert

The Marketing of Financial Services: A Book of Cases

*Planning the Development of Builders, Leaders, and Managers for
21st Century Business*

Why Some Firms Perform Better than Others: Toward a More Integrative Explanation
With John U. Farley and Scott Hoenig

The Asian Marketing Case Book
With Wilfried Van Honacker

Marketing Management in the 21st Century
With James M. Hulbert

Marketing Management in the 21st Century (Chinese)
With James M. Hulbert and Willem Burgers

Key Account Management and Planning

Total Integrated Marketing
With James M. Hulbert and Nigel Piercy

The Marketing Mavens

Managing Marketing in the 21st Century
With James M. Hulbert
www.mm21c.com

The Virgin Marketer
www.mm21c.com

Managing Global Accounts

Managing Global Accounts

Nine Critical Factors for a World-Class Program

Noel Capon, Dave Potter, Fred Schindler

BRONXVILLE, NEW YORK
www.keyaccountmanagement.com

www.wessex21c.com
www.keyaccountmanagement.com

Managing Global Accounts: Nine Critical Factors for a World-Class Program
Noel Capon, Dave Potter, Fred Schindler

2nd Edition

First edition published in 2006 by Texere, an imprint
of Cengage Learning.

Composed by: Integra Software Services Pvt. Ltd

Printed in the United States of America by
RRD-Crawfordsville
1 2 3 4 5 08 07 06 05

This book is printed on
acid-free paper.

ISBN 978-0-97973-443-4

Library of Congress Cataloging in Publication Number is available. See page 259 for details.

CONTENTS

DEDICATION

To those dedicated individuals who are propelling their organizations into the 21st century by building global customer relationships.

Noel Capon

To our colleagues from The Global Forum, and the many great GAMs with whom we have worked.

Dave Potter and Fred Schindler

ACKNOWLEDGEMENTS

Noel Capon acknowledges the contributions of members of The Columbia Initiative in Global Account Management for their role in educating him in the complexities of the topic—Tim Hammond and Michael Graff (3M), David Bowerin, Gary Greenwald and Arnold Ziegel (Citibank), Peter Kirk (Milliken & Co.), Dick Potter (Deloitte & Touche), Mike Cohn and Alan Nonnenberg (Hewlett-Packard), Luc Grapotte (Inergy Automotive), Michael Rec, Bill Radwill and David Heckman (Lucent Technologies), Richard McGregor (Maersk Sealand), Tim Love and John McNeel (Saatchi & Saatchi), Brigitte Walkenbach (SAP), and Geoff Williams (Square D/Schneider Electric).

Dave Potter and Fred Schindler wish to acknowledge the cooperation and insight of their colleagues at Xerox and IBM respectively. Over the years, many individuals have significantly added to their global account management knowledge bases. They also wish to acknowledge members of The Global Forum: Eric Drewery (ABB), Charley Elias (ING), Dave Oulighan (Dun & Bradstreet), Tom Muccio and Steve Goodroe (Procter & Gamble), Tom Ryan (Xerox), and Alex Hungate and Doug Mehne (Reuters America) for the experiences and ideas they have shared. Dave Oulighan is a founding member whose initial interest in benchmarking gave birth to the Forum.

All three authors thank Beth Seidler Rehman for her many contributions as research assistant and enforcer in keeping them on track with their writing schedule, and Olga Dorokhina who helped with last-minute additions.

Who Should Read This Book?

The challenge of developing an approach to dealing with the increased global complexity of customer relationships is the subject of this book. If your company has determined it must shift to a focus that embraces globalization, we believe you will gain important insights. We include not only B2B companies but also B2C companies that deal with downstream manufacturing and distribution organizations. Further, we embrace executives around the world. Although we, the authors, are based in the U.S., we accept that the U.S. has no monopoly on globalization. Neither do large companies, and we write also for the increasing numbers of medium and relatively small companies competing in today's global marketplace.

If you are not completely satisfied with your global account program, you should read this book. If your company has decided it must shift from a domestic (or multinational) focus to a global perspective, you should read this book. The book is as relevant for Swedish, Swiss, Chinese and Brazilian executives as for those based in the U.S. You may work for a large corporation, but our approach is just as relevant for small- and medium-sized companies.

Global account personnel—global account managers, managers of global programs and international marketing personnel—will resonate with the issues we address and benefit most directly from this book. Hopefully, this book will equip all of you to confront global challenges more effectively. It will also give you ammunition to challenge your global account management system and improve its overall functioning. Further, other executives whose responsibilities concern global business will benefit from the concepts and ideas we present.

Finally, corporate procurement executives will find value. After all, an effective global account management system should benefit both suppliers and their global customers. Global customers will learn the art of the possible, and how their suppliers could behave. They will learn how to prod global suppliers to push the envelope for the benefit of suppliers and customers alike.

Finally, CEOs and COOs must understand the message we are delivering. Only with top executive understanding and support can corporations accomplish the changes that must occur. As we see later, successful global account management must be fully supported from the top. Get a copy of this book in the hands of your senior executives!

Who Should Read this Book?

Managers of global programs
Marketing personnel with international responsibilities
Global account managers
Corporate procurement executives
CEOs and COOs

Does any serious CEO today really believe that their firm can survive and prosper in the 21st century without addressing the many challenges of globalization? Despite some minor setbacks, globalization forces are trumping localism. We believe these forces are inexorable and that the firm must come to grips with globalization challenges by developing appropriate strategies, organization structures, and business practices to take these forces into account.

Of course, since early in the last century, leading firms have operated outside their home countries and many have been very successful. But the approaches on which they built these successes simply will not work in the 21st century. The game has changed, and changed dramatically. Just being an international or multinational company will not bring success. The future is global.

The future winners will be truly global firms. Yet these firms face many and varied globalization challenges. These include, for example, building new plants abroad, entering new national markets, import/export issues, local, regional and global branding, governmental regulations, failure of some economies, and the risks of "going global."

These are all important challenges, but globalizing firms often overlook perhaps the most critical challenge of all—the globalization of customers. As organizations now "go global," they make major changes in their procurement practices. Rather than purchase the products and services they require to operate their factories and manage their organizations on a domestic basis, they increasingly make these decisions on a global basis. Winning suppliers will be those that are able to successfully develop and manage relationships with global customers.

Now, it is certainly true that, increasingly, senior executives in companies large and small are realizing that the future health of their organizations, indeed their very survival, depends on success with major customers. Indeed, during the past 20 years, strategic (or key) account management has become a critical area of focus for many corporations.

Unfortunately, these same senior executives have not given proper attention to developing and maintaining the people skills, completing the planning, exercising the discipline, and gaining the top management commitment necessary to implement a strategic account program. Many firms are guilty of maintaining misguided measurement and compensation systems, outdated management information systems, decentralized and parochial field organizations, making poor account selection and setting unclear objectives. In short, practice has lagged significantly behind managerial intentions.

Many firms face this state of affairs on a domestic basis. This unfortunate state of affairs is the situation for addressing domestic customers. The problem ratchets up in an order of magnitude when customers shift from making procurement decisions on a multi-domestic basis to making them on a global basis.

During the past several years, leading corporations, based in many countries, have attempted to leverage their strategic account programs into global account management. A few have succeeded, but more have failed in many aspects. Successful global account management is not simply strategic account management ratcheted up a notch. Just as doing business globally is qualitatively different from operating in a national context, successful global account management is qualitatively different from managing strategic accounts within a single nation state. Planning and field implementation must be much more rigorous, and top management commitment even more substantial.

This book will help you with the difficult challenge of developing and managing relationships with your global customers. Your competitors are already working to improve their global account management practices. We have consulted with some of them—they are taking global account management very seriously. Many have joined such associations as the Strategic Account Management Association (SAMA) where they learn global relationship-building techniques. Others are attending courses at Columbia Business School, the Carlson School (University of Minnesota), William Paterson (New Jersey), the University of St Gallen (Switzerland) and other institutions that address global account management. They are eagerly embracing the concepts we discuss here. Unless you heed the messages we present and strive to enhance your own capabilities, the competitive result is an unfortunate foregone conclusion!

In this book, the authors lay out a framework for building a successful program for managing global accounts. They highlight the critical success factors necessary for a global account program to satisfy the needs of both global accounts and global suppliers. In addition, each chapter that focuses on a critical success factor, and concludes with some diagnostic questions designed to help you assess your own global account program. A fuller set of questions is accessible on a Web site that will also show how you stack up against other companies.

This book represents a unique partnership of academe and business practice. Noel Capon is the R.C. Kopf Professor of International Marketing and past Chair of the Marketing Division at the Graduate School of Business, Columbia University. He is also author of the highly acclaimed book *Key Account Management and Planning* (The Free Press, 2001), and director of senior-executive Strategic Account Management Programs at Columbia Business School and the Global Account Manager Certification Program (GCP) offered jointly by Columbia and St. Gallen University, Switzerland.

Dave Potter had a 34-year career at Xerox, a company known for significant managerial innovation. After holding a variety of domestic sales management and quality officer positions, he filled numerous Asian posts, including: Director of Marketing, China South Pacific; General Manager, Southeast Asia; and Vice President of Marketing, Fuji Xerox Asia Pacific. From 1995 to 2002, he was Director of Marketing Global Account Management.

Fred Schindler had a similar 33-year career with IBM during which he consulted with IBM account teams and customers to improve global account management. For 7 years, Fred was Program Executive for IBM's Global Customer Management program, encompassing its top 150 global clients. He consulted with multinational client teams and with team leaders of various IBM infrastructure groups—the international special bids group, relationship management process owners, services support groups, and brand divisions.

Schindler and Potter are founding partners of *The Global Guys, LLC* (www.theglobalguys.com), a consulting practice dedicated to improving the performance of global account management programs. Each author has pushed forward the field of global account management. Schindler and Potter are driving forces in *The Global Forum*, an organization that meets several times annually to benchmark and discuss critical issues in global account management. In addition to IBM and Xerox, current and past members include ABB, ING, Cable & Wireless, Dun & Bradstreet, Reuters America, Procter & Gamble, Nokia, Young & Rubicam, and DHL. Noel Capon hosts The Columbia Initiative in Global Account Management, a similar group based at Columbia Business School; members include 3M, Citibank, Deloitte & Touche, Inergy Automotive, Hewlett-Packard, Lucent Technologies, Maersk Sealand, Milliken & Co., Saatchi & Saatchi, SAP and Square D/Schneider Electric. Schindler and Potter served as board members of the SAMA. All three authors are regular presenters at its annual conference.

Managing Global Accounts in the Real World

In the set of prologues in this book we follow four characters, based on real-life encounters. Each character comes to global account management from a different perspective. Each character's organizational position has been strongly influenced by recognizing that increasing globalization has led to the emergence of a new type of customer— global accounts that make procurement decisions on a global versus domestic or multi-domestic basis. Each character accepts that global account management is the way for firms to address these accounts, but each has to deal with a different set of issues.

PROLOGUE

Back Bay, Boston

Todd rushed to the apartment door, paused and looked around in a vain effort to see what he might have forgotten. Things always seemed to be rushed since **Todd** became a global account manager. As he flopped into the airport limousine he contemplated what faced him: four connecting flights to Japan and crappy coach class all the way. Cut-backs, huh! The company acts like they're doing me a favor just by letting me travel internationally, but then all of our global account managers are in the same rocky boat! No matter, this trip I will get the Japanese customers even more on board. Then, just maybe, my management will get the bean counters to stop giving me such a hard time. Sometimes I think management just doesn't get it. I wonder why we seem to be cutting back on the global account program when we're losing business to other firms.

Prudential Center, Boston

The intercom buzzed—"**Constance**, your car is waiting; whenever you're ready." Her assistant's voice on the intercom always caught her off guard. Since becoming CEO, **Constance** had so many things on her mind. She scanned her email for anything that couldn't wait until after the Board meeting, gathered her travel gear, and headed for the office door. Being tied up in meetings for the next couple of days doesn't give me time to think about strategic issues. But Jack Simpson has been trying to get me to focus on our global account program. Better alert my assistant.

"If Jack Simpson calls, it's about our global account program, but it will have to wait until I get back." In the elevator, **Constance** remembered the phone call she received from a global customer. The message was all too clear. *"You're not a global company; you just do business internationally— but not very well or consistently. And your global account manager—he's a nice guy and understands our business but has no authority to make things happen outside the U.S. I just can't view him as a 'trusted advisor.' "* As she stepped into the limousine and headed for Logan, **Constance** shook her head. *Nowadays everything seems to be global; running a company is so much more complex than it used to be! I really need Jack to bring me up to speed on our global account program.*

American Airlines Check-in, Logan Airport

Jace took a small step forward; the check-in line was finally beginning to move. Normally, she wouldn't be checking luggage for such a short flight but her final consultant reports were too cumbersome for a carry-on bag. She could have sent them ahead but she wanted the satisfaction of putting her report in the CEO's hands. Her clients always liked that and she got a sense of satisfaction from delivering her recommendations in person. She mused, *My job is all about observation. It sounds so simple before you have to write the report. They're having so much trouble building the internal values for global account. They can decide what they want at the top, but you've got to get everyone on the same page or it just won't work.*

American Airlines Departure Lounge, Logan Airport, Boston

*"**George**, just listen to me."* Bill, one of his more outspoken global account managers, seemed more upset than usual. *"I'm spending a quarter of my time reconciling revenue with my team's compensation. Country management is not giving me the support I need to win deals. The company hired me to win and we both know I'm damn good at winning! Come this November, if things don't change, I'm going to have to think about moving on."*

George held the cell phone close to his ear. *If Bill screamed any louder his fellow travelers would be sure to hear him.* Since **George** had been promoted to global account director it seemed there'd been nothing but pain and irritation. *Bill doesn't mean it, he thought. He won't leave. I know things are a mess. Still, the thought of losing his best global account manager was scary. Good global account manager material was hard to find.* *"Bill, when I get back, let's talk . . . You know I back you all the way. I'll talk* *to the country managers and area heads and get this straightened out. Trust me. Going global is very important to top management. They really do want it to work effectively. Listen, I gotta go, they're calling my flight."*

Soul Mates!

George and *Todd*

*As he leaned forward, **George** noticed the wry smile from the man in the next seat. He recognized the smile—the "eavesdropping" smile. Although they hadn't met, something was oddly familiar about this man. "Sure it was just a white lie," **George** said to the eavesdropping stranger, "But I had to get him off the phone so I could have some time to think. He really was uptight and I can't afford to lose him."*

*Todd recognized the conversation. "I know where he's coming from. I had a similar conversation last week. You and I have a lot in common— **Todd Jenkins**." George looked puzzled. "**George Marshall**—good to meet you. You're a global account program director?" **George** asked; perhaps he had found a soul mate. "No, I am a global account manager." So that's why he looked familiar, the knowing look of a global citizen.*

*"I was a global account manager up until a few months ago. Then the executive team asked me to manage our global account program. Where are you off to **Todd**?" "Japan," **Todd** said almost braggingly, "but I have to take four connections." Four connections! **George** thought that was unusual. "They have direct flights from here. I know, I've taken them myself," **George** offered. **George** should have guessed **Todd**'s response. "Well, the squeeze is on us these days. I'm used to flying coach but a 32-hour trip in coach is a lot, even for me."*

***George** saw an opportunity to hear views on managing global accounts from someone outside his company. "What seat are you in **Todd**? Maybe we could chat on the flight. I would be interested in your views."*

Constance, George and *Todd*

*As **Constance** stood nearby, she couldn't believe the conversation she'd just heard. This global account stuff seemed more prevalent than she had thought. Maybe she better call Jack when the plane landed and get him on her calendar.*

Listening to these guys triggered some of the doubts she had on the value of a global account program. There were so many competing claims on her time and valuable firm resources. **Constance** sometimes wondered if it was smart to set up the global program in the first place. *Yeah, better call Jack. But, maybe I can get some insight from these guys?*

Jace, Constance, George and Todd

The woman seated next to **George** seemed to be taking in all the conversation. **George** turned toward her and commented, "And are you getting all this?"

She responded coolly, "Well, I was listening, not sure if I really 'get it' either, but I am working on some answers related to managing global accounts." **Todd** laughed, "Are you a global account manager or global account director?"

"None of the above," **Jace** replied, "**Jace Cleardon**, I'm a consultant. I help design and fix companies' global account programs. Right now I'm headed to a client whose program really needs help—I think I've a few suggestions."

Constance had remained silent up until now. She had to challenge this consultant. "And you have the magic five-minute answer?" said **Constance** sarcastically. "I'm very wary of consultants. It seems to me that global account management may mean different things to different companies." **Jace**'s reply was expected. "I couldn't offer firm recommendations without looking at your company. But, at the least, I believe there are some general principles to follow."

Constance was impressed at the straightforward response. This could be another source from which to gain some insights. **Constance** introduced herself to the group. She pulled out business cards and offered one to **Jace**. "My name is **Constance Bennett**. I'm CEO of Bennett Industries International. Where are you seated? Maybe we could chat some more." Then there came an announcement.

> We regret that American Airlines flight 147 to New York's La Guardia Airport has been delayed due to mechanical problems. We are hopeful that this will not take too long to fix. Please do not leave the terminal and listen for updated information.

"Hey, let's go get a drink," said **Todd**, cheerily smiling at **George**, "My global account director is paying." With that invitation, the four new acquaintances headed for the bar. Each was thinking this could be an opportunity to gain greater insight into managing global accounts.

CHAPTER 1

GLOBALIZATION AND GLOBAL CUSTOMERS

Fundamentally, this book is about achieving corporate success and organizational survival in the 21st century. In particular, it focuses on developing and sustaining mutually beneficial relationships with your most important global customers. Not just the global customers you have today, but also those potential global customers that are right now developing their strategies for expanding into global markets.

That said, many firms now find they are deriving an increasing proportion of their revenues, and profits, from fewer and fewer customers. These fewer higher-value customers thus become increasingly critical to corporate health. Indeed, these customers are your "real" core assets, even though they do not figure explicitly on your balance sheet. Because they are more important than "average" customers, the firm must place increased emphasis and resources against them.

During the past 20 years, many firms have stepped up to the challenge of customer asset management by developing strategic (or key) account programs. These programs are an organizational response to increasing revenue and profit concentration. Many firms have secured great success in focusing their efforts on major customers (actual and potential) and developing the appropriate strategies, line organizations, systems and processes, and human resources to serve them. Typically, these efforts have been conducted within domestic country organizations. Strategic/key account management achieved great success so long as customers made their procurement decisions on a domestic basis.

But suppose these critical customers evolve their procurement decision-making into a different model. For example, the customer wants to place a single global order for the firm's products, to purchase similarly designed products, and to negotiate a single price, or at least a set of prices with high transparency and comparability. These products will be delivered to the customer's various sites in many countries around the world, and the customer desires equivalent service regardless of whether the delivery point is in an advanced Western country or less-developed country (LDC).

In this scenario, the domestic strategic account management model simply does not work. The supplier has no framework, strategy, organization or processes with which to negotiate an arrangement with this global customer. Who would conduct the negotiations? What process would the supplier use to assure equivalent service levels around the world? Who would negotiate-price? Indeed, does anyone have the authority to set a single global price? To put it bluntly, the multi-domestic (or multinational) supplier cannot satisfy this customer's need for conducting business globally, even though the supplier itself may operate in many countries around the world. The supplier will lose this business to a competitor that has invested in addressing its customer on a global basis.

Consider the following illustration from Xerox. A "Print-for-Pay" customer wanted to expand internationally in an aggressive manner. The customer was very happy with the domestic U.S. Xerox relationship but was "having trouble" with Xerox's foreign operating companies. The customer wanted to leverage its global buying to secure better product prices in various countries. The "trouble" included being told by the managing director in Xerox, South Africa that there was no reason why it should get better pricing than the largest domestic customers (even though global billings were significantly greater). In addition, Xerox prices for servicing customers in Japan were three to four times higher than in the U.S.

Or consider the experience of a European firm with annual revenues of about €150 million. Top management decided to introduce a new management process focused on those accounts that were shifting from multi-domestic-focused procurement to global procurement. The response from middle management was very clear: "We have 10-year contracts and excellent, long-term relationships with all of our major customers. There is absolutely no need for a costly program to address these global accounts. Our business is different and we know all about it." Seven months after top management's directive (not implemented), the firm's leading customer switched to a competitive supplier. Overnight, the firm faced a 26 percent loss of business in its core division and a 12 percent overall corporate revenue loss. The CEO was quite unhappy when he met with financial analysts and business journalists.[1]

The focus of this book is on developing and managing global customers. In the following chapters, we present a framework for developing a global account program in the form of nine critical success factors.

---

[1] Personal communication from Professor Christoph Senn, University of St Gallen, St Gallen, Switzerland.

To be successful in global account management, and deliver value both to your customers and to the firm, you must address each of these critical areas. We do not pretend that this will be easy. Senior management will have to be involved in matters that historically it has left to others. You will probably have to reformulate your line organization and accept all of the personnel dislocations that accompany such changes. Without question, your domestic or multinational systems and processes will not be adequate—you will need to make considerable investments in new systems and processes designed to serve global customers. And where will you secure your global account managers, the focal point of all global customer activities?—the complexity of the global account manager job is so enormous that the human resource implications are quite staggering.

If you decide to seriously address your global customers, and we believe that a failure to do so may ring the death knell of your firm, much will have to change. But we believe that in the pages that follow, you will find the constituent elements that will allow you to construct your own road map to address what we believe is one of the critical managerial challenges of the 21st century. Quite simply, global customers are here to stay; to survive and grow, you must "get with the program!"

As we enter the 21st century, business organizations in all nations face many forces for change. Perhaps none is greater than globalization—"the inexorable integration of markets, nation-states and technologies to a degree never witnessed before in a way that is enabling individuals, corporations and nation-states to reach around the world farther, faster, deeper and cheaper than ever before."[2] Notwithstanding the anti-globalization movement and the dangers of terrorism for global business, we expect the path of globalization to continue largely unchecked.[3]

So what does globalization mean for companies in the 21st century? Should we refocus completely and concentrate solely on international business? The answer, of course, is no! We do not suggest that meeting your client's "local" needs is dead. Rather, as Friedman points out, "The challenge in this era of globalization—for countries and individuals—is to

---

[2] Thomas L. Friedman, *The Lexus and the Olive Tree: Understanding Globalization*, New York: Anchor Books, 2000, p. 9. See, also, Friedman's follow-on book, *The World Is Flat: A Brief History of the Twenty-First Century*, New York: Farrah, Straus and Giroux, 2005.

[3] The more recent growth of the countervailing anti-globalization movement, most evidenced by demonstrations in Seattle, Genoa, and New York at the turn of the century, is of itself an affirmation of the strength of the globalization trend.

find a healthy balance between preserving a sense of identity, home and community and doing what it takes to survive within the globalization system."[4]

The bottom line is that the globe is getting smaller and companies must learn to operate in this new environment. Many firms that, in earlier times, would never have contemplated moving out of their home markets are now forced to do so. On the one hand, they face increased competitive pressure domestically; on the other hand, new opportunities beckon abroad. Of course, operating overseas is not a new experience for many large U.S., Japanese, and European companies. They have traded abroad and operated overseas subsidiaries for many years. But, even for these old international business hands, they cannot manage today's global customers by yesterday's models.

Customer strategies are now increasingly global in scope, and demands placed on their suppliers are ever more complex. Many customers seek supplies and suppliers worldwide and want to make global supply arrangements. As a result, managing global accounts is increasingly a requirement for suppliers. Customer pressures have risen to new levels and they demand ever-greater efficiency in field operations and work processes. Quite simply, the new environment of emerging global customers requires a very different approach from the past.

When corporations started to operate internationally, they developed organizational structures and processes to manage their increasingly far-flung organizations. Initially, many formed international divisions. When foreign operations increased in importance, geographic regions and global product divisions became very popular. Later, some of these morphed into complex matrix organizations. Depending on the circumstance, these structures were more or less viable for firms becoming increasingly multinational in scope. To a very large extent the *raison d'être* of these systems was to manage the firm's business in individual countries. In many cases, country management was the fundamental organizing unit and, regardless of the overarching structure, profit and loss (P&L) resided with the country manager. Indeed, in many firms, country managers are "kings," and geographic-area heads are powerful executives in the corporate pantheon.

Unfortunately, very few corporate organizations anticipated the transformation required to satisfy the needs of global customers. Rather, the

---

[4] Ibid., p. 42.

evolving organizational approaches just discussed were largely concerned with addressing *differences* in customer needs across various geographic markets. For example, Brazil is different than France. Generally speaking, these approaches were not concerned with potential *commonalities* in customer needs across markets.

An underlying reality of globalization is that *individual customers wish to be treated similarly no matter where in the world they operate.* A few years ago, most customer headquarters had little information on supplier relationships in remote operations. That state of affairs has changed dramatically along with vast improvements in information technology (IT) infrastructure. Customers now have increased visibility to their own activities. They also know more not only about your products and services, but also about competitive alternatives. And, they have a much better handle on the prices of all offers globally. For these and other reasons, they increasingly want to make procurement decisions on a global basis.

As noted above, in recent years many companies have implemented some form of account management—variously described as key account management, national account management, or strategic account management—to address the needs of important customers. All of these programs share one common denominator. They focus on building relationships and placing selling effort at the account's headquarters location. These programs have generally brought suppliers and customers closer together by addressing a host of strategic, structural, human resource, and process issues. And, most of these programs operate domestically, within a given nation-state.

Globalization requires a new approach to strategic customer management. Generally speaking, programs for global customers "grafted onto" existing organizations bear bitter fruit. Rather, practices for operating globally must be melded with the developing practice of key/strategic account management to develop a new synthesis. Firms must develop strategies, structures, processes, and human resources that are responsive to the challenges presented by major customers as they increasingly make their procurement decisions on a global basis. In the pages that follow, we develop the meaning and methodology for managing global accounts. And, we present a blueprint for addressing global accounts by identifying the critical success factors for developing and operating a successful global account program.

Some major changes occurring today that must be addressed by a global account program are captured in Table 1.1.

Table 1.1   The Changing View

Old Way	New Way
Supplier focuses on client's local needs	Customer requires focus on global needs
Supplier offers differentiated products around the world	Customer demands identical products and services worldwide
Supplier discriminates price by geography	Customer demands price transparency worldwide
Supplier focuses on sales revenues and profits in current year	Customer treated as an asset with a lifetime value
Supplier has strong sales capabilities in local markets	Customer requires strong headquarters relationship
Supplier accountability for client is fragmented by geography	Customer demands single point of accountability
Supplier focuses on individual products locally	Customer requires value with solutions globally
Supplier differentiates on product and price	Customer evaluates differentiation via global relationship and worldwide business experience with supplier
Supplier utilizes transaction pricing and bid response to gain business	Customer pursues long-term global contracts to lock in preferred partner status
Supplier focuses complete attention on its direct customer	The direct customer is well served when the supplier helps grow the customer's relationship with its customers

The New Challenges of Globalization[5]

The growth in globalization has critical implications for suppliers.

- Customers are more demanding and more sophisticated.
- There is a new look to competition.
- Global business is more complex and fast changing.
- Highly competent global account managers are in short supply.
- When it comes to global account management, not everyone "gets it."

---

[5] For other literature on global account management, see, Kevin Wilson and Nick Speare with Samuel J. Reese, *Successful Global Account Management*, London: Kogan Page, 2002 and H. David Hennessey and Jean-Pierre Jeannet, *Global Account Management*, Hoboken, NJ: Wiley, 2003. See, also, Julian Birkinshaw, Omar Toulan and David Arnold, "Global Account Management: Linking External Demands with Internal Abilities," in J. Birkinshaw and P. Hagstrom, eds, OUP, 2000; Julian Birkinshaw, Omar Toulan and David Arnold, "Global Account Management in Multinational Corporations: Theory and Evidence," *Journal of International Business Studies*, 32(2-2001), pp. 231–248 and Julian Birkinshaw, "Global Account Management: New Structures, New Tasks," *Financial Times Online*, © 2001.

Customers are more demanding and more sophisticated

Your customers, particularly your strategic customers, are your firm's most critical assets. The complexity and change wrought by globalization have a major impact on your interface with these customers. Global customers place demands on suppliers that are qualitatively different, and much greater, than demands placed on domestic suppliers. The global customer wants to be treated exactly the same in every place it operates. It wants to purchase identical products regardless of destination country—the global customer has little patience with local variations. And it wants the same price, or at least high transparency of price differences. And it wants those products serviced with the same high standards wherever it chooses. If the global customer decides to do business in Paraguay or Benin, it expects the same level of service that you provide in France or Japan. What? You don't have an operation in Paraguay? Well, you'd better figure it out!

This increased pressure comes from significant change in your global customers' procurement processes. These changes lead inexorably to greater scope and power for procurement executives. In particular, customers are refocusing on core competence and seeking flexibility by reducing operating leverage. They may reduce fixed costs by vertical disintegration such as General Motors' and Ford's spin-off of parts suppliers Delphi and Visteon respectively.[6] Alternatively, they may simply buy in parts or complete products—carrying their own brand names—that previously were produced in-house. Regardless, the proportion of total company costs controlled by procurement is increasing.

Two implications follow. First, customers implement centralized procurement to manage costs downward. For the global customer, this means global procurement and multi-year global contracts. Second, this is not a job for traditional purchasing agents operating in a backwater characterized by dull operating routines. With increased procurement dollars on the table, top management needs a new breed of procurement executive very different from the purchasing officers of old. Today's procurement executives are highly visible corporate superstars, charged with making critical strategic decisions having a major impact on their firms' bottom lines. None are more highly ranked in the corporate pantheon than *global* procurement executives. For global suppliers, the implication is very straightforward—the intellectual horsepower across the table has greatly increased.

---

[6] Unfortunately for General Motors and Ford, these spin-offs have been less successful than they anticipated.

Global procurement executives want to deal with a global supplier organization that has the clout to commit to global contracts, yet can also make things happen at the local level. Sometimes they want a deep supplier relationship. Other times they use the Internet to conduct reverse auctions and/or join buying organizations to increase their firm's purchasing power. They want timely, accurate and comprehensive management reports on such agreed metrics as customer satisfaction, billed revenue by category, product populations, repair response time, and uptime. They also want product-design input so your offerings are customized for their unique requirements. On a global scale these technical demands can make life very difficult for suppliers. Not only have the procurement executives' demands become progressively more complex and comprehensive, but their ability to monitor your performance has become more sophisticated. Using the Internet, they can now secure real-time information about procurement and supplier performance around the globe.

These pressures are heightened by a secular shift of global customers to reduce their numbers of suppliers. The old purchasing rules of asking many potential suppliers to respond to a request for proposal (RFP) then selecting the lowest bid (or bidders) have been replaced. Under the new mantra, procurement executives know that closer relationships with fewer suppliers offer greater benefits. In addition, prices (from scale economies) may also be lower, and they demand global price equivalence and transparency. Some global customers may even drive for sole-source agreements. As the global customer reduces its supplier base, the demands placed on those remaining increase, but so do the risks. The consequences of not making the cut can be devastating. As an illustration, in late 2000, prior to consolidating its public relations (PR) efforts, IBM reviewed relationships with 50 PR agencies worldwide. New York-based TSI Communications, an important incumbent agency, expected revenues to double. Rather, IBM chose British-based Text 100, an agency with offices in over 30 countries. TSI's revenues dropped by 65 percent and it laid off 70 percent of its employees.

Finally, figuring out how to deal with your customer is not enough. Increasingly, customers want your assistance in dealing with their customers, so that they can secure differential advantage over their competitors. For your global accounts, you must answer such questions as: Who are our customer's customers? What value proposition does our customer offer? How can we enhance this value proposition and help our customers deliver on it? Increasingly, your customers are looking for supplier partners to share the risks and rewards of competing in the evolving global environment.

There is a new look to competition

The competitive landscape is shifting. Depending upon your industry, competitors may range from new entrepreneurial start-ups to savvy global players. Global players present an especially significant threat. Many wish to increase global market share by gaining significant presence in major markets around the world. Where they have no presence, they may partner with local firms—the partner often remains in the background—giving customers the illusion of working with a single global supplier. Or, your competitor may be a channel intermediary—in high tech, it could be a systems integrator or consulting firm (for example, Electronic Data Systems [EDS] or Ernst & Young) that controls the project and places business with its favored supplier. Even traditional competitors join forces to facilitate large global deals. For example, to secure outsourcing contracts, IBM services non-IBM hardware and software. The client may operate primarily IBM equipment but use Hewlett-Packard (HP) in remote countries. IBM supports these products, and may procure new HP hardware when current hardware becomes obsolete.

Competitors may be based anywhere but they operate everywhere. As global customer demands increase across the board, suppliers are developing global account programs to better address their needs. But global customers are so complex and so demanding that a mere handful of global suppliers are doing this well. For most firms this is a new competitive dimension. Some suppliers will effectively manage demanding global customers—most will not, or will do so ineffectively. Firms that provide consistently positive customer experiences around the globe will be winners in the increasingly tough competitive conflict.

Global business is more complex and fast changing

What sort of a world are we operating in?—One full of change and complexity. For example, the economy shifts from the 1990s boom to the early 2000s bust and the 2003 rebound. Technological change is exponential and the Internet brings quantum leaps. Governments around the world embrace widely ranging perspectives—from a free-market focus and relaxed regulation on the one hand, to tighter control and regulation on the other. Privatization of state-owned enterprises is a continuing trend. Regional trading blocks such as the Association of Southeast Asian Nations (ASEAN), the European Union, Mersocur, the North American Free Trade Agreement (NAFTA), and supranational global entities like the

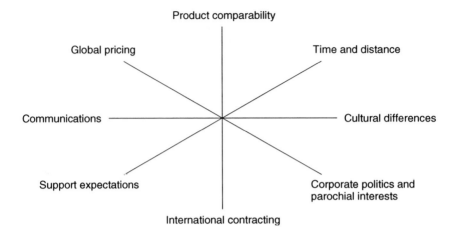

Figure 1.1   Customer-related Complexities

World Trade Organization bind nations closer together. And China is emerging as a major global economic power.

In other times, domestic firms dealt with their external environments in more or less satisfactory manner. Today the game is played on a different field with a different set of rules or, perhaps in some cases, no rules other than Darwinian principles. Operating domestically has never been more difficult but to compete in a global market is something else again—domestic challenges pale in comparison. Forces in the global environment impact both suppliers and their customers. Global suppliers face an environment whose scope of change and complexity is so vast it is difficult to know where to start. And their survival is based on a relatively small set of global customers facing their own similar challenges. We highlight just a few critical complexities, some relating directly to customers (Figure 1.1), others more concerned with internal functioning (Figure 1.2).

Customer-related complexities

Product comparability

Historically, many companies gave significant autonomy to geographic region and country heads. Customer firms offered products tailored for their domestic environments. Suppliers were happy to oblige with specially designed versions of their offerings. These offerings may have been localized versions of products developed centrally; or they may have been developed independently by individual geographic organizations.

Centralized global procurement organizations do not like multiple versions. In general they prefer standardization. Standardization can present suppliers with enormous problems. At a minimum, such requests cannot even be entertained unless the supplier has a centralized product database. For example, at Xerox, specifications of various versions of products produced in factories around the world are not centrally tracked. The situation is somewhat better at IBM's personal computer division (now Lenovo) where it frequently receives requests from global customers for a standardized *ThinkPad*. Some progress has been made in reducing models but, for example, a single byte design will not work with Japanese or Chinese alphabets. Meeting global customer requirements is a complex operation. For some global contracts, IBM configures total systems, installs software, and adds special features at a central location. The total tested system is "shrink wrapped" and shipped to destination countries ready to plug in.

In addition, global customers often demand concurrent global product availability. Historically, product-launch timetables were frequently sequential. Now customers demand that new products be available on a global basis simultaneously. During the 1980s, Xerox typically launched products in Europe 9 to 12 months after launching them in the U.S. However, Xerox Turkey launched a recently introduced color copier within 90 days of the U.S. launch.

Global pricing

Traditionally, suppliers used geographic segmentation to set prices around the world. For example, a U.S. supplier might price low in its domestic market, higher in Europe and Organization for Economic Cooperation and Development (OECD) countries, and even higher in the Third World. Pricing methodologies involved cost mark-ups for transportation, duties and tariffs, and exchange rates. More often, they were driven by opportunism regarding what prices were acceptable in different countries. Where product was scarce and competition weak, companies would tend to increase prices. Alternatively, some companies priced high domestically but lower in foreign markets—especially if they sought a toehold. (The large number of anti-dumping cases is testament to this practice.)

Pricing is far less simple when the customer procures globally. Global procurement executives want identical or, at least, highly similar prices around the world. And they can do the math. They understand transportation costs, exchange rates and import tariffs. They wonder why, accounting for these matters, prices for similar products delivered in different countries are not the same or, at least, very similar. In general, the global customer is uninterested in the cost or location of manufacture. Quite simply, it wants similar prices for similar products, no matter where manufactured and delivered. Setting global prices is a tricky proposition. And lowering prices for large global customers, but keeping them high for local clients, will quickly sink your ship. Finding the right formulae and making sound business trade-offs in pricing is a critical customer-related global complexity.

Time and distance

Suppose one morning your national account manager in Boston, New York, or Atlanta wants to communicate with a colleague or customer in San Diego, Los Angeles, or San Francisco. He only has to wait until lunchtime to make a phone call. Or, he can be face-to-face with the manager after a 4- or 5-hour plane trip. For local personnel and their domestic colleagues in most other countries the situation is even simpler.

It is a very different story for global account managers. Assuming an 8-hour working day, two-thirds of the world is out of sync. Further, for countries on the other side of the world, night and day are in complete opposition. And to travel from New York to Hong Kong (or pick your own two cities) may require a 24-hour trip with all the attendant problems of jet lag and sleep deprivation.

Quite simply, communication within a global company and with global customers is just much more difficult than it is domestically. Of course, the Internet, e-mail, chat rooms, and videoconferencing have eased communication difficulties, but they still remain a formidable challenge. Quality customer relationships still demand the personal touch that "high tech" solutions cannot provide. This is just much harder in the global environment.

Communications

In addition to time and distance challenges, the world does not speak a single language, even though English is becoming the language most widely used. The global supplier must make special efforts to aid communications within the firm and across the supplier/customer boundary. It may be difficult to find personnel with the required language skills. And when translators are required, it may be difficult to secure technical fluency. With even the best translators, the possibilities for miscommunication are legion for both verbal and written communications.[7]

---

[7] Consider, for example, the scene in the movie "Lost in Translation," when the Bill Murray character is taping a commercial.

Cultural differences

We all know that cultural differences can cause tension or problems in international business transactions. Although there are increasing numbers of "internationally savvy" business people, most individuals remain tied to their native cultures. Some critical cultural factors comprising business etiquette such as tone of speech and social behaviors are very culture-specific. And they can "make or break" a deal. For example, a U.S. technology firm was well placed to win a major contract from a Chinese firm. However, at a banquet given by the Chinese company, a senior U.S. manager started eating before the host, a cultural no-no. A French firm won the contract: its technology was inferior, but the Chinese felt more comfortable.

Support expectations

As your relationship with global customers grows, they realize the increasing importance of their business to your revenue base. They may demand your "best people" for every task. They do not want to be covered by agents, dealers, or concessionaires. They expect easy access to your senior management and they want high-quality global account managers who can solve problems and meet their needs quickly and effectively. In short, they expect to be treated commensurate with their status as one of your most important accounts.

International contracting

Global customers increasingly want global contracts. The logistics of creating a global contract are often complex. Your firm must develop a legal and business practices system so that offering a global contract is a matter of course. In the mid-1990s, IBM had a major contracting problem. Its aggressive service strategy coupled with customer-requested changes in how to contract left it unable to quickly deliver executable contracts. When customers requested a single global contract, it could take the legal and business practices team several months to secure sign-off from local countries. Requested terms might conflict with local country laws—warranty liabilities often differed across country. Typically, the lead country received amended contracts from individual countries. The reams of paper stapled together were unintelligible. Customers were dissatisfied and opportunities were lost.

IBM dealt with the problem by forming a worldwide legal and business organization. Staffed by legal specialists, the team developed a single global

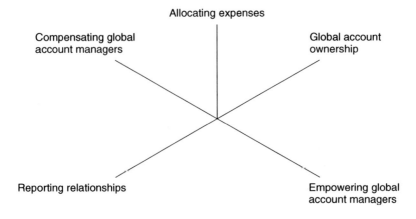

Figure 1.2   Supplier-related Complexities

contract. The language was simpler, and redundant language was reduced into a global set of terms and conditions. And the team responded quickly to specific country requests by adding the necessary terms and conditions in a country-by-country exceptions section.

Corporate politics and parochial interests

Despite the shift to global procurement, it may not be universally accepted within the global account. The global account manager may find himself or herself stuck in the middle of a power struggle between the customer's corporate procurement organization and local management. Headquarters expects him or her to "enforce" a global agreement. Local management resists, believing the global agreement is not in its interest. The relationship is strained locally, and headquarters management is disappointed. The global account manager cannot win. Even a simple headquarters request to "keep us informed" of global business activity may cause local management to view the global account manager as a "corporate spy."

Supplier-related complexities

Allocating expenses

In the multinational firm, revenues and expenses are typically accrued at the country level. Sales activity and customer management is typically focused by country, and country managers develop plans and budgets for their geographic jurisdictions. Typically, these plans and budgets are aggregated to a geographic region. Budgets for global activities present a problem for companies managing customers on a global basis. In a typical case, the global account manager has worldwide customer responsibility but is based in an individual country and reports to the country head.

Suppose that the global account manager needs to visit the global account in another country, perhaps in a different geographic region. Who should pay? The firm may secure increased business but the revenues accrue to a different county manager. For the host country manager, measured by revenue and profitability, this trip is quite negative. She loses the global account manager's time and probably has to pay for the trip. Or, she refuses to pay and the needed trip does not occur. For example, Xerox's global accounts group planned a global account conference in Rochester, New York. European management decreed that Europe-based global account managers could not attend—corporate was not paying and they could not be spared from Europe.

To solve this issue conceptually is not difficult. The problem relates to the complexities of internal planning and budgeting systems, and in-place organizational structures and processes. These sorts of issues typically consume an inordinate amount of executive time and energy and may never be satisfactorily resolved.

Compensating global account managers

One of the more emotional managerial issues is compensation. Decisions around compensation levels typically relate to responsibility, culture, control and power, and may occur at many levels. A critical compensation problem in global account programs is under-valuation of the global account manager. Some firms simply take national account managers and shift their role to global. They do not recognize the considerably greater job complexity, and do not build this into the compensation package. The newly appointed global account manager is disillusioned and dissatisfied with his or her financial compensation.

Culture plays a major role in forming compensation attitudes. Highly leveraged commission and bonus plans typically motivate the average American salesperson. European representatives are less interested in leverage—they want predictability in salary and benefits. The Asian model is geared more toward loyalty and respect. Culture and money issues are not easily solved. Uniformity in compensation is not the answer, but neither are plans that vary widely from country to country. Finding the happy medium is an art form. Further, a $3,000 bonus in

New York may seem insignificant—in some countries this is enough to quit and start your own company.

Typically, a global account team supports the global account manager. Who should decide the compensation levels for global team members? Who decides on special recognition? And what is the size of the payment? An American-led team may wish to pay team member bonuses. In China, local managers may see this practice as infringing on their power, leading to a loss of face. And how do we compensate an executive whose home location shifts from a high-wage to low-wage country, and vice versa?

Global account ownership

A critical yet contentious issue in addressing global customers is: who controls the business relationship? More specifically, who sets the overall strategy, sales direction, pricing, contract-specifics, and relationship management activities around the world? Frequently, this issue is focused on disagreements between headquarters global account managers and local country representatives (and managers). Other times it concerns disputes between global account managers and business units over product positioning. The fundamental underlying problem is individual employee resistance to actions designed to serve the "greater good." Personal and/or parochial interests must be subordinated or they will interfere with your firm's ability to effectively satisfy customer needs. The challenge for senior management is to align goals and objectives and focus the enterprise on serving the global customer.

Reporting relationships

Many firms use some form of global account management to address global customers. A critical issue is the reporting relationship for global account managers. This comprises two sub-issues—reporting location and reporting level. One naturally reporting basis (for many firms) is geographic. This can cause several problems—a peer support network does not develop, creating a practice community is very difficult, and administrative problems with travel expenses and the like get in the way of serving the customer. Reporting level has a critical impact on getting things done. For example, at many firms, employees gauge a person's influence level by position on the organization chart. This is a critical issue for management to get right as it embraces both the ability to secure competent global account managers and their ability to function effectively.

Empowering global account managers

Closely coupled to the reporting relationship issue is the empowerment of global account managers. What authority should global account managers enjoy—how much and over what areas? This is not a simple question, for the answer differs depending on such issues as reporting structure, company culture, and support network. For example, if global account managers have senior management mentors their authority is on the high side—similarly if global account managers are senior executives. Regardless, you must develop a system such that the customer can be assured that commitments made by global account managers will be honored.

Highly competent global account managers are in short supply

As a managerial practice, in general, key account management evolved out of the sales force. Firms decided that some customers were sufficiently important that only higher-quality/better-trained executives should be given responsibility for such critical revenue streams. Key account manager positions were created, but firms found that good key account managers were difficult to secure.

Global account management *ups the ante*. Customer demands, time and distance, language, cultural hurdles, legal and contractual issues, and greater customer and firm complexity combine to narrow the talent pool. It is one thing to decide strategically to manage customers globally, and another to secure the human resources that will become good global account managers. Simple approaches such as taking key account managers and giving them global responsibility just does not work. Both Xerox and IBM discovered that newly promoted global account managers might not possess passports.

There are many challenges in securing high-performing global account managers. To start with, the firm must clarify the general criteria for effective global account managers, and the specific criteria required for individual global customers. Then it must figure out where to find these scarce human resources. Few executives have the knowledge, skills, abilities, and experience to hit the ground running as global account managers. Those that do may be found in many different organizational positions, or they may not be found at all (or in sufficient numbers). And that is just global account managers—many other organizational positions must be filled to support the global account effort, each with its own criteria for effective performance.

If these human resources cannot be found within the firm, where can they be found? At competitors, customers, or other firms with estab-lished/successful global account programs? And when we get them, how do we make them effective? And how do we hang on to those that make the grade? Our experience is that "outside" hires generally have a very difficult time "working the system" for their global accounts. Understanding the idiosyncrasies of company culture and the political power structure takes time. And "behind the scenes" efforts may not be successful in the absence of an "old friends" network.

When it comes to global account management, not everyone "gets it"

The essence of this chapter is that as globalization takes hold several things happen; customers are more demanding and sophisticated, competition gets tougher, business is more complex and fast changing, and highly competent global account managers are in short supply. The managerial challenges of competing in a global world are more difficult by orders of magnitude than competing domestically. Life is especially tough when the corporation is not centrally focused on the global customer—when corporate personnel across functions and around the world do not "get it." To "get it" means under-standing at a visceral level that success or failure with global customers may be synonymous with success or failure of the entire enterprise.

In many industries, the competitive focus is shifting from products to services to experiences. In account management, the customer experience reflects the quality of the relationship between supplier and customer organ-izations. Unless all employees are focused on the firm's relationship with its global customers, competitors that do "get it" will surpass them. Indeed, competitive advantage based on building global supplier–customer relation-ships may be longer-lasting than competitive advantage based on products or services. Companies cancel products but they less easily cancel people, espe-cially those that have served them well. Is building powerful relationships easy to do? No! It is very difficult. But its difficulty makes it tougher to emulate. Paradoxically, as globalization has vastly increased the challenge for global firms, it has provided the opportunity to build long-run sources of competitive advantage.

But the promise of long-run sustainable competitive advantage can be secured only if the firm truly focuses on serving the global customer. No matter where they are located, all firm employees must understand they are competing in a global world and that success with global customers is the

Holy Grail. They must throw off the shackles of ethno-centrism and nationalism acquired in their youths, and embrace the global challenge. Not only should they defend their turf against global competitors but they must do what they can to make their global customers succeed. In pursuing this goal, they may develop a global account management system that in itself becomes a competitive advantage.

Essentially the firm must implement a global cultural realignment. All employees, as individuals and as members of cross-functional, cross-national teams, must align together in the common task. Achieving this alignment is a very difficult challenge.

Key Messages

- The world is fast globalizing and the relationships with emerging global customers must be addressed in a different manner.

- The firm must be reoriented to serve the global customer.

- The firm must extend its customer focus to its customer's customers so as to secure advantage for both firms.

- Global customers are more complex to address than their domestic counterparts. They are also more demanding and sophisticated.

- Competition is increasingly nontraditional and tougher.

- Traditional sales management models and processes are no longer sufficient.

- Globalization creates challenges that require innovative and flexible responses.

- A well-formulated global account program is the means of addressing emerging global customers and the increasing challenges that this implies.

CHAPTER 2

CRITICAL SUCCESS FACTORS FOR MANAGING GLOBAL ACCOUNTS

PROLOGUE

At the bar

George was impressed by *Jace*'s comments. Giving her credit might secure more information. *George* opened, *"I think you hit a chord in all three of us when you said something about focusing on general principles as being key in a global account program."* He added, *"Are you saying that these principles operate across different global account programs? It does sounds like we deal with similar issues, though we're with different firms and each involved with different aspects of our global account programs."* He was also impressed with *Constance*'s dedication to her program. *George* turned to *Constance*, *"I wish my CEO felt as strongly about global account management as you seem to. It's like pulling teeth to get on the senior management agenda."*

"Let me ask you something," said *Jace*, *"Did your companies think through the global account program before they started, or did it just 'happen' and evolve? What I mean is, did someone in each of your companies put in significant design effort, make a conscious decision of its initial size, have a plan for how many global accounts would eventually be in the program— you know that type of thing."*

"Well," *Constance* replied, *"I was in a rush to jump on the global bandwagon and we practically had to devise a program overnight. We had customers threatening to leave unless we serviced them using all our global resources. For us it was more of a necessity than a well-thought through initiative."*

"What amazes me is that virtually all our major customers became global accounts at about the same time," *Todd* remarked. *"I mean, when I was promoted from Strategic Account Manager to Global Account Manager I thought I was going to do something new. It turns out that they decided every account should be 'global' and assigned a global account manager to each—even to some accounts that will never do any significant business overseas."*

George turned to *Todd*. *"We really didn't do all the things we should have—in fact, I'm not sure we know what they are. But we do have some great global account managers who seem to succeed despite our lack of planning and systems."*

*"Go on, **George**," **Constance** encouraged, "I need all the tricks I can get."* **George** *wasn't sure he wanted to share too much information with his new-found team, but nothing ventured, nothing gained. "Well, when my firm started the global account program I had a lot of say in who we hired as global account managers. I didn't have this job then, but I had a good history of hiring into the sales force generally. If I say so myself, I do know how to pick 'em. I got involved in practically every hire. Well that was the story in the early years but then I was given an overseas assignment and by the time I got back, senior management had let things slip through the cracks and many of my hires had moved on. The top people seem to have so many other priorities and today's global account managers aren't what they used to be. It's a big challenge for me right now; it's like pulling teeth to get them to complete their global account plans."*

*"I have my own set of frustrations," **Todd** interjected, "our global account program doesn't seem to fit into the organizational hierarchy. It even starts with my reporting line—it's not clear to whom I report." **Todd** was about to go on when **Jace** cut him off. "If I'm hearing you guys right, there are a few 'critical' things that contribute to your global account program's success or are necessary for it to be successful, right?" "Guess you could look at it that way . . . kind of like the basics," said **George**. **Todd** nodded his head in agreement, "Maybe we should make a list. That might help each of us quite a bit."*

__Constance__ thought for a second. "There's one thing we haven't talked about. I've been in direct contact with our biggest global customer and he just doesn't seem to understand how our global account program is helping him. He just seems interested in getting the lowest price. It's more or less the same when I talk to my own Board of Directors—they don't seem to understand how the global account program is helping the company. They only seem to pay attention to the resources I give to the global program. In fact, one of them suggested that 'GAM,' our short hand for global account manager, stands for 'Give Away Money.'"

*"Sounds like you need a way of demonstrating the global program's value to the company and to the customer," said **Jace**. "And then, when we get all these factors, we've got to make sure they all pull in the same direction and empower each other, so to speak." **Jace**'s statement seemed to hit a chord with each of the other three, but the loudspeaker interrupted their conversation:*

"American Airlines Flight 142 headed to New York's La Guardia Airport ready for boarding."

*"Hey, let's exchange business cards," said **Todd**, as the group members downed their drinks and headed to the boarding area.*

Critical success factors (CSFs) are those areas that the firm must "get right" to be successful. CSFs are "the limited number of areas in which results, if they are satisfactory, will ensure successful competitive perform-ance for the organization . . . If results in these areas are not adequate, the organization's efforts for the period will be less than desired."[1] Management should pay particular attention to CSFs.

We apply the CSF process to managing global accounts. As with many managerial issues, design, and process weaknesses in global account programs often emerge only when the "limits" are tested. Based on our experience, we develop eight individual CSFs and one integrative factor. In this chapter we introduce these factors and subsequently devote a chapter to each. Taken together, these nine CSFs form a solid blueprint for successfully managing global accounts. We conclude this chapter by discussing the rewards and risks of global account management.

Critical Success Factors for Managing Global Accounts

The eight individual CSFs concern planning, developing, executing, and assessing the global account program. The integrative factor ensures that the CSFs are properly aligned.

The CSFs for an effective global account management program are:

CSF1   Establishing the scope—size and boundaries—of the global account program

CSF2   Securing senior management commitment

CSF3   Nominating and selecting the "right" global accounts

CSF4   Designing the line organization for managing global accounts

CSF5   Securing effective global account managers

CSF6   Developing effective global account plans

CSF7   Establishing the supporting organizational infrastructure

CSF8   Demonstrating the global account program's incremental value to the firm and to the global account

CSF9   Aligning critical success factors in managing global accounts

This is not a long list! Certainly, individual detailed CSFs could be added for specific companies; details may also vary by industry. However,

---

[1] J.F. Rockart, "Chief Executives Define their own Data Needs," *Harvard Business Review*, 57 (March–April 1979), pp. 81–93.

we believe that firms that get our nine basic factors "right" will operate high-quality global account programs. Because global account programs are a major endeavor for the firm, they must be carefully planned in the early stages. "Getting it right" the first time is important. Scarce company resources are at stake and it is difficult to recover from a botched introduction.

You should certainly consider these nine factors if you are initiating a global account program for the first time. But they should also be a guide as your program evolves. For example, a global program with six key accounts will look very different from a program with 60 accounts. As your program evolves, you should use the nine CSFs as criteria in guiding the growth of your global account program.

Following is a brief glimpse of the nine factors. We clarify their context and demonstrate inter-relationships.

CSF1: Establishing the scope—size and boundaries—of the global account program

You should address the scope of your global account program in the initial design stage. Scope is also an important element in evolving a successful small program or re-engineering a program that has gone off track. Simply put, you must resolve the question of how aggressive you want your program to be. The driving feature of scope is the number of accounts in the global program, and the percent of corporate revenues involved. But scope also embraces supplier–customer global account relationships, the line organization, human resources and reporting relationships, empowering global account managers and funding.

The number of global accounts and the percent of revenues are relatively easy to understand. Less easy to define and frame are philosophical, political, cultural, and policy-related issues. For example: Who "owns" the global account? What level of empowerment should global account managers (GAMs) enjoy? Where should GAMs be placed in the organizational hierarchy? To whom should they report? What special privileges and pricing considerations should global accounts receive? Where does the global account program rank among the various organizational priorities?

Establishing the scope of a global account program entails achieving a shared understanding among all executives about conceptual and practical aspects. For example: Who should be the main beneficiary of tough decisions that will have to be made—the customer, the company as a whole, or individual business units within the firm?

CSF2: Securing senior management commitment

We define senior management commitment as the overall level of company financial and human resource investment in the global account program. When senior management commitment is high, many elements of the global program are affected, including among others, funding levels, human resource policies, functional procedures, employee attitudes, managerial decisions, organizational design, and active senior management involvement with global customers.

Top management commitment goes a long way to resolving often-conflicting interests. It can help cut through much of the ambiguity inherent in matrix organizations. For the global program to be successful, captains that own company turf may have their power reduced and redistributed. Geographic-based managers and/or product/brand leadership may have to cede authority to customer-facing executives. Only strong leadership from the top can make that happen. In addition, when the organization focuses on the global customer, senior management can play many different supportive roles.

Particularly important supportive roles are those requiring direct global account contacts. Perhaps the most visible role of this type is the Partnership Executive (PE). The PE is assigned to one or more global accounts for the purpose of establishing senior-executive-level relationships with the customer. By virtue of their executive status, PEs raise the contact level at global accounts. They make commitments that the GAM cannot. Further, PEs may act as GAM mentors as well as internal champions for the global account and the account team. At a broader level, the PE role helps solidify a customer focus within the firm.

CSF3: Nominating and selecting the "right" global accounts

Accounts ultimately selected for the global account program absorb significant levels of company resources. If in the early stages of a global account program you select the wrong accounts, you build in failure before the program is able to prove itself. Later, incorrect account selection leads to two major problems. First, company resources are wasted on accounts that should not be in the global program. Second, accounts that should be in the global program do not receive the attention they deserve. Incorrect selection jeopardizes the program's credibility and wastes firm resources. You must get account selection right.

A root cause of downstream problems with global account programs concerns those accounts that are in the program and the method by which they gained membership. To choose global accounts appropriately, you must develop a formal nomination and selection process. You must decide on a set of admission criteria for your global account program and on the relative importance of each criterion. Once your criteria are established, you should examine candidate global accounts and select those offering the best fit. Unless this process is formalized and carried out professionally, the integrity of the "account roster" is suspect. In the worst case, political considerations lead ill-suited customers to be force-fit into a well-developed profile. When this occurs, the likely result is dissatisfied customers, frustrated GAMs, and business results that distort potential program benefits.

Sometimes companies confuse global accounts with key (or strategic) accounts. Your firm may have a national account program or even a key account program that encompasses domestic, regional, and/or global accounts. Performance at these accounts may be critical for company success, but it does not make them "global." *Global accounts are a subset of the firm's strategic accounts.* Other strategic accounts do not need the same type of resources as global accounts—the uniqueness of global accounts requires special considerations. Selecting the "right" global accounts is a critical challenge for defining the global account program.

CSF4: Designing the line organization for managing global accounts

The line organization for your global account program must interface with the firm's current organization structure. How the global account element relates to that structure—especially to the geographic organization and the product groups—has important ramifications that may not be immediately apparent.

For many companies, the existing line-organizational design for interfacing with customers is based on geographic-area divisions—for example, North America, Latin America, Asia Pacific and Europe, Middle East, and Africa (EMEA). This structure gives rise to some basic issues for managing global accounts. To whom does the GAM report go to? A country manager, a senior person in the global account organization, or both? If both, what is the nature of the reporting relationships—solid line to the global organization, dotted line to the country organization; or dotted line to the global organization, solid line to the country organization; or a true matrix structure?

Or, should the firm develop an organizational design more focused on managing global accounts where the geographic dimension is given less weight? For example, should the firm create a separate division for global accounts distinct from the geographic organization(s) that deals with less important customers around the world? Or, should the entire customer-interface organization be located within industry segments?

The line organizational structure and reporting relationships for the global account program, including relationships to the rest of the corporate organization, are challenging issues. Company culture, current go-to-market strategies, and current company organization exert heavy influences on global account program design and incorporation into the firm. For example, a culture of highly empowered geographic regional executives or a strong product- or brand-led organization will not easily accept a new design developed around customers. In their myopic view, the cost in lost authority may be far too great.

Besides the major question of where GAMs should report, many other questions must be answered before your program can be launched: Who "owns" the account, determines the overall strategy, sets priorities, and provides operational direction? How much, if any, input does the GAM have in local representatives' annual performance appraisals? Do local representatives participate in the global account team bonus? How much authority does the GAM have over the daily activities of local representatives? Even if the GAM reports elsewhere, do local operations receive revenue and profit credit for sales activity with global accounts within their geography.

CSF5: Securing effective global account managers

Global account managers have day-to-day responsibility for revenues (and frequently for profits) earned at the global account—both in the short-term and for the long run. They must develop global account plans and seek out opportunities to add value to the firm–global account business relationship. They must develop sets of relationships with individuals at the global account, as well as manage a supplier team dedicated to serving the global account—across functions, across geographies, and across managerial levels. This is not a trivial task.

Put very simply, there is no question that the GAM assignment is extremely challenging. The GAM must deal with a multiplicity of corporate, business, geographic, political, and legal issues on a regular basis. The position requires an exceptional breadth of intellectual scope, energy, and perseverance. To secure effective GAMs you must use the full set of recruiting, selecting, training, rewarding, and retaining tools and processes. Unfortunately, most companies have not taken advantage of research and selection tools that are generally available—users of fact-based competency profiles and formal selection processes are a minority. Has your firm shifted from a national account model to global account management and simply re-titled the national account manager—the NAM, as GAM? If so, you are assuming the only change is territory expansion—this is way off the mark!

The GAM's job is very different from, and significantly more difficult than, its domestic counterpart. The GAM faces tremendous additional pressures requiring a host of upgraded skills—for example, time management, interpersonal and communication skills, strategic thinking and planning, international business acumen, and implementation coordination. Securing the right people requires a correspondingly more professional and thorough approach. GAMs are responsible for millions of dollars of revenues and profits. You cannot afford to put any but the very best people in your management team into these positions. You have to make sure that you have the right collection of potential GAMs in waiting. Then, you must place the "right" people, with the "right" competencies, in the "right" place, at the "right" time in the "right" numbers. Getting this right is one of the most significant management challenges of the next 10 years.

CSF6: Developing effective global account plans

If you have spent time in sales, you have probably developed some form of sales plan for a territory or individual account. Many service providers and consultants offer customer relationship marketing (CRM) processes and systems that have elements of account planning. But global account planning is different. Developing the global account plan is more complex by orders of magnitude than a domestic account plan. Among the issues that must be addressed are integration of cross-cultural perspectives, communication problems, language barriers, infrastructure weaknesses, and related financial and budget issues.

An effective global account planning process, based on solid situation analyses, develops a road map for addressing the firm's portfolio of individual global accounts. Because the global account environment is so complex, this is a challenging task. It is one thing for an individual GAM to develop a global account plan. It is quite another to develop a system and infrastructure that operates across the entire global account portfolio and allows for account-to-account comparisons. Global account planning is more than just plan creation. Critical elements in a quality global account planning process concern many issues—How the plan is developed? How and to what extent are the global customer and your worldwide team involved? How and to whom is the completed global account plan communicated? How does the GAM use the plan? How is progress tracked against the plan?

Successful global account planning requires an agreed-upon process that functions across global accounts on a worldwide basis. It should be sufficiently flexible to allow "roll-up" of individual plans. It should also embrace multi-purpose use to avoid extra "form-filling" by GAMs and account team members.

CSF7: Establishing the supporting organizational infrastructure

The supporting infrastructure for managing global accounts embraces a host of systems and processes. (Because global account planning is so critical, we treat global account planning as a CSF in its own right.) In a sense, the supporting infrastructure is the glue that holds the global account program together. It contains many elements such as IT and administration, human resources, business practice, global contracting, training, communication, and financial systems. To change the metaphor, these systems and processes function as links in the global account program chain. The chain is as strong as its weakest link! When account profitability systems are ineffective, when communication systems do not function effectively, or when a host of other things go wrong, the firm will not achieve the global account program's potential.

Effectively addressing infrastructure issues is not "business-as-usual." The firm must develop creative solutions to meet growing customer expectations, competitive actions, and to establish positive marketplace differentiation. Developing these infrastructure elements involves detailed and sometimes very tedious work. Management must consider the many "mechanical" details that are crucially important to an effective and efficient program. "The devil is in the details" and any individual detail can derail the train.

CSF8: Demonstrating the global account program's incremental value to the firm and global account

A successful global account program creates incremental value for the customer and for your firm. Many sources define value creation—we shall not formulate a new theory of global account program value. Much depends on your business model and the customers you serve. Value creation for transactions between P&G and Wal-Mart differs significantly from value creation for transactions between IBM and Wal-Mart. Regardless, the global account program must create incremental value for the customer and for your firm. This CSF focuses on building a model and culture that demonstrates the incremental value of your global account program.

What value can you assign to an improved customer relationship? How do you measure success in relationship building? All too often our targets for success relate directly to the ease of securing data. Candidate measures include year-on-year revenue growth, customer satisfaction, share of wallet, and a number of transactions. There are no easy answers to defining and creating value. But, for a global account program to survive and prosper, the firm must develop clearly defined objectives for incremental value creation and a consistent method to demonstrate success and failure.

Tracking company performance with global accounts on multiple measures in multiple countries is a challenging task. Add in the complexity of product flows through multiple distribution channels and it may seem well-nigh impossible. Is the data collected on your global accounts accurate? Is the cost of tracking programs too high? These are legitimate concerns, but foregoing the monitoring and assessing function is not an option. Your firm succeeds or fails based on its metrics—the same is true of your global account program. More significantly, your global account program is one of many claims on corporate resources. Unless you can demonstrate that it provides a worthwhile return, you do not deserve to have a global account program. Even more to the point, senior management would be failing its shareholders if it funded a global account program without appropriate accountability. You must be able to demonstrate the wisdom of top management's investment in the global program.

Measurement is a difficult challenge. All too frequently firms fail to put in the appropriate systems. The result is management by perception. This is not very satisfying for a firm that jealously guards corporate resources and demands that its initiatives deliver a target return on investment. Most of the other CSFs are, perhaps, inherently more interesting—but CSF8 is where the rubber really hits the road.

CSF9: Aligning critical success factors in managing global accounts

Each CSF is important in its own right. But, in addition, the alignment of all eight CSFs plays a crucial role in the success of your global account program. What do we mean by alignment? It is making sure that the entire set of decisions about the global account program forms a coherent whole, and interfaces appropriately with other organizational dimensions, both within the firm and with global customers. If one factor is "out of alignment," the firm cannot compensate by doing well on another.

In Chapter 11 we label the types of alignment as *Intra-CSF*, *Inter-CSF*, *Holistic*, and *Cross-Boundary*. *Intra-CSF* alignment, as the name implies, deals with how you formulate the specific aspects of each CSF. For example, are the various individual elements necessary for securing GAMs well aligned? *Inter-CSF* alignment, on the other hand, deals with how well each of the eight CSFs work together to form a coherent global program. For example, are your processes for securing those GAMs consistent with the scope of your global program?

Holistic alignment addresses how the global account program interfaces with those organizational functions, systems, and processes, within the firm, that interface with the global program. Good *holistic* alignment supports the program; poor *holistic* alignment means there may be significant problems in implementing a global program. Finally, *cross-boundary* alignment deals with how well the program aligns with your global customers.

Each of these forms of alignment is important, yet we believe that most problems arise with *holistic* alignment—making sure that the global program "fits" into the rest of the organization. For example, compensation plans that drive GAMs to focus on monthly sales activity undermine their critical roles of strategist and relationship manager. Ineffective financial reporting systems that cause GAMs and team members to spend hours reconciling "the numbers" kill productivity and customer face time, and eventually lead to diminished performance. By contrast, a well-designed team bonus based on overall global account performance rewards each team member for their support and cooperation, and can be highly motivating.

Rewards and Risks in Global Account Management

In this chapter, we have presented eight individual CSFs, plus the alignment factor. Whether you are starting a global account program, or upgrading a current in-place program, you should focus on these nine elements.

Why should you prepare so extensively? Why not just begin and correct problems as they occur? Of course, if you pursue such an incrementalist approach you may enjoy some degree of success. But, the benefits of "getting it right the first time" are very substantial. If you are able to improve your relationships with a few global accounts, the rewards in additional revenues and profits should by far exceed your investment in the global program. Further, it is always more difficult to change processes and procedures once implemented, especially if the proposed change is perceived as "taking back" some firm or customer benefit.

The benefits of implementing a successful global account program can make the difference between company success and failure. It can mean improved profitability through better global coordination; increased opportunities by developing global customer partnerships; better competitive positioning by building stronger global relationships; and greater long-term global dependency of your customers on your products and services. You will also increase internal efficiencies and build new "executive" career opportunities.

Customers also benefit from a successful global account program. From an improved focus and superior relationships, the supplier more thoroughly understands customers' global requirements. They receive improved products and services tailored to their global needs. They may also gain process efficiencies due to your improved service levels, and solve global supply chain issues more effectively. Further, benefits from successfully implementing a global program should spill over to customers not included in the program.

However, managing global accounts is not a risk-free endeavor. You may create expectations in your sales team and their customers that you cannot meet. Now that they are your "global accounts," customers may subject you to additional price pressures. You may need to invest heavily to improve inconsistent service levels in remote locations. Corporate culture may interfere with redistributing authority from country management to GAMs. Understanding and anticipating these potential problems will allow you to avoid some of the major showstoppers. As with any major change, you will not be able to anticipate all the issues, but we shall do our best to warn you what lies ahead.

This book provides a road map for your journey into managing global accounts. For new players, it will help you "get it right the first time." For those with experience, it can function as a tool to assess your current program, and allow you to make mid-course corrections.[2]

---

[2] For an up-to-date review of global account management in the food and grocery industry, see *Global Account Management: What Next?*, Watford, Herts., Great Britain: Institute of Grocery Distribution (IGD), October 2004.

Key Messages

- A successful global account program requires intensive focus on a limited number of CSFs.

- Nine CSFs define a successful global account program—eight individual factors and one alignment factor.

- If not given proper consideration, any single individual CSF can derail a global account program.

CHAPTER 3

ESTABLISHING THE SCOPE OF THE GLOBAL ACCOUNT PROGRAM

PROLOGUE

On the plane

When they boarded Jace was surprised to find she was sitting next to George. Jace said, "Well, that was a fluke they put us next to each other." George smiled then responded, "actually I fixed it—thought I might get some free consulting." "Well, it'll be worth what you paid for it," joked Jace.

Jace had been thinking about their earlier conversation. She wondered what other issues George might be facing. Jace addressed George, "So, is lack of good global account managers your only problem?" "Well, I don't know about that," responded George, "but it is one of the issues that concerns me the most. We have well over 50 global accounts and finding managerial talent to cover them all is a big deal."

Jace wanted to know more. She asked George, "Is it a question of a lack of talent or that the position is not sufficiently attractive to attract the right caliber person?" George thought awhile, "Actually, Jace I think it may be a combination of both. We may be trying to cover too many accounts too soon, and most of the really good candidates are concerned about the position description and level."

"Well George," replied Jace "I guess it's too late to suggest that you start out small and then build up your roster. But it's not too late to tell you that you won't attract the right talent if you don't position the role appropriately. For one thing, you've got to get the empowerment level consistent with the role responsibilities." George listened but thought there might be some other underlying issues to which he had not given proper attention. "You know Jace, it does seem that there are quite a few important issues that keep popping up in implementation. For example, I'm not at all sure we are structured properly. Many of the functional and business-unit organizations we need to support the program are not on board. Maybe we tried to go too fast too soon."

Jace had heard this from other clients. "George, this is not a surprise to me. Several of my clients have had a similar experience. I believe the gut issue is that they gave insufficient thought and planning to establishing the program scope." George was not quite sure what Jace meant by scope, *but he was sure his firm hadn't done enough planning before initiating the program. Perhaps scope was something he could explore with **Jace** and maybe gain some insight.*

Global account program *scope* is one of the more important CSFs in managing global accounts. We identified several definitions of *scope* to provide a context to help you understand what we mean:

> *Scope* is the way that we describe the boundaries of the program. It defines what the project will deliver and what it will not deliver . . . It can include the organizations affected, the transactions affected, the data types included, etc.[1]

> Defining the *scope* of a program: How to promise what you can do, and deliver on what you promise.[2]

> A project *scope* defines the tasks and outcomes for a project, based on the determined needs and expectations. It is necessary to clearly identify which tasks will be included in the process and, no less importantly, to determine those which fall outside of the scope.[3]

To deliver on the promise of a successful global account program you must determine its boundaries. Early on, you must plan for the global account management scope you expect to achieve when the program reaches a steady state and has become part of your firm's overall management system. There are many issues to consider. Specifically, you should focus on such topics as:

- *Program roster size:* How many accounts should be in the program? What percent of total firm revenues should customers in your global account program represent? (How you conduct the selection of global accounts is dealt with in CSF3.)
- *Supplier–global account relationships:* How hard will you try to establish true partnerships? When will you be satisfied with a quality supplier relationship?
- *Designing the line organization:* How will global account management fit into the firm's organization structure?

---

[1] R. Max Wideman, "Wideman Comparative Glossary of Common Project Management Terms," March 2002 http://www.maxwideman.com/pmglossary/.

[2] Project Management Course, Mindconnection, www.mindconnection.com.

[3] www.Applied-Research.com Article 34—November 4 1999 PROJECT MANAGEMENT—DEFINING PROJECT SCOPE.

- *Human resources and reporting relationships:* Who will be your global account managers, and to whom will they report?
- *Empowering global account managers:* For what sort of issues will global account managers have the power to make decisions?
- *Funding the global account program:* What levels of financial and human resource investment will the firm commit to the global program?

The answers to these questions are crucial. The scope of the global account program sets the parameters for many other CSFs. For example, senior management commitment, line organization design, and establishing the supporting organizational infrastructure all relate directly to decisions about program scope.

To take one issue, your global account program scope should be tied very closely to the level of senior management commitment. (We address this CSF in Chapter 4.) If you secure strong senior management commitment up front, you can be aggressive in developing your global account program. *Strike while the iron is hot* if you secure a shared value among your senior executive team about the conceptual and practical aspects of a full-scale global account program. On the other hand, weak senior management commitment calls for a less aggressive program.

When you introduce a global account program there will be significant organizational change. This is never easy to accomplish. Too much change or too much change too quickly, without the right level of senior executive support, is a sure recipe for disaster.

Certainly, if senior executive support is weak, or even if it is strong, your most prudent approach may be to begin slowly. Start initially with a narrow scope embracing just a few clients. If executive support is strong, these clients provide a market test—you can quickly scale up if test results are positive. If executive support is weak, and program results are positive, your first few global accounts provide the convincing data you need to solidify support. They allow you to build a stronger business case and secure greater commitment for later program expansion.

If you start with too broad a scope, there are several issues to watch out for:

- Infrastructure, human, and financial resources are untested and probably inadequate. This causes potentially serious operational issues and will likely lead to customer disappointment and/or frustration.
- Introducing the global account program causes such organizational dislocations that internal political resistance kills the program before it gets off the ground.

- The global account program does get off the ground, but very slowly and with tremendous organizational effort. Ultimately it fails because the environment is so fast changing and the program is unable to adapt. It never gains the traction required to be successful. If this occurs, global account management may be buried for many years.

On the other hand, if your introduction is too *low key*, you limit program benefits. The new program is not really differentiated from the old way, and you limit your ability to solve problems and deliver incremental benefits. Your program may address symptoms rather than underlying causes. For example, suppose your firm has a problem in responding to special price requests—you are too slow for one specific customer. One potential solution is to put in a temporary bid process for this customer. But this solution would not resolve the underlying issue of responding to all global bids. Perhaps, the corporate pricing process should be overhauled.

We have developed a six-stage framework of global account program maturity. Depending on the stage of your global account program, the material in this chapter will have different meaning for you. For example, if you have never had any form of global account program, this chapter can function as a blueprint for initiating global account management. On the other hand, if you have had a well-functioning global account program in place for several years, the chapter content may help you with fine-tuning.

To categorize the six stages, we define the global account program in terms of *breadth* and *depth*. *Breadth* refers to overall program size, for example number of customers, percentage of revenue, and number of GAMs. *Depth* is the degree of organizational commitment, for example support from senior executives, investment in information technology, and GAM education and development.

Following are our six stages:

- *No global account management:* These firms have not addressed global account management in any form whatsoever. They may have various domestic key account programs but, regardless of customer procurement behavior, have not introduced any form of *global* account management. If you are in this stage, this chapter will help you get your program underway with the proper scope.
- *Global account management skunk works:* Somewhere in a key account management program, one enterprising key account manager (KAM) has realized that her customers require servicing globally. This KAM has formed a global account program for her customer with wile and

guile. The KAM has made things happen by forming relationships with colleagues based in other countries. Even the KAM's own manager may have little understanding of what she is doing. If your firm is in this stage, you can benefit from what this KAM has learned about the issues we raise in this chapter. Since you have no formal program, you are in the same place as *no global account management*, but you have the benefit of this key account manager's input.

• *Global account management—limited in breadth and limited in depth:* This stage of managing global accounts is where many companies begin, and is the most limited formal entry into global account management. This firm is probably testing global account management by placing a few customers in a start-up program, but has not made any serious commitment to this initiative. As a whole, international operations continue much as before. If this is your stage, then the scope issues outlined here will help you analyze your program more effectively, allowing you to transition into a broader and deeper program.

• *Global account management—broad in scope but limited in depth:* This stage is dangerous for the firm. Someone in senior management got the message—global account management is important! "Right, we'll name our top 60 key accounts as global accounts and rename the relevant key account managers as GAMs. Now go to it!" Extra resources, "No!" Education and training for the newly appointed GAMs, "No!" The firm may experience escalating tensions as it attempts to develop the embryonic global customer organization side-by-side with an in-place geographic structure. Problems are likely because the program has been insufficiently thought through, and the firm has not secured broad agreement on individual roles and responsibilities.

• *Global account management—limited in breadth but deep:* The firm understands the importance of managing global accounts and knows it must invest in this initiative. It also understands the complexity of managing global accounts. It wants to move cautiously to develop the right systems, procedures, and line organization. This firm may have substantially changed previous organizational arrangements to develop a new global account structure separate from geography, with a well-documented and agreed-upon set of operating principles. The focus is on testing program scope, but success will be limited to those few accounts in the program. If you are in this stage, the information in this chapter can help you inventory the areas you are testing. This is a good stage to add additional structure and support in preparation for adding more accounts.

- *Global account management—broad and deep:* The firm has successfully tested global account management. It has made significant investments, and these are paying off. The global account program has become integrated into the fabric of the organization, probably with a separate infrastructure for global accounts. Managing global accounts is here to stay as a corporate priority. If you are at this stage, the information on scope should help you enhance your program with additional capabilities as you expand its success. Notwithstanding the fact that this stage is the most advanced of our six stages, global account management continues to evolve as new challenges emerge and the organization responds.

IBM transitioned through most of these stages during the past 20 years. In the 1980s, global account management began primarily as a skunk works—leading sales people on international accounts worked out deals with their managers to recognize their efforts with international accounts. As information technology systems became more integrated with telecommunications, and customers needed more global coordination, IBM began a limited formal program. It designated customers as "international" and initiated the Selected International Account (SIA) program. IBM built an international operations organization to coordinate sales activities and built software to track global revenue streams—it also began to compensate sales representatives on global revenues. As customer demand for global consistency increased, international operations grew. IBM's international sales organization placed a limited number of large global accounts in what it called the "Top international account program." This program selected accounts primarily on the basis of revenue contribution. IBM published an internal list of Top accounts and sent out several executive letters asking sales people and management around the world to treat these customers with *special interest.* Essentially, IBM broadened its global focus but did not add much depth. There were few formal operational guidelines, limited training, and only limited executive involvement.

As the 1990s approached, IBM realized it needed a more formal structure—both *breadth* and *depth* needed review. IBM restructured the global sales organizations by industry, and assigned executives to *own* industry sales strategy worldwide. Senior industry executives realized they needed closer account coordination across countries. Such clients as Citigroup were placing increased demands on coordinating product/service delivery around the world as well as requiring industry knowledge in remote locations. IBM's Global Customer Management (GCM) program began as a project involving the Finance industry and the international sales operations group. As program operations guidance evolved, GCM increased *breadth* by adding accounts and global account sales executives. IBM built *depth* by adding supporting infrastructure and executive involvement. GCM found its way into other industries, and product, services and software organizations evolved to provide support to named accounts. In 1995, IBM assigned coordination responsibilities to industry executives—they ensured GCM worked across geographies.

By 2000, customer demands evolved from buying products and services globally to a concern with solutions and outsourcing. Both *breadth* and *depth* needed review. A new sales coverage model was designed to put global customers in tiers. IBM reduced the first-tier large GCM accounts to around 40 (from 150)—later built up to 60. The second tier comprised approximately 4000 large customers—the final tier covered the remainder, the vast majority of IBM's several hundred thousand customers. Account team resources for the 60 first-tier accounts increased significantly. IBM assigned senior executives to lead these teams and delegated a broad range of authority including setting global policy, prices, and customer support. Sam Palmisano, IBM's CEO, reviews each of these accounts on an annual basis. IBM's top executive team supported the new organization and built infrastructure around the new model. IBM increased authority for second-tier GAMs, and the various brand organizations provided added support. The new approach continued under the industry structure, but IBM added more service organizations to support these accounts.

In 2005, IBM's global account program continues to evolve as IBM earns higher wallet share at its global accounts than at other customer groups. Senior management views the program as highly successful, but IBM's plans do not include increasing the number of accounts in the global program. IBM does intend to increase the number of top-tier accounts from the current 60 to 100. The process for managing global accounts is now highly integrated into the geographies. Because both the geographies and industry sectors are rewarded for success with global accounts, and the geographies now view their role very much as driving revenue growth and securing resources. IBM continues to put major effort into the nomination and selection process for global accounts—these decisions are made by the industry sector general managers, based on significant information from the finance function on growth, share, customer satisfaction, percent of outsourced business, and input from the geographies. IBM has backed off having GAMs report into the industry leaders worldwide—they now report to geographic heads in Europe, and industry heads elsewhere.

To summarize, IBM took a decade to go from no program, to skunk works, to a limited breadth and limited depth programs. Then IBM accelerated into a *broad* and *deep* program in less than two years. IBM continues to broaden and deepen its global program to meet more demanding customer needs.

In 1989, the Xerox Global Account Program began with six accounts. Its introduction is best described as an *official skunk works* at corporate headquarters. Visionary executive, Howard Katzen, developed the initiative with the backing of a couple of senior executives. Each of these executives had significant international experience and predicted emerging global customer requirements. Additionally, Katzen was the Xerox Focused Executive for American Express, an active global player and a very demanding customer. The confluence of four factors—a common vision of internationally experienced executives, insight into emerging customer needs, deep involvement with a global customer, and recognition of a great opportunity for substantial competitive advantage—shaped the 1989 pilot. Finally, Katzen's personal relationships with senior Xerox geographic heads, including joint-venture subsidiaries (Fuji Xerox and Rank Xerox) secured global program endorsement to operate as an overlay to their organizations.

By the mid-1990s, the program had grown to 65 accounts but was still relatively unknown within Xerox. During this period, the program was limited in scope but gaining depth. For example, a management information system covered over 60 countries, GAM quality improved, a rudimentary contracting process was in place, and senior management attention increased. Katzen's *old boy* network drove global account management and provided the leverage for individual GAMs to get things done for their customers.

By the late 1990s, Xerox's global account roster had grown to 125 accounts. But, although largely successful, the program was not living up to its potential. Customer demands were straining the program and testing the commitment of Xerox's geographic-area structure. Lack of a broadly agreed program scope and clear senior management support frustrated

GAMs and customers alike. Quite simply, Xerox's program was too broad, in part because inappropriate accounts had been allowed to join, thus diluting the effort. Promises to customers had outstripped Xerox's investment in program depth—the program was ahead of Xerox's capabilities.

In 1999, Xerox introduced a two-tier structure, permitting a deeper approach to a limited number of accounts. Unfortunately, Xerox had limited success in securing the culture change necessary to treat these customers appropriately around the world. In 2003, in an attempt to *get it right*, Xerox focused on *the Global Fifteen*—five accounts each from Japan, the U.S. and Europe, as a pilot within the existing program. In 2005, Xerox is expanding this program to "the Global 35."

The Xerox program faces some continuing challenges. It continues to have a problem with top-management commitment, broad-based shared value for the strategic importance of the global program, and lack of field support. For example, two very senior and well-respected GAMs, responsible for two of Xerox' largest customers, were each asked to manage a second global account. Both are concerned about their ability to take on these additional responsibilities. On the positive side, the CEO of the British subsidiary of one of these GAM's accounts continues to make Xerox the benchmark for account management.

Xerox's experience is different from IBM's and ultimately less successful. Of course, during the late 1990s, Xerox had many other things on its mind—deteriorating market share and profit performance and a very public CEO firing. By contrast, IBM's grim period was in the early 1990s. By the late 1990s, when IBM made major program changes, its evolving business model with a focus on services was quite successful. The core message from these two illustrations is that your global account program can evolve in many different ways, some less desirable than others. But, if you are very clear about your program scope you will have a better chance of a successful global account program development.

Elements of Scope for the Global Account Program

Now we turn to those issues having greatest impact on the scope of a global account program. These characteristics are comprehensive and will stimulate your thinking on the appropriate design elements for your global account program. Of course, your specific business or industry may have unique characteristics. At a minimum, we believe the factors we discuss will give you a good start.

Element one: Program roster size

From the outset you should ask yourself: How many customers should be in our global account program? What percent of total revenue should the global account program cover? You should think long and hard about these questions— there are no magic answers. Often, the decision on number of global accounts is made as part of a broader process of tiering all of the firm's customers and developing different coverage models for each tier. For example, HP has five tiers, ranging from the top 100 *corporate* accounts to millions of individual consumers.

Some questions you should ask yourself in deciding on the number of toptier global accounts are:

- *Objectives:* What are our overall objectives for the global account program?
- *Aggressiveness:* How aggressive do we need to be? How aggressive do we want to be?
- *Executive Support:* What level of executive support have we been able to garner? Can we expect to garner?
- *Urgency:* How urgent a matter is this? Are customers clamoring for a global account program? Are competitors securing advantage because we do not have a global account program? Is the point of introducing a program now to preempt competition?
- *Internal Resistance:* How much internal resistance are we likely to face when we implement a global account program? What will be the major success of this existence? How much change can the organization digest during the next few years?
- *Risk:* How much risk, and what type of risk would we face by introducing a global account program?
- *Information Technology:* How adaptable is our IT infrastructure to support a global account program?
- *Investment:* How much of an investment in global account management can we commit to, and for how many years?

The decision on global account program size must combine the rewards you anticipate, with the investment and risk level you are willing to incur. There are really three decisions:

- How many accounts will you start with?
- How many accounts do you plan for in steady state?
- How fast will you scale up?

Most global account programs with which we are familiar start with a subset of the desired number of global accounts. No matter how well you plan program introduction, somewhere along the line something will probably not go as planned! Limiting the starting number lets you build and test your global infrastructure, assess your processes, and gauge customer satisfaction. A useful modification is to start with a set of clients from a single industry—this is especially viable if your customers are currently managed by industry. In any event, start-up issues can be resolved without impacting the broad scope of your customer base.

Limited entry and later scaling up is the most common approach for companies that develop successful global account programs, but it is not the only way to go. You can also be successful with a more aggressive introduction with more accounts.

Regardless of the initial number of global accounts, as with any managerial innovation, you must be very clear about your objectives both initially and for the long run. When you introduce your global account program, you must be very clear about what you are trying to achieve:

- What do you expect to gain?
- What do you want your customers to gain?
- How will the global account program be managed?
- What do you intend to learn?
- What part of the global infrastructure are you going to test?
- How will the customer's experience change, and how will you know?
- What time limits are you setting for reaching your objectives?

In several global account programs we have observed, objectives were not clearly established and the global program's success could never be demonstrated. Other firms spent so long testing their programs with a few clients that momentum dissipated and senior management lost interest.

A French public relations firm serving the high-tech sector decided to expand by servicing some clients globally. Initially, it pitched a pan-European offering with the goal of eventually servicing these clients worldwide. But objectives were not established and many senior personnel considered the global account program "a waste of time." The firm hired extra personnel and expended considerable resources. After four years, the results were disappointing and the program was abandoned.

You must be very clear about expectations. Rarely do you get instant results from introducing a global account program. You may not see a measurable payoff until a year or two after the start of implementation. During this period, your infrastructure, corporate culture, customer expectations, and management systems must develop and adjust to the new model. If development and adaptation do not occur, you will fail. And you may lose your chance to establish a global account program for a long time to come.

Regardless of whether you start small and expand later when the bugs have been worked out, or you decide on a more aggressive approach, you should have a good idea of steady-state parameters. Essentially, program size depends on your firm's current and projected revenues, and on the current and projected degree of globality in your customer base. We have no hard data, but anecdotal evidence suggests a median of 50–70 accounts in mature programs. Larger companies may reach the low hundreds. For example, Schneider Electric has almost 100 global accounts representing somewhat less than 15 percent of overall *tracked* business.

Of course, there will be exceptions. For example, among its institutional clients, Citibank probably has one of the most diverse customer bases of all organizations, both by industry and by geography. As a result, its Global Relationship Bank comprises upwards of 1700 global accounts.

Finally, settling on the "right" number of global accounts is not a simple matter. For example, HP's global account program has a considerable history. During the 1990s, HP's program contained around 100 global accounts and seemed to be in steady state. It then expanded to around 200, but today is back to the former level. The appropriate number of accounts for your global program must continually be tested against the net value that the global program delivers. We address value specifically in Chapter 10.

Element two: The nature of supplier–global account relationships

We may view supplier relationships with individual global accounts as potentially falling on a single dimension with end points *vendor* and *partner.*

- *Vendor:* These relationships are characterized by a lack of loyalty between supplier and buyer. The emphasis is on such purchase criteria as price and delivery. This type of account is not generally accepted into a global account program unless there is sufficient potential to try to change the customer's philosophy.
- *Partner:* These relationships are characterized by close collaborative supplier–customer working relationships with an emphasis on value delivery. These are ideal candidates for your global account program.

- *Preferred-supplier:* These relationships fall somewhere between the two extremes. These accounts may be accepted into the global account program with the understanding that they could be "moved" into the *partner* category in the not-too-distant future.

A critical element of scope relates to distribution of accounts among these categories. More highly scoped global account programs have a larger percent of global accounts in the partnership category. You can reap many benefits from partnership accounts. Closer relationships lead to greater developmental activity and opportunities for value creation, higher switching costs, and decreased emphasis on price in contract negotiations.

But, developing meaningful partner relationships requires significant firm investment both in dollars and in human resources. You must make a serious decision about how many partnership global accounts you can afford. The global account must also make significant investments. Not all potential global accounts will invest sufficiently to make it worthwhile for you to pursue a partnership. You probably should not accept accounts into your global program unless you feel that you can *win them over* within a reasonable time period.

What constitutes a reasonable time period depends on required program investment, individual account potential, and the current quality of the firm/account relationship. If the cost of supporting an individual account is not too high, the potential large, and your current relationship strong, you may adopt Schneider's liberal position (below). An alternative approach is to work with the customer to gain their agreement to truly partner—then accept them into the program.

> When Schneider attempts to grow a global account relationship from transaction-oriented into a partnership, the developmental process can take from one to three years. In early efforts, teams of Schneider experts worked with global accounts. Nowadays, Schneider account managers are sufficiently experienced that they facilitate these transitions themselves.

Element three: Designing the line organization

Whether you start out conservatively or aggressively, you must decide how to organize around your global customers. Initially, there is one major decision—Will you graft the global account organization onto the existing line organization, or will you develop a totally different structure for managing global accounts?

- *Graft onto the existing organizational structure:* Most companies expand their global presence via some form of geographic-area structure, at least in the selling organization. For example, senior executives may be responsible for North America, Latin America, EMEA and Asia Pacific. Their direct reports are responsible for individual countries. Frequently, the organization for managing global accounts is matrixed with this structure. An individual GAM reports both to the global account organization and to a country head within a geographic region. Depending on political and practical issues, reporting relationships to global and geographic managers may be any combination of solid or dotted.
- *Separate organizational structure for global accounts:* Other companies separate out global accounts from the traditional geographic structure and form dedicated organizations for global customers. These organizations may be more powerful than the matrix structure. A higher-level executive is more likely to be directly responsible for global account performance, and revenue and profit data are more easily separated out.

In general, we view grafting global accounts onto an existing organizational structure as a lower commitment approach. Certainly, it is a less expensive and less dislocating option than developing a new organization focused expressly on global accounts. Nevertheless, along with lower expense comes the problem of managing within the matrix. This takes enormous skill, and the inherent ambiguities may lead to less than optimal support for global customers.

Element four: Human resources and reporting relationships

Human resource choices, particularly the quality level and experience of GAMs are a critical element of scope. If your GAMs are relatively junior employees and correspondingly report at a low organizational level, you are severely limiting the scope of your global account program. By contrast, if GAMs are senior executives reporting at a high organizational level, we can say the global account program is "highly scoped." Of course, the two factors, employee experience and reporting level, are not independent. A low-reporting level for the GAM is unlikely to attract high potential applicants. Conversely, a high-reporting level may attract your organizational superstars.

As we write, a relatively new trend is emerging. Some firms are appointing senior-level executives to serve as GAMs and are elevating the reporting structure—not for all global accounts, but for the core set of global accounts that is especially critical for the firm. These firms really seem to *get it*. They truly understand that their major customers are critical firm assets and should be treated as such. Hence, they are investing their highest-quality human resources in these relationships.

> For many years, IBM's GAMs were experienced client managers with sales responsibility at IBM's largest accounts—but they were not senior executives. In 2001, IBM made a significant shift for its top 40 (ultimately around 60) global accounts. Client responsibility is now filled from the senior executive cadre. Previously, GAMs reported to regional or country sales managers. These new senior executives reported significantly higher—to Global Industry General Managers. As noted, IBM has backed off this reporting structure in Europe, but is reevaluating the reporting relationships as we go to print.

Ratcheting up the GAM position gives your firm greater influence on the customer. Correspondingly, the GAM has greater leverage within your firm and the influence to get things done. By placing client-relationship responsibility in the hands of senior executives and elevating the reporting structure, many internal issues that GAMs traditionally face are defused. Re-engineering the global account position for your most important customers sends a clear and powerful message both to your customers and to your various internal units and functional areas. This initiative may be highly effective in shifting the entire organization toward a more external orientation.

Of course, this version of managing global accounts is not without its issues. Creating a pool of high-level executives who agree to go into (back into) the field can be challenging. Reluctant executives, shortage of global skills, and traditional resistance to change combine to create potential "show stoppers."

Element five: Empowering global account managers

Empowering GAMs by delegating authority is crucial to the scope of your global account program. Many companies pay lip service to this issue. Many GAMs hear the *pep talk* designed to sell them on their new positions of power—unfortunately, most are not given sufficient authority to be fully effective. This discrepancy between *expectations* and *actual* can absolutely kill your program's effectiveness. When expectations are set for GAMs to go forward and conquer the world, but they lack the adequate authority to do their jobs appropriately, they become very disappointed and disillusioned. They come to resent the *bill of goods* the company sold them.

You should delegate the type and amount of authority based on several factors. These include the importance of the individual global account, the reporting level of the GAM, and corporate policy on price setting and committing firm resources. In addition, consider how much legal involvement is necessary to formulate global deals, and the power of executives who are delegating.

> At Machine Co., a corporate executive delegated pricing authority to GAMs, but did not have the authority to do so. Individual countries claimed they had the last word and that corporate pricing had no power to change their decisions. It was very confusing to figure out who had pricing authority. GAMs lost credibility and their relationships with country organizations suffered. To resolve the confusion, a special pricing unit with proper authority was formed. GAMs used this group to price global deals.

So, what level of authority should you give? Here are a few simple rules to keep you out of trouble but, in the end, delegation of authority must be based on your firm's unique circumstances.

- Give GAMs broad authority to decide human resource issues. Hiring and firing their own team members is very important to GAMs and crucial to their success. Because employee laws vary widely among countries, GAMs should be linked into human resource organizations in relevant countries. Of course, an employee removed from the global account team may simply be reassigned elsewhere in the local organization.
- GAMs should allocate resources to remote territories, and should be held responsible for the results.
- GAMs should have the authority to set performance targets for all team members. We have seen many arguments and debates over how to measure and reward performance, and who should be measured and rewarded. Authority should reside with the GAM but the corporate compensation team must advise. As we noted earlier, a U. S. $3,000 bonus may seem relatively small in the U. S., but is substantial in other countries. The compensation team advises on the appropriate levels of reward, but the GAM should retain authority to decide to whom, when, and where the bonus should be given.
- GAMs should have budget and spending authority to support their customers.
- In general, decisions involving pricing, legal issues, service-related matters, and product availability should not be delegated to the GAM.

You should think seriously about forming an international support team of *pricers*, global service experts, and legal advisors to help the GAM structure and close global deals, and prepare global contracts.

Element six: Funding and the global account program

Funding for the global account program plays a significant role in defining its scope. Funding can be a problem under any organizational model, but especially so when the global account program is grafted onto an existing geographic structure. When operating units take on additional global responsibilities, they need additional funding. If budgets are treated as business-as-usual, it is as though the firm gives weapons to the GAMs, but not any ammunition.

Here is the essential problem. Traditional financial staff tend to be neither visionary nor strategic thinkers. They often fulfill their role as *guardians of the bottom line* by keeping a lid on expenses. But GAMs (and their teams and support personnel) must incur expenses to do their jobs. They need to visit customers around the world, conduct global team meetings, hold global account planning sessions, make international conference calls, and on and on.

If budgets for global accounts are based on similar assumptions as for their domestic counterparts, the global account program will be seriously under-funded. GAMs and their teams will be constantly challenged to defend their "exciting" international travel. The message will be very clear— spending is bad for their careers. They will stop making important investments in building global customer relationships!

A common manifestation of this problem is the following. The firm gives the GAM authority to make remote coverage decisions. When she tries to exercise her authority, funding is a major roadblock. Local management may say: "I can't assign a full-time sales representative to this account—I don't know about the rest of the world, but the revenue generated in my country just isn't sufficient to justify it." Negotiations to secure sufficient funding can take months or even years to resolve.

Funding for global teams should be separate and apart from traditional budgets. The firm should view these expenditures as investments and track them against firm performance with global accounts. We have observed several successful funding methods:

- Provide a global fund from which GAMs can draw.
- Separate budgets for global accounts from geographic-region and country budgets. For example, take the expenses for German-based global accounts out of the German budget.

- Pay all GAM expenses centrally. Charge back each country commensurate with the percent of the total global account revenues generated in that country.
- Delegate travel and investment requests to an international support team. GAMs make travel requests to the support team.
- Relate funding to specific global opportunities. The firm holds GAMs accountable for closing those opportunities.

Many funding options are possible but one fact is indisputable. Restricted funding will restrict the scope of your global account program.

Scoping Your Global Account Program—Total Company or Sub-unit

The organizational positioning of your global account program is a critical decision. Should this be at the corporate level or in one or more of the businesses? The decision depends on the firm's customers. If the firm is highly diversified in products/services and there is no synergy among business units, then separate programs located in various businesses may be justified. For example, Siemens Information Technology group focuses on a different customer set to the Siemens Rail Automation and Electrification group. As a result, Siemens has global account programs in each of these business units.

By contrast, if customers for the firm's various products and services have considerable overlap, a single corporate-level global account program may be appropriate. Indeed, forming separate product-focused global account programs may be counterproductive.

IBM (and HP) serves many different industries, but has a similar customer set for each of its business units. By the mid-1990s, IBM had a well-established corporate program. At that time, IBM's Personal computer (PC) Division formed its own global account program. Later, IBM Services planned a similar program, separate from the corporate program for software and hardware. The PC program created significant sales force confusion—customers that secured global account status for the PC division did not have global account status in the corporate program, and vice versa. And, the Service Program did not get off the ground.

We do not recommend these types of structure. They create confusion both internally and externally, cause inefficiencies, and increase program costs. Internally, they divide executive support and individual units will not honor each other's programs. Ultimately, these programs fail.

Another illustration concerns single-industry firms. For example, P&G customers are such retail outlets as Wal-Mart, Carrefour, and Target. P&G's global program covers 10 customers accounting for a highly significant portion of their revenues. It would make little sense for individual product category organizations, for example laundry and dish care, to have individual global account programs.

Not all business-unit separation is as cut and dry as these examples. For example, at one major specialty chemicals firm, the relatively young global account program comprises around 30 global accounts, each assigned to one of four business areas. For 25 accounts, the firm earns over 95 percent of revenues from a single business area, and GAMs are dedicated to a "home" business area. But, for five accounts, revenues are distributed among the four business areas. The supplier struggles with whether to broaden the responsibilities of these GAMs to additional business areas, or to introduce a corporate program. In the latter case, a corporate GAM would manage these five accounts. Regardless, the decision has significant implications for breaking down the current "silo" mentality among business units, and hence the skill requirements for the GAM. It also affects the GAM's job, reporting relationships, and measurement and control systems.

The bottom line is that a global account program may start life in a business unit, and then transition to a corporate program as its value is demonstrated to the firm and to customers that purchase from multiple business units. Indeed, for some companies, it may take significant analysis and deep understanding of customer decision-making to determine whether or not a single program can deliver synergies. Ultimately, customer sets and customer decision-making processes drive the corporate versus business-unit decision. Even when separate business-unit global programs are chosen, some level of corporate coordination is better than having each unit go its own way. Experience has taught us that there are enough common issues across business units that central responsibility and best-practice sharing can avoid repeating mistakes in multiple business units.

Implications of Different Levels of Global Account Program Scope

We now present two scenarios as one way to gain insight into the impact of global account program scope on the firm's relationship with its global accounts:

- *Scenario 1:* Your firm has many global accounts. You expend significant resources on the program overall, but resource commitments to individual accounts is not high. Your global account organization is grafted onto a conventional geographic-region structure.

Because of interplay between separate line organizations, responding to global customers generates significant internal conflict. Objectives of the product/brand organizations conflict with the geographic organization. Further, because country managers report on a strictly geographic basis, global account teams are insufficiently funded for seeking out global opportunities. In addition, you have no mechanism for quoting global prices in a timely manner. Several competitors are challenging your firm's market leadership position. They are making inroads on critical strategic accounts by being more responsive to customers' global needs.

In this scenario, your major problems are internal. A well-designed global account program can address these issues and make you more responsive to the needs of global customers. Unfortunately, the required resources have not been committed and your organizational arrangements are dysfunctional. What should you do?

A major announcement you are going to be more responsive globally would probably be a mistake. Indeed, it may trigger a global-price discussion. Because you do not have appropriate internal mechanisms to offer a global price, you really do not want this discussion. You are losing on responsiveness not on price, nor on a lack of product/service offerings. You should totally re-evaluate how you are addressing your major global accounts.

- *Scenario 2:* You enjoy respectable market share and are a leader in supporting your global accounts. You allocate significant resources to the global account program and to individual global accounts. Your line organization has shifted from a geographic basis to be more globally responsive. Internal barriers are creating some productivity problems for your global teams, but these do not seem to affect your clients. Recently your competitors have been making promises to some important global clients. If these clients were to increase business with your competitors globally, they would receive global price discounts and additional services not available to other customers.

In this case, you may need to include enhanced offerings and benefits in your global account program. Value creation is another subject, but clever alignment of service support, pricing, and global terms and conditions can improve the benefits customers receive from your global account program.

Design as a matter of balance

Designing an effective global account program means achieving a balance between *ambition* and respect for the *status quo*. If your program design is too conservative, you will not accomplish your marketplace goals. If your design is too ambitious, you may never gain the internal agreements to put it in place. The key is to spend considerable time and effort on *balancing* your program. You can make enhancements after program launch. If your program is incorrectly scoped, you will spend too much time and effort defending the program from insiders and trying to keep it on track.

Implementing the Scope of Global Account Management

Deciding the appropriate scope of your global account program is one thing, making it happen is another. Wherever you start, the journey to implement your chosen global account program design is a significant business transformation. Before starting on your journey, you have to make sure that *you can get there from here.*

Business Transformation is holistic, purposeful, and managed change from your current business design and operating model. You are seeking a new design and operating model that is more effective, more efficient, and more adaptable. When you decide the appropriate scope for your global account program, you must include a change management component. If you merely attempt to develop your global account program as just one more initiative to be managed in a traditional way, you will probably fail.

Implementing an effective global account program will alter the current *regime* in your firm. The authority of important people will be changed. Some will find their roles enhanced but perhaps even more will find their roles diminished. The new program may threaten corporate heroes and people will be displaced.

Traditionally in IBM, one of the more coveted positions was country manager. These executives were *kings* in their countries—cabinet ministers returned their telephone calls. When IBM shifted global operations from a geographic structure to one based on industry, the country manager role was significantly downgraded. These positions no longer had budgets for global accounts and managers operated in more of a public relations (PR) role. There was considerable angst among this group and many left the company.

When Deloitte and Touche (D&T) began its global account program, senior partners found their roles had to change. Traditionally, D&T partners spent about half their time on client service work. Over a three-year period, some senior partners transitioned into dedicated relationship-development managers. Others focused entirely on client service responsibilities. For the former group, shedding client service work for their new roles was a major challenge.

As your firm becomes more customer-focused, traditional organizational processes may have to be discarded. The firm must develop new processes and may undergo a dramatic transformation in the way business is conducted. Rules that are part of your corporate culture may change and you will have to apply business methods across previously uncrossed cultural boundaries. For example, if your geographic structure is discarded, some local representative in a far-off country now has to take direction from a distant manager. Based in a foreign country, this new boss may neither speak the local language nor deeply understand the local culture. Many people may be confused and angry. The problems you may encounter trying to implement change on both a national and an international basis can be very daunting. Fortunately, a consulting industry has emerged to help companies through such transformations.

Deal and Kennedy put the issue quite succinctly: "Change always threatens a culture. People form strong attachments to heroes, legends, the rituals of daily life, the hoopla of extravaganzas and ceremonies—all the symbols and settings of the work place. Change strips down these relationships and leaves employees confused, insecure and often angry."[4]

Many difficult issues in transforming organizations cannot be avoided, but the worst side effects can be managed. If you treat introduction (or enhancement) of your global account program as a significant business transformation, you can ensure that senior managers give it appropriate attention. They will also likely be sensitive to the impact of the change.

How to Transform Your Global Account Program to a Different Scope

We have spelled out many factors relating to the scope of the global account program. You may be thinking that figuring out the right scope for you, then implementing on that scope, is a daunting task. Very true! Putting a

---

[4] Terrence Deal and Allen A. Kennedy, *Corporate Cultures: The Rites and Rituals of Corporate Life*, Reading, MA: Addison-Wesley, 1982.

global account program in place is very difficult. But, by thoughtfully approaching program development, you can build a new program based on what is currently in place. Without delving any more deeply into *change management*, some approaches we have seen used effectively are:

- *Establish an oversight or steering committee:* All functions likely to be affected by the change should be represented on the committee for the new global account program. These functions should include, at a minimum, finance, pricing, sales management, information technology, human resources, compensation, country management, and product divisions. An early task for the steering committee is to add other functions its members think are necessary, for example international legal expertise. A large committee slows down the planning process but pays significant dividends at execution time.
- *Appoint an executive review team:* This body provides strategic thinking and may help resolve issues when the steering committee gets stuck.
- *Test the proposed design:* Test the proposed design on senior executives with global customer responsibility. These experienced executives will be quick to tell the committee that some approaches may be *pipe dreams*, and alert the committee when important issues have not been addressed.

Announcing your global account program

So, now you have defined your global account program scope and are ready to implement. You are ready to tackle whatever problems you may encounter. Should you proceed with a full-scale announcement of your new program? Or, should you gradually and informally invite customers to join the program? To put it more bluntly, should you broadly publicize the existence of your global account program, or should you let it be known only within your organization?

Many companies we have studied chose not to announce their global account programs. Sometimes not even to customers in the program! They worry about the consequences such an announcement may have on price negotiations. They fear their customer's first reaction would be: "What do I get for being a global account, global discounts?" Reduced price may be a significant program benefit for a global account. More likely, you have other benefits in mind.

Other companies decide to make major announcements regarding their global account programs. They include tangible benefits such as reduced prices and/or special terms and conditions in their contracts. If you develop your global account program to rival a competitor's program, you may gain some competitive advantage by formally launching the program and "spreading the word." The flipside is that a formal launch can be an invitation for criticism and a PR problem if your program encounters unforeseen difficulties. A test-phase offers protection against such problems.

How Does Scope Affect the Firm and its Global Accounts

In this chapter, we spent significant space on the scope of your global account program. A reasonable question you may have is—so what? When we get down to the bare essentials, what is the big deal about scope? How does scope affect the firm and its global customers? Why should the firm want a broadly scoped global program versus one that is more narrowly scoped? And what about the firm's customers—should they care whether the program is broadly or narrowly scoped?

Broad versus narrow scope: The firm's perspective

The firm needs a broadly scoped program to achieve meaningful competitive advantage. Such a program touches more customers and offers greater benefits/value. A broadly scoped program provides a greater variety of vehicles by which to "delight the customer," add value to the relationship, and differentiate the firm from competitors. This capability makes it easier for the GAM to execute (more arrows in the quiver), and customize her responses to the customer. Broader scope also gets more individuals and functions involved with global accounts. Greater participation improves the program, creates a learning environment, raises morale, and increases the volume of innovative solutions offered to solve customer problems. When customers recognize you are delivering value, your chances of jointly developing new opportunities, gaining wallet share, and improving margins are considerably enhanced. The bottom line is that broader scope delivers greater opportunity for improved client satisfaction, stronger revenue/profit growth, and higher probability of achieving partnership status.

Broad versus narrow scope: The account's perspective

A broadly scoped program offers more customer benefits. Among these benefits are access to your senior management, special contracts, enhanced information system options, higher caliber account managers and account teams, greater likelihood of customized products, and customer council representation. What customer would not enjoy a greater spectrum of available "perks" for being a part of their supplier's global account program. The broader the scope the better the chance that the supplier's approach will surface a "perfect fit" for a particular customer need. Narrow scope limits these benefits, options and possible solutions to customer's problems.

Key Messages

- Global account program scope is a critical design variable comprising multiple dimensions.

- The scope of the global account program embraces critical decisions around numbers of customers and percent of revenues, the nature of supplier/customer relationships, designing the line organization, human resources and reporting relationships, empowering GAMs and funding.

- Global account programs may be designed with different levels of breadth and depth. They may also be located at the business-unit level and/or at corporate.

- Organizational transformation to global account management is a difficult process that must be managed carefully.

CHAPTER 4

PROLOGUE

On the plane

Todd was anxious to get *Constance*'s perspective on securing commitment *from senior managers. As a global account manager, he knew this was a difficult task. He would have to influence several layers of management and the possibility of stepping on someone's toes was very high. He secured a seat across the aisle from her:* "So, **Constance**, how did the global account program get so solidly on your agenda?"

*Constance didn't want to tell **Todd** she'd been ducking her key global account executive. She was increasingly realizing the importance of her involvement and wanted to give **Todd** some worthwhile input. She also wanted to take this opportunity to get a global account manager's perspective on senior management.* "Well, **Todd**, direct contact with key customers really got my attention. They told me we weren't doing the best job globally. They said my competitors had better-functioning global programs. That got my attention."

Todd enquired, "I've been trying to get senior executives to visit my global account, but they always seem too busy. Can't seem to get on their calendar. Any tips on how to get them interested?"

*Constance thought before responding. She wondered if her global account managers were getting the executive attention they needed. She thought, I really need to get Jack on the phone when I get to New York. Then, to **Todd**,* "**Todd**, do your managers think managing global accounts is important? Maybe they can help get you to senior executives."

"It's chicken and egg," said **Todd**. "My management isn't interested because executive management isn't interested. Nobody is willing to take the argument up the hill. Executive management isn't concerned because my management isn't raising the issue. Sometimes I think I should get in their face by creating a customer situation—maybe that would get their attention."

*This discussion began to hit home for **Constance**. Her global account managers were directly responsible for millions of dollars of revenues. She hadn't realized how difficult it could be for a global account manager to get senior management's attention. Here was an articulate global account manager, seemingly doing a good job, but unable to get his voice heard. She* *thought to herself, Maybe I should get Jack to form a representative group of global account managers as an advisory board. Jack does a great job, but with so much revenue on the line, I can't afford not to be involved.*

*How to help **Todd**? "Look **Todd**, I think your CEO and executive management would be very interested in your views on the global customer. I think you should put your concerns into a presentation and start working it up the line. 'We've done a pretty good job but I know we can do better.' I'm convinced that without your CEO or someone at the top driving global account management you'll come nowhere near to fulfilling the promise. Creating a customer issue may get their attention, but they may also look for a new global account manager!"*

***Todd** considered **Constance**'s advice. Maybe she could help him get the right issues into a presentation. But **Todd** wasn't sure what burning issues would get senior executive attention.*

Senior management commitment is critical to the success of your global account program—lack of commitment may spell failure. Senior management commitment sets the stage for developing a global account program that can have a major impact on your firm's fortunes. If you do not secure this commitment, it is unlikely that you will be able to develop a successful broadly scoped program. In this chapter, we discuss several forms of senior management commitment, and the various roles senior management may play in a global account program. Of course, since global accounts are the firm's most important customers, not only does senior management commitment enhance the global account program, feedback from global accounts may impact the firm's corporate strategy.

Senior Management Commitment: What Does it Mean and How Does it Work?

The belief that senior management commitment is instrumental to the success of any serious organization-wide initiative is not new breakthrough thinking. Any savvy project or program leader has committed senior executive support at the top of his wish list. In most cases, the *bosses* programs get attention and take priority. So why do we think it is so important to take time to explain to you senior management's involvement and commitment for global account management? Quite simply, we believe it is a deal breaker. Senior management commitment is *the* critical ingredient in a successful global account program. We do not recommend any attempt to implement a global account program of any significance without solid support from your firm's senior executives. In this chapter, we show why this should be your number one priority. We also clarify the difference between global account programs and domestic key account programs.

The global account management model must contend with business complexities that are more difficult by orders of magnitude than those facing national account management. The firm must overcome territorialism at both the country and the geographic-region levels. Significant management issues cross product (brand) and divisional boundaries. Solutions to clashes among individual national cultures must be hammered out and well-entrenched corporate cultures changed.

As the firm moves toward globalization and takes on a variety of globalizing initiatives, some part of the organization must consider global customers and act as their voice in corporate decision-making. And, the firm must identify gaps between the needs of global customers and the ability of the firm's global infrastructure to focus on these needs—and deliver gap-closing solutions. Quite simply, the only way to successfully grapple with these complexities, issues, conflicts, and problems is with deep personal involvement from your senior executives.

We should be clear that senior executive contact with the customer is not unambiguously positive. Some CEOs take the view that they have account managers to take care of customers, and that their customer contact can be idiosyncratic and not subject to any particular process. Consider the situation we found in several global suppliers. The CEO meets with the global customer CEO on an infrequent basis. The CEO is never briefed by the GAM or any other senior executive, and never debriefs either. The potential for undermining his own GAM's efforts is quite significant.

When we mean support from the top, we do not mean making a few customer calls—we mean deep involvement. Consider Marriott International; J.W. (Bill) Mariott, CEO of Marriott Corporation, is the partnership executive (PE) for major global customer, Accenture. Once a quarter, Mr. Marriott meets for an hour with the GAM on the Accenture account to review the situation and think through strategy. Larry Ellison, CEO of Oracle, says, "I am Oracle's point person for GE—I spend an awful lot of time at GE management meetings."[1]

---

[1] "A Bad Boy and His Business Grow Up," *Fortune*, July 25, 2005.

Overall, our research has shown that firms with successful global account programs have garnered support directly from the "top."

Then incoming HP CEO, Carly Fiorina, declared that a restructuring of the company's global account program was a priority almost immediately after her appointment. She quickly diagnosed difficulties in the reporting structure due to clashes between product-oriented and geographic-oriented units. She gave full support to a program overhaul that has continued to evolve.

Henri Lachmann, Chairman and CEO of Schneider Electric, identified further development of Schneider's global account program as a top priority. He affirmed Schneider was willing to accept more risk to service global accounts than national or local accounts.

What Roles should Senior Management Play?

In the global account management model, senior management must play several different but related roles. A large enterprise may choose a different individual in each role. In smaller enterprises, a single individual may play multiple roles. Cost, talent, urgency, and size are considerations for how your organization chooses to staff these roles.

Senior executive champion

The senior executive champion provides leadership from the top. Ideally, the CEO or COO should play this role—it could also be the senior sales executive. This person communicates the global account program's importance to the entire senior management group—she also ensures it has high visibility throughout the firm. The senior executive champion provides strategic thought leadership to global account program owners (see below), incorporating the developing strategic vision for the corporation as a whole. The champion provides direction to the operating units supporting global accounts, and is the source of the program's authority. During his tenure at IBM, Lou Gerstner played this role; Sam Palmisano has inherited this position.

Executive sponsor

The executive sponsor is deeply involved in the global account program. The program's success has a major impact on his personal success. The sponsor ensures the program is on track and provides direct support to the executive owner (see next role). There may be significant value in appointing the executive sponsor from outside the company headquarters country. For example, a U.S.-based firm may assign the key European sales executive to be the executive sponsor. Such an appointment overcomes some of the almost inevitable resistance from personnel based outside the firm's home country.

Executive owner

The executive owner manages day-to-day global account program operations. He is directly responsible for the global account program's success or failure. Specific role responsibilities are numerous. They include:

- Developing the global program's vision, overarching strategy, and operating principles
- Branding the global account program within the firm as a way of securing organizational buy-in
- Tracking milestone progress
- Reporting on measurements that determine program success or failure.

The executive owner resolves program issues and provides day-to-day support to client teams. If the global program exists in a business unit, the executive owner manages the relationship with global programs in other business units. The executive owner's critical responsibility is to present a cohesive global program to the firm's customers. Depending on firm size, desired program scope, and funding level, the executive owner may act alone or with a team. Beginning, January 2004, for the first time, the Executive Owner of Xerox's Global Account Program began reporting to CEO Anne Mulachy.

Executive steering committee

This group provides additional leadership to, and involvement in, the global account program. Executives who manage geographic regions, critical individual countries, product/brands, and key operating divisions typically constitute committee membership. The steering committee is a powerful method for involving a broader executive team in the global account program, providing support to the executive owner and resolving top-level conflicts. The executive sponsor should chair this committee.

Partnership executive

The roles just discussed operate at the level of the overall global account program. The PE is directly involved at the individual global account. The PE's job is to facilitate long-term, supplier-to-customer, executive-to-executive relationships. Some firms insist that the global account also appoint a PE to deal with its supplier. For a specific global account, the PE can be any company executive who provides value-added services to the GAM. This role focuses on relationship building, including developing alliances and partnerships, and helping to resolve tough global customer issues. Linking corporate executives to global accounts is critically important in gaining customer mind share and ensuring executive buy-in to critical program principles. Although the PE is a senior manager in the firm with multiple responsibilities, in this role they "work for" the GAM.

Examples of Senior Executive Involvement in Global Account Programs

IBM: As discussed in Chapter 3, at IBM, the global account program has been through much iteration. In the early 2000s, the global account *Senior Executive Sponsor* was the Corporate Senior Vice President of Sales—all sales executives in IBM worldwide reported to this executive. He communicated broadly about the global account program, set the rules of engagement, and provided guidance to other IBM executives. He also chaired the *Sales Executive Committee*, which met regularly to discuss and set direction for sales program and productivity issues. The global account program was on this committee's agenda.

At this time, IBM organized its global account program by industry— IBM had several *Executive Sponsors*, one per industry. For each industry, sales executives worldwide reported to this person. Each industry also had an *executive owner* who developed and ran the global account program for that industry—this person had overall program and day-to-day operating responsibilities.

A dramatic example of the PE's importance occurred at Xerox in 2001.

Xerox: Xerox was experiencing severe cash flow problems, and— media speculation was fueling concerns about potential bankruptcy. Customers postponed orders, delayed contract renewals, and had many questions for account managers. Frequently, assurances from GAMs were insufficient to calm customer concerns. To address this problem, Xerox's financial staff developed a briefing document outlining "Operation Turnaround," together with answers to frequently asked questions. This material was provided to all GAMs and their Focused Executives (PE in Xerox's terminology). These two-person teams visited

Xerox's important global customers, dramatically reduced their concerns, and earned highly positive responses for "keeping customers informed." The "Xerox Focus 500 initiative" expanded this program to Xerox's top 500 customers worldwide, and achieved similar results.

Global account manager

The GAM has the day-to-day responsibility for managing the global account. The PE supports the GAM by shifting some account responsibility to a senior corporate executive. As we noted in Chapter 3, IBM has appointed senior executives as GAMs for its top 60 accounts. If relatively few global accounts bring in a high percent of firm revenues and profits, perhaps they are important enough to be worth continuous senior management attention. Even so, IBM's "super" GAMs also have PEs.

> Consider a firm with $25 billion in revenues and a profit/sales ratio of 10 percent—annual profits equal $2.5 billion. Assume the firm's largest customer is responsible for five percent of the firm's sales and profits—$1.25 billion and $125 million, respectively. If the firm's cost of capital is 10 percent, lifetime customer value is $1.25 billion (assuming no growth). Perhaps it is worth allocating a senior executive to the account!

Deep involvement of key senior executives as stakeholders in developing and managing the global account program vastly increases the likelihood of success. These stakeholders provide critical resources and important information, and help resolve conflicts. Further, critical expertise on global business resides in the organizational units that these people direct. Of course, other than the *Executive Owner*, all these executives have a myriad of other responsibilities. Involving them directly in the global account program does not assure enthusiastic support—in some cases, for example with geographic executives, it surfaces simmering conflicts. Nonetheless, participation of your senior executives in these identified roles will leverage your global account program to a stronger position.

How Does Senior Management Develop and Sustain the Global Account Program?

Maybe we have not yet convinced you of the importance of securing senior management commitment. To bolster our position, we now identify the types of value created by securing senior management commitment in developing and sustaining the global account program.

Elevating the global account program's stature

Overt backing and regular supportive communication from the firm's most senior executives (preferably the CEO) demonstrates the global account program's importance to the firm, and places it above initiatives sponsored at lower executive levels. Senior executives may have forgotten how things work in the trenches and not understand the way people react to power. They may take some convincing, but you need support from executives with significant organizational stature for your global account program to be truly effective. For example, Citibank shows senior executive support by awarding an annual prize to its best global team. Industry heads nominate teams, and a senior executive committee makes the final decision.

Reinforcing authority of the organization or person who is driving the program

The executive owner is responsible for driving the global account program. A global account program that is one among many programs may not stand out. However, if the authority of, and overt support for, the executive owner comes from the very top of the organization, it increases her effectiveness.

Demonstrating company support to your global account manager

The GAM's job is exceptionally complex—according to one study, the second most complex after the CEO. Further, GAMs are typically responsible for a significant portion of current and/or potential firm revenues and profits. Managers with these pressures should feel they are members of a select group. Supported by, and regularly communicating with, senior executives, GAMs have the confidence and reassurance that the firm will backup their decisions.

Reducing resistance to change that all organizational transformations must address

How many times have you been in a meeting and heard "Does the CEO support this?" or "This area is my responsibility, not yours!"—or how about "Why don't we set up a meeting next month to discuss this matter?" Resistance to organizational change is normal and often healthy for surfacing issues and sharpening discussion. Senior management involvement can help to manage the normal resistance and like behaviors, and lessen their impact.

Reducing the time and effort to implement the global account program

A program closely associated with a senior executive will almost certainly run more efficiently than one with no such association. Employees are apt to become very cooperative when they learn a high-level executive is shepherding the global account program. The official approval that senior executives bring typically clears away time-consuming roadblocks.

What Specific Benefits Does Senior Management Commitment Deliver?

The benefits associated with senior management commitment can be classified into two types: benefits to the firm at the global account (external), and benefits to the organization as a whole (internal).

External benefits

These benefits are difficult to quantify. They are essentially perceptual benefits related to the impact of senior executive commitment on key actors in the global account arena.

The customer's perceived reputation with your company is enhanced

For most firms, pronouncements made by their key supplier's senior executives are of great interest. Customers know that a key supplier's actions can have significant impact on their business. Suppose senior supplier management speaks publicly about its global account program. It also identifies the customer as one of few organizations accorded global account status. In all likelihood, top customer managers will believe they are important global partners.

It strengthens the global account manager's reputation

When senior management speaks out publicly about the global account program's importance, the GAM secures new stature in his customer's eyes. Simply put, the customer's key contact with the supplier, the GAM, is associated with a program personally endorsed by the supplier's senior management.

Of course, these external benefits depend on public announcements about the global account program and on company policy for notifying customers about their membership. As we noted earlier, many firms we studied chose not to announce their global account program; and, in some cases, they did not even inform customers of their global account status. In such cases, these specific potential benefits tend not to be realized. (Of course, the firm could assign a PE without telling the customer about the global account program, but these initiatives typically occur in tandem.)

Internal benefits

Internal focus is a major element of most global account programs. This apparent paradox arises because long-standing management structures and internal processes create most of the difficult issues that GAMs face. In many cases, the in-place structures and processes that drive company decision-making were originally introduced to address very different environments. Almost certainly, they had little regard for managing global customers. When senior management is deeply involved in the global account program, it understands these conflicts at a deep level and can make appropriate changes happen.

The global account program influences corporate strategy

A global account program can have a significant influence on other elements of the firm's strategy. For example, one goal of the global program is for the firm to move closer to its customers and become more responsive to their needs. This process inevitably influences the firm's product/market scope. A successful global account program delivers market intelligence that would have been uncollected or overlooked in the program's absence—this will likely lead to strategic changes.

Global strategy becomes a marketing priority

In many firms, marketing plans are developed relatively independently of sales force input. There are many reasons for this state of affairs, but one in particular is crucial—no single customer is responsible for a significant share of firm revenues. By raising a limited number of customers to global account status, these significant customers must be integrated into the marketing planning process. Senior management commitment to the global account program ensures this occurs.

Senior management moves closer to the customer

Even the most dyed-in-the-wool senior operations executive cannot fail to realize that customers are critical firm assets. Global accounts are first among equals. The *PE* role ensures that senior executives, from multiple functions, engage directly with global customers. The corporation's entire senior management cadre, and hence the organization, is thus closer to the market. PEs are one more voice inside the company communicating customer requirements. They add a layer of credibility to the *Executive Owner's* message on customer serving global customers.

Increased senior management involvement in performance reviews

This benefit represents the other side to senior management commitment and the resources accompanying that commitment. Senior management is highly interested in the return for its investment in the global program. It will also want to know how specific global clients are performing. Indeed, all business-unit reviews should include a section on global account performance. This is an important step for gaining internal global account program support.

Suppose We Do Not Gain Senior Management Commitment for a Global Account Program— What Are the Consequences?

What happens if senior management cannot, or will not, commit to a global account program? Because you fail to gain senior management commitment, what happens if you choose not to implement global account management? What is the worst that could happen? Well, the worst that could happen is very serious: Your firm may become less competitive and start to lose global business.

Lack of a global offering

Increasingly, your customers compete in many countries around the world. They want to rationalize procurement and require seamless global support. In Chapter 1, we showed how a PR firm was decimated because it could not offer global coverage. This pattern is occurring in many service industries. Without direction and support from the top, territorialism can take over and fracture the enterprise into competitive groups.

> In the mid-1990s, ABB launched two initiatives aimed at developing global account programs. Both were unsuccessful, essentially, because they did not have top-level support. In 1998, incoming CEO Goran Lindahl asked the former president of ABB Germany to lead a taskforce to implement a global account system.[2]

---

[2] Julian Birkinshaw, "Global Account Management: New Structures, New Tasks," *Mastering Management Online, The Financial Times,* August 2001.

Van Leer Packaging supplies steel drums to the oil and chemical industry. In October 1995, Van Leer lost a major contract (in France) with the French oil company, Total. The major cause was the refusal of Van Leer's British subsidiary to offer price concessions for a Europe-wide agreement. Van Leer (Britain) had a close relationship with Total (UK)![3]

Here is the reality. Your products may do a fine job in your global customer's applications. However, increasingly, your competitors can match you on product benefits. Your customers want more than competent product performance on a multi-domestic basis. They want the benefit that comes from a supplier's global infrastructure and understanding. For example, Siemens' top management believes understanding individual national cultures is critically important for successful global account management. Siemens has developed a forum in which local contact managers from 80 countries meet with GAMs. They make presentations on culture, market strategies, and the appeal of Siemens' products.

Turf battles

Global customers want seamless global service. They also want answers in short order. Without a well-supported global program, internal company barriers make the firm less responsive to customer needs. For example, customers' globally driven procurement organizations increasingly require global pricing. We have seen instances when the response to a global request for price has taken several months. Securing responses from multiple countries and negotiating price concessions can be a daunting task. A significant consequence of not receiving senior executive commitment is the escalation of turf battles that consume precious time and other resources.

Budget battles

Failure to respond promptly to customer requests may make the firm lose business. A more insidious consequence of time-wasting internal disputes is the opportunity cost of not spending the time building customer relationships and loyalty. Bickering and battling over funding for every dollar, euro, and yen is a huge time sink for global account personnel. How often have your GAMs spent time trying to convince internal money managers that international travel to participate in global activities is different from leisure/vacation travel? (Maybe they should try traveling 18 hours without

---

[3] Van Leer Packaging "Worldwide: The Total Account, A, B, C, D, E," 598-(018-022)-1, Fontainebleau, France, INSEAD, 1996.

sleep across a dozen time zones for a 2-hour customer meeting—then turning right around to travel home and put in long hours executing the deal they just sold.) By contrast, a senior-executive-sponsored global account program budgets for such essentials as international travel, global account team meetings, and remote location coverage. And, moreover, the firm "buys itself out" of this opportunity cost.

Global escalation

Do some of your managers exhibit petty behaviors, if they do not have to face the customer or senior management? These behaviors may detract from customer satisfaction and continue for long periods if there is no clarity to the escalation process. Customer teams can find themselves in circular debates, unable to respond to customer requests. We have seen account teams squander months of customer response time trying to escalate global issues to the appropriate executive(s). Global issues are important and solutions must be approved at a high organizational level. Senior management involvement in the global program adds significant clarity in dealing with many issues in global account management.

In our experience, most escalated decision requests (90 percent or better) result in favorable decisions for the GAM. The significance of the problem is the time taken to fight internal battles. Not addressing this issue can result in the customer losing confidence in your ability to provide ongoing global solutions. Slow response to escalated decision requests damages your reputation and image as a global player/partner. A properly supported global account program can significantly reduce your firm's response time to escalated decisions.

Lost in the shuffle

Without senior management backing, your global program will be lost in the swirl of other "strategic" programs. Sustaining a global account program requires day-to-day emphasis and management. Senior executives can keep up the pressure and the global account program can become a catalyst to drive global innovations.

OK, I Am Sold! How Do I Go about Getting Commitment from My Firm's Senior Management?

Securing senior management commitment may be a complex task, or it could be simple. If there has been a global customer disaster, or if an incoming CEO is already sold on global account management, your global account program may get off the ground very quickly. If you do not have these conditions, then securing support will depend on a variety of factors such as organization structure, corporate culture, and bureaucratic processes. Other factors include the politics of reaching and convincing senior management.

Some of the successful techniques for enhancing global account management that we have observed include:

Customer councils

This organizational device is a good means for presenting the voice of your customers to senior executives. You assemble a core group of senior customer executives for open dialogue with your senior executives. Council members will communicate the urgency of satisfying their global needs to your senior management. These meetings should occur on a regular basis, for example bi-annually. They can be extremely valuable on multiple dimensions, including relationship building and helping to set your firm's R&D agenda. For example, Vodafone's global account program focuses on six segments—its Customer Advisory Council includes one account from each of the six segments. The organizational positions of regular attendees from Vodafone include the CEO, COO, and CMO.

Global account forums

These groups typically comprise several noncompeting companies. Senior executives involved in global account management meet on a periodic basis to discuss issues of common interest. These forums can be directed by company groups or may be held under the auspices of a major business school. For example, for several years, two of us (Potter and Schindler) have been instrumental in directing the Global Account Forum—ABB, ING, Dun and Bradstreet, Reuters America, P&G, DHL, and Xerox. At Columbia Business School, author Capon has hosted The Columbia Initiative in Global Account Management—3M, Citibank, Deloitte and Touche, HP, Lucent Technologies, MaerskSealand, Milliken & Co, Saatchi & Saatchi, SAP, and Square D/Schneider. Professors Christoph Senn of St. Gallen University (Switzerland) and George Yip of London Business School host similar forums.

These forums offer a place where members share information, best practices, and future challenges regarding their global account programs.

They provide anecdotal and market research data on global account management issues. Gaining senior management support is just one of many possible topics. Of course, senior executives sometimes attend as invited guests—they may be surprised at what they learn!

Associations

These organizations allow you to share and learn from the experience of others. For example, the Strategic Account Management Association (SAMA) <www.strategicaccounts.org> hosts an extensive library of information on national and global strategic account management programs. It also hosts an annual conference where many strategic and global account management issues are discussed. The Chief Sales Executive Forum <www.salesforums.com> is another organization where senior sales executives meet annually to discuss critical issues of the day, including managing global accounts.

This book

Finally, we believe this book presents a convincing argument for the critical role of senior executives in global account management programs. You might just send copies to your senior executives.

Skunk works

Maybe you have tried all of the above but senior managers are just too focused on other matters—they seem unable to pay attention to the needs of global customers. Do not *give up*, the globalization pressures we discussed in Chapter 1 are just too great and will ultimately impact on your firm, if they are not doing so already. Unless your company becomes responsive to customer requirements, these accounts will go elsewhere, and you will lose revenues and profits. In addition, you will never gain new global customers. If you are in this situation, then *work* the organization. Find like-minded managers across the company and do your best to be globally responsive. Without senior executive backing, this will be a tough challenge, and you may fail more often than you succeed. Nevertheless, when you do succeed, do not be bashful. Advertise the basis for your success and suggest how many more successes you could have if only senior management were on board!

Key Messages

- Senior executive commitment is critical for a successful global account program.

- Senior executives can play several related yet different roles in supporting the global account program.

- Senior executive involvement offers several benefits to global customers and to the firm.

- Lack of senior executive involvement can lead to significant negative consequences for the firm.

- There are a variety of approaches for gaining senior management support for a global account program.

CHAPTER 5

NOMINATING AND SELECTING THE "RIGHT"
GLOBAL ACCOUNTS

PROLOGUE

In the cab

George and *Jace* stood together in the taxi line. *George* said: "I'm glad our meetings are in the same neighborhood *Jace*, it gives me a chance to ask you a few more questions."

"Well *George*, you pay the cab fare and you can ask away." "It's a deal *Jace*, I'm hoping for heavy traffic!"

Once settled in the taxi, *George* steered the conversation to global account selection. "*Jace*, something that has bothered me since I took this assignment is inconsistency in the profiles of accounts in our global program. Is this the case with your clients?"

Jace didn't want to give away too much free consulting, but *George* had hit on one of her hot buttons. "*George*, all my clients seem to have difficulty with account selection but I've been able to set most of them on the right path. In the beginning, most firms think they can pick their most important global customers intuitively and just put them on the list. They end up with someone's idea of the perfect list, but it seldom leads to a successful program. A global account program should be a reflection of the firm's goals for building its global business. The process for nominating, selecting, and maintaining the global account base must be planned very thoughtfully. Typically, I advise clients to use a rather formal process for account nomination and selection—this tends to produce a pretty consistent account profile." *Jace* went on, "That doesn't mean that profiles are consistent across companies. From one client to another, criteria for program membership can be quite different."

Jace could see her comments had *George* concerned. She asked, "*George*, do you have a formal process and agreed set of selection criteria and that you apply consistently?"

"You know *Jace*," *George* replied, "you just confirmed my suspicions. We have a reasonable set of selection criteria but I think the problem is in execution. Somewhere along the line, politics seems to have polluted our process."

*"Polluted is a strong term **George**. Are you saying that politics alone caused your problem? In my experience there is never a single reason," **Jace** questioned.*

"You're right, it's probably not politics alone. I traced back the process on a couple of global accounts. It was obvious an 'executive decision' was made to accept them in the program rather than adhere to the criteria. I've also noticed some customers that don't fit in the program at all. They remain because no one seems to know how to remove them. Then, senior executives lobby me to add specific accounts—some of their reasons have little relationship to our global account program objectives. Any suggestions?"

***Jace** knew she couldn't solve this problem by the end of the cab ride. "**George**, I hate to seem like a consultant, but I think you need help putting together a formal process. I could do an initial assessment of your program and suggest some action steps. Give me a call next week and let's see what we can set up."*

Selecting the *right* customers is one of the most important factors for developing a successful global account program. Enthusiastic senior manager support and great GAMs can partially compensate for poor account selection, but never completely. Establishing and maintaining a global account program is always challenging. Focusing on the wrong accounts makes the process more difficult, more expensive, and less productive. A poorly selected global account roster will increase your costs, frustrate your people, fall short of business expectations, and most likely drive customer dissatisfaction. The global account program should include your most important current and potential customers. You must take the time and effort to choose the right accounts. Our purpose in this chapter is to help you do just that.

Some of the questions we shall try to answer in this chapter are:

- What are the consequences of getting global account selection *right* and getting it *wrong*?
- How should you nominate accounts for global account program membership?
- Who should be accountable for the integrity of the program selection and membership process?
- What criteria (customer characteristics) should you use to assess program nominees?
- What kind of selection process should you use and who should you involve?

- How many global accounts will your infrastructure support?
- How should you align account selection criteria with global account program objectives?
- How should you communicate information about your global account program—internally and externally?
- How should you monitor global accounts for suitability to remain in the program? When and how should you make decisions to de-select global accounts?

Global account selection should be ruthless.[1] The thrust of global account management is to allocate corporate resources for managing and developing the firm's most important current and potential global customers. There are two dangers. First, corporate resources should not be spent on accounts that are not in this category—to a large extent these resources are wasted. Second, if deserving customers are not receiving these resources, you are losing significant opportunities.

Global account program credibility largely depends on selecting the *right* customers. Suppose some of your global program accounts have the following characteristics. They:

- Cannot execute global strategies—for example, write global contracts
- Do not make decisions globally—for example, they do not select preferred global vendors, and
- Are unwilling to work intimately with you on global issues.

When you have accounts like these, your resource allocation is sub-optimal. These customers should not be in your global account program. Further, they provide internal critics with ammunition to undermine your global account management efforts.

Most firms err on the side of selecting too many accounts rather than too few. As a result, at launch, global account programs often include borderline customers. If this is your situation, perhaps you did not develop rigorous selection criteria or, if you did, you did not implement them consistently. Regardless, your resources and support capability are severely strained and your global account performance will be sub-optimal.

Nominating and selecting customers for the global account program are distinct activities. But, they share one common feature—each must be a formal process. For each process, you must develop a very strict set of

---

[1] One of us makes this same point for key accounts, Noel Capon, *Key Account Management and Planning*, The Free Press: New York, 2001.

filtering criteria. Further, formal processes require a set of organizational arrangements. Typically, a Program Office runs the day-to-day activities of managing global accounts. The Program Office is responsible for managing the nominating and selecting process—it sends recommendations to the Executive Sponsor or Executive Steering Committee. The office is typically small (two to six persons)—staffed by people with major account sales experience and/or significant international responsibilities. Other than the roles we describe in this chapter, the Program Office has many additional global program responsibilities. These include developing the GAM competencies profile, setting the training agenda, establishing compensation plan elements, setting financial targets, managing the annual meeting for all GAMs, managing customer council agendas, publishing best practices, auditing websites, updating all processes, procedures, and operating principles, benchmarking for continuous improvement, setting operational review schedules and format, and solving operational issues (Chapter 9).

Now you may be thinking, "What's the big deal? Certainly we know which customers are most important. And, if we overlook one, surely it will be quick to remind us!" If you had unlimited resources in general, and unlimited funds in particular, you could probably include all the important customers you do business with internationally. But, in reality, resources and funding are scarce and you cannot support a wide-open roster. If you include all your important customers in the global account program, many will be under-funded and customer service will deteriorate. The results will inevitably be unsatisfactory. We strongly believe you should carefully and rigorously select the portfolio of customers for your global account program.

Lack of a formal process exacerbates the problem. Once the global account program is announced and funding secured, organizational politics commences. Believe us—there will be more candidate customers than you have room for. The human dynamics of account management guarantees that field managers will want their accounts in the global program, regardless of whether they meet your criteria. Highly skilled field sales managers will always present a good case to support a particular customer's membership. However, you must adhere to the selection criteria you established— a single individual's agenda should not sway your decisions.

Later, when your global account program is successful, sales managers may flock to present accounts for membership. Membership creep will strain your process capability and diminish program effectiveness. We want to be very clear—a random, uncontrolled nominating, and selecting process will produce random, uncontrolled results. If you develop a solid set of selection criteria, the Program Office will minimize the time it has to spend defending its judgments.

Nominating Customers for the Global Account Program

We discuss the qualifications for nomination and the nomination process.

Qualifications for nomination

To be nominated for the global account program, candidate customers should qualify on three distinct screening criteria.

Globality

Many firms engaged in strategic/key account management seem to believe in an important hierarchy for individual accounts. In increasing importance, this hierarchy is regional accounts, national accounts, multi-national regional accounts and, finally, global accounts. Taking this perspective, the firm's most important customers should be placed in the global account program.

The problem with a global account program developed on the basis of this perspective is that it may contain important customers that are not global. At its most absurd, the important customer may operate in a single country. Slightly less absurd, the customer may operate in a few contiguous countries, for example Sweden, Finland, Norway, and Denmark, or Canada, the U.S., and Mexico. No such customers should be nominated for a global account program.

In an early iteration of BOC's (formerly British Oxygen Company) global account program, one account was British Steel. At the time, all British Steel's manufacturing operations (95 percent of revenues) were in Britain. Clearly, British Steel had no place in BOC's global account program. Xerox had a similar situation with Lloyds Bank. Lloyds Bank was in Xerox's global program, yet 95 percent of Lloyds' business was in Britain.

The message is simple and straightforward. Your global account program should be a subset of your strategic account program. British Steel was a very important strategic account for BOC, Lloyds Bank was a very important strategic account for Xerox. But, neither were global accounts. Because British Steel and Lloyds Bank each operated in a single country, they did not need the global managerial attention, coordination, and systems and processes necessary to manage global accounts.

Each firm must set its own criteria for *globality*. Some firms demand the customer have significant operations in at least two continents. Others may prefer regional programs for such customers and require at least three continents for the global program. Some firms require the firm's non-home-country business with the account to reach a fixed percent of total revenues, and to be growing.

Customer Appropriate for Being Managed Globally

An appropriate customer candidate for the global program would require global suppliers to provide a single point of contact and accountability for global coordination. Ideally, the customer would provide an internal champion responsible for the relationship. Particularly appropriate candidates are those whose purchase decisions require complex multinational decision-making.

Inappropriate customers come in several types:

- Highly global business activities, yet unwilling to share information.
- May view global account program membership simply as a means of extracting price concessions.
- May have a presence in many countries, yet operate in a highly decentralized manner such that all critical decisions are made at the local level. Consider, for example, oil-field drilling. Major exploration companies purchase some products/services globally, for example pipe. But, in the late 1990s, drilling chiefs at individual fields purchased oil-field services locally. At the time, Schlumberger, a major supplier of oil-field services, elected not to introduce a global account program.
- May be global and receptive to being a global account, yet its internal systems and decision-making processes make global account management currently infeasible and/or without value. Further, this customer is not investing in globalizing its processes.

Notwithstanding these impediments, you may decide it worthwhile to place a customer in your global account program as a preemptive move. The account may not be ready for global treatment but you may believe that change is inevitable. By including the account, you will be well positioned when the shift to a global posture does occur.

Staying Power

Certainly potential global accounts should be creditworthy, but you should consider the possibility that the account may be acquired. We indicated in Chapter 1 that the pace of mergers and acquisitions, especially cross-border, increased substantially in recent years. When a merger/acquisition occurs, the new firm must rationalize two procurement organizations. All things equal, the stronger of the two original organizations is more likely to retain its major suppliers. Global account effort on the weaker organization may be wasted. By the same token, selecting potential acquirers as global accounts may bring long-term benefits.[2]

Of course, nominating situations are rarely cut and dried. Introducing a global account program is often fraught with difficulties, and you must be sure that your firm has the global capability to serve any potential global account. Similarly, customer movement to global procurement frequently encounters *bumps and snags*. Local subsidiaries, measured on bottom-line profit, are often unwilling to surrender procurement control to a global group. In many cases, you may have to make reasoned judgments whether to nominate a particular customer for your global account program.

The nomination process

There are two broad approaches for nominating customers to the global account program—top-down and bottom-up.

- *Top-down:* The Program Office identifies candidates. These candidates are presented to the field for validation and testing with the customer.
- *Bottom-up:* Candidates are nominated by the field and approved by the Program Office.

In our experience, the most common nominating method is field-driven, responding to customer requirements. Sometimes, managers dealing with a specific customer in different country environments (probably operating as a virtual account team under the "leadership" of the home-country account manager), perceive an opportunity to enhance the business relationship. But, if you are just starting a program, we advise handpicking the first wave of global accounts. There are several arguments in favor of this approach.

---

[2] Additional criteria include share of the account's relevant procurement budget, ability to use a broad spectrum of the firm's products, long-run market growth rates for the account's markets, technological sophistication, management longevity, and centralized decision-making.

Snags and problems

In its early days, your new global account program will hit snags and problems. These may require special handling and centralized control. Program Office nomination ensures you have the best accounts to work with. Better to have a customer that forgives your attempts and inevitable errors, than one with a short fuse.

Setting standards

The Program Office sets the bar high and establishes the standard for future nominations. By setting high expectations on required characteristics for entry into the global program, potential internal political problems may be diffused.

Avoid disappointment

Field nominations would require the Program Office to implement a thorough and rigorous selection process. Inevitably, egos will be bruised and customers disappointed. The result will be a sub-optimal politically driven process that is designed to avoid such problems.

To produce a list of qualified candidates, the Program Office must spend time and effort to complete the due diligence on your customer base. A *high and wide* view allows the Program Office to compare candidate customers rigorously. The Program Office should have easy access to your business opportunity models and apply them evenly across your customer base. Once the Office has developed a candidate customer set, it must secure more granular input from the field. The field has a deeper understanding of customers' current situations and its own perspectives on managing global accounts.

Once the global account program is well established, you should take more of a bottom-up approach. Bottom-up processes have a major advantage in that they originate closer to the customer. Only local/national account teams clearly understand the depth of advantage you may gain from granting particular customers global account status. Account team members *own* customer relationships and are best placed to assess future customer behavior. Only an account team can discreetly *feel-out* a customer's interest in global account status and its willingness to invest in a partnership. Moreover, since the field will most likely pay additional expenses for global account membership, we wholeheartedly recommend securing its support. The Program Office should maintain an oversight role—ultimately it performs its own reviews and makes recommendations regarding each nominated account.

How and when the Program Office receives nominations is an important issue. You will almost certainly wish to *grow* a small, successful program. Even when your global program reaches steady state, you will probably wish to drop some accounts and add others. You should operate the nomination process on an annual cycle, for example, during the second or third quarter, rather than on an ongoing basis. Occasionally, you may need to make exceptions for unusual circumstances.

> Square D/Schneider conducts its filtering phase between January and April. Account plans are developed in May and June. Final decisions to accept new accounts are made in July when the steering committee meets.

The nomination process should be tightly linked with the annual business planning process. Newly selected global accounts are considered in next-year's budgeting cycle—this ensures they receive appropriate funding and resources. Further, when all nominations are submitted simultaneously, you can make inter-account comparisons and identify the total required investment.

> IBM aligns the nomination process with its fall planning activity. During the planning cycle, senior managers evaluate global account teams—these teams typically include specialists from the hardware, software, and services organizations, together with individuals with financial and contracting skills. They may also include sales people assigned to large customer divisions. As a result of these reviews, the most promising-global accounts receive additional resources. During this process, IBM also makes a serious attempt to evaluate candidate customers for its global account program. Because global accounts receive additional resources, IBM tries to identify additional revenue opportunities resulting from those extra resources. These resources include special funding for travel, and relationship-building expenses for senior customer executives. By only allowing entry to the global program during the planning cycle, IBM ensures proper adjustments to financial objectives and minimizes the probability of needing mid-quarter or mid-year adjustments.

Your company's organization structure will determine how nominations are processed. Suppose you have a geographic-region organization. Individual countries where potential global accounts are headquartered should complete the nomination package—the package is sent for regional approval. Regional endorsements are forwarded to worldwide operations, and then to the Program Office. The Program Office (Executive Owner) completes its review and forwards a recommendation to the Executive Sponsor or the Steering Committee (see Figure 5.1).

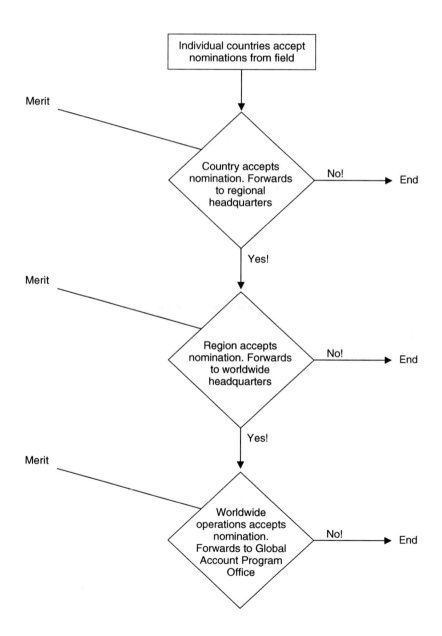

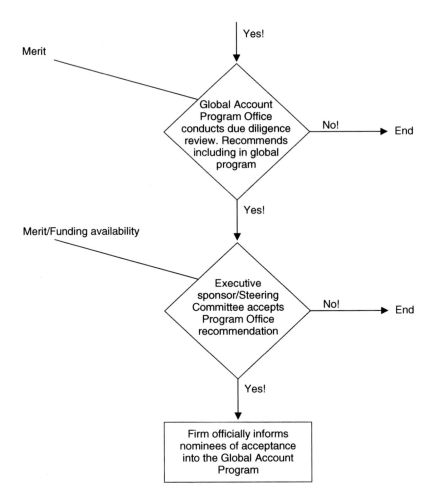

Figure 5.1   Nomination Process for Global Accounts

At Xerox, the steering committee comprised senior functional, indus-try and geographic representatives. This committee made the final decision on program admission. Early in the program's life, the steer-ing committee method worked quite well. Individual functions had to approve nominees—sister geographies agreed to treat the nominating geography's customer especially well within their regions. This process produced solid nominees—individual regional directors did not want to be embarrassed in the committee by *shaky* nominations from their regions. Over time, the Program Office matured and the steering committee became a rubber stamp for its decisions. Eventually, the steering committee was disbanded.

Identifying Selection Criteria for the Global Account Program

The nomination process provides an initial screen for potential customers that may enter your global account program. We discussed above that potential nominees are screened on three major factors—globality, customer appropriateness for being managed globally, and staying power. We consider these criteria as absolute. Any customer that does not pass this three-item screen should not be considered for membership, and does not move to the selection process.

The purpose of the nominating process is to identify which of your customers may be strategic for the firm on a global basis. In the selecting process, you evaluate successfully nominated accounts using more fine-grained selection criteria. There are two reasons to develop these criteria. First, they will guide you with individual selection decisions. Second, they show customers that your selection process is not arbitrary. For both internal and external constituencies, you must avoid any perception that global account selection is a political process.

Specific selection criteria will vary across suppliers based on idiosyncratic firm factors. A key discriminating factor is firm objectives for the global account program. For example, if your core objective were to protect large customers from competitive attack, key selection criteria would probably focus on revenues from current business. By contrast, if the core objective were to improve account profitability, size would be less meaningful than account profitability. And if business growth were the most critical factor, opportunities for developing value-added services and willingness to share business problems would be important criteria.

> The major goal of 3M's global account program was to identify opportunities to use its numerous technologies. 3M commenced its search with the global *Fortune* 500, then focused heavily on a single criterion—*bias for innovation and creativity*—measured by R&D spending as a percent of sales. Nature of the current relationship was essentially irrelevant—for some selected global accounts, 3M had no prior relationship. Each item in the entire criteria set was weighted in a formal decision model.

Screening criteria for *nomination* deal largely with suitability for a global account program *per se*. Selection criteria for *global* accounts are similar to those for *strategic/key* accounts. We present three major categories of potentially useful selection criteria—direct sales revenue and profit, organizational interrelationships, and opinion leadership.

Direct sales revenues and profit

Two of the most important global account selection criteria are current sales revenues and current profits. We also consider the future revenues and profits, and financial security.

Current sales revenues

Current sales revenue is the most frequently used criterion. For example, Saatchi & Saatchi has two clients that together account for around 22 percent of global revenues—including these customers in its global program is a no-brainer. The loss of an account meeting the current-sales-revenue criterion would be extremely serious—total revenue and associated profits would decline immediately. This criterion may be valid even if specific products are unprofitable—high volume products typically carry a significant share of overhead. Loss of *unprofitable* volume would require this burden to be carried by other products sold to other customers—overall firm profits would decline.

We recommend that you do not automatically apply this criterion. Some high volume accounts may be truly unprofitable. Indeed, firms that start measuring customer profitability often discover that excessive price discounting and high support costs make high volume customers unprofitable. Finally, some accounts may be very difficult to deal with—they make excessive demands and/or have poor business practices. Despite their high volume, we advise that they not be selected as global accounts.

Current profits

Some customers selected as global accounts may provide significant revenues but little profit—other customers may provide relatively low revenues but significant profits. Large customers frequently have significant bargaining power and drive prices down—smaller customers may be less price-sensitive. Perhaps these customers value your additional services, whereas larger customers provide these internally. Regardless, mid-size customers may be highly profitable and so warrant global account status.

Future sales revenues and profits

Many firms incorrectly use high current revenues as a global account criterion to the exclusion of all others. They often fail to consider *potential revenues and profits*. By relying exclusively on *today's* criteria, they are guilty of ignoring *future* revenue and profit opportunities. Indeed, in some industries, customers may be highly global, yet relatively small. Nonetheless, their potential may argue for global account status, although they may be treated in a different manner from the firm's larger customers.

But, the firm should be cautious—some customers may represent significant but *unattainable* potential. For example, a small customer for the firm may purchase large volumes from a competitor. Potential may be high, but this firm's close long-term relationship with the competitor may argue against significant effort. Regardless, demonstrated requirements for specific benefits may spur a supplier to develop competitive advantage that surpasses any switching costs.

Xerox's key criterion for global program acceptance is current revenues coupled with an element of potential future business, currently annual billings of $10 million, or the ability to reach $10 million within 3 years. The growth window must be supported by an opportunity matrix that specifies the source of increased revenues. In this process, *rising stars* are less likely to be passed over.

Tunnelers are a subset of global account prospects that Citibank has decided to target for development effort. Citibank believes these accounts have significant potential but does not expect revenues within the next 2 years. Citibank has an ongoing inventory of about 20 prospective customers that are going through an intensive tunneling process. The operational goal is to give *tunnelers* a new idea every 2 months.

Financial security

Global accounts must be financially secure. After all, suppliers want to be paid for the products/services they deliver. Also, they do not want to waste long-term relationship development investment on global accounts that will fail or be acquired. To this end, some firms set industry leadership as a criterion—others set cut-offs based on financial metrics.

Organizational interrelationships

In this category, you should consider whether or not the customer's strategy is coherent with your strategy, whether the customer values you as a supplier, and whether there is a cultural fit between the two firms.

Coherence with your firm's global strategy

Global account programs do not exist in isolation from overall firm strategy. Regardless of where critical choices are made—at corporate or business-unit level—global account selection is a strategy implementation decision. Each higher-level strategy should have a well-formulated market strategy(ies) with which global account selection must cohere. For example, if your market strategy requires a broad product line, you may want your global accounts to purchase multiple products. If innovation were critical, you may select only those accounts with a *bias for innovation and creativity*.

Your firm valued by the customer

A selected global account should value your global offer. This sounds like a fairly basic criterion but, actually, it is complicated and, ultimately, judgmental It must be assessed against your worldwide value proposition. If your offer is highly valued, the account will be committed to you. Indeed, it may be willing to develop a global strategic partnership relationship, allowing access to senior management, and sharing business issues and critical success factors. The customer's organizational structure and decision-making processes should allow you to maximize the value that global account management provides. New opportunities, greater wallet share and, possibly, sole vendor status may follow.

Cultural fit

Some customers are difficult to do business with. They may institutionalize gatekeepers and exclude you from important decision-makers. They may operate with ethical principles very different from your own. Other customers are easy to work with. They embrace your global account process and are open to and/or have experience with partnership relationships. *Cultural fit* captures such interface issues. If *cultural fit* is poor, you may want to exclude a potential global account from consideration, regardless of its attractiveness otherwise.

Opinion leadership

In many industries, specific firms are well known for the care they exercise in selecting suppliers. Frequently, these firms are industry leaders and qualify for global account status under current and/or potential sales revenue criteria. Smaller firms may also play this role—they exercise influence on other industry firms and so impact significant revenues. These firms have high public relations value as showcase accounts. They may also serve as Beta (development) sites for new technology. Their high performance standards and encouragement of supplier excellence make them highly valuable as supplier launch platforms. Indeed, they may require complex problems to be solved and are thus extra valuable for building the firm's intellectual capital.

Using the Selection Criteria

Some examples of global account criteria in practice:

> For potential global accounts, Citibank requires a financial services wallet of over $5 million p.a. and at least 30 percent of activities outside the home country. Citibank also evaluates the customer's *management mindset* to determine if it values the relationship Citibank's program provides.

> Xerox requires current billings of $10 million and a presence in at least two (of four) geographic regions. Potential global accounts must also show a willingness to partner.

> Lucent requires global accounts to have a presence in a minimum of five countries in two different geographic regions. Lucent only selects as customers for its program those with the perspective, "I cannot be successful unless Lucent is on my side."

In the previous section, we identified potential criteria for global account selection. We also emphasized that chosen criteria should be related to your firm's objectives for the global account program. There is no cookie-cutter solution—you must select those criteria making the most sense given your objectives.

We now offer some general principles for deciding how many criteria to use in the selection process. We also suggest some methods for using the criteria. In general, fewer criteria are better. A single criterion is too blunt, yet 15 criteria are too many! No matter how many criteria you use, top candidate accounts are typically no-brainers—a single criterion, typically current revenues (unless the candidate is seriously unprofitable or in bankruptcy), ensures their selection. After all, it is rare that securing revenues from current customers is more difficult and costly than from new customers.

Multiple criteria become useful when you get further down the potential candidate list and hard choices must be made. Your instrument must be sufficiently sharp edged to distinguish among comparable candidate customers. But, it must not be so sharp that the extra complexity makes it too difficult to use or yields no additional value. You must also consider the use of these criteria around the world. What may be simple criteria in one country may be viewed differently in another country. The complexity you choose should be linked to the task at hand. If you have to select a few accounts from a limited nominee pool, a simple approach may do the job. But, if the task requires sorting through hundreds of comparable accounts headquartered in multiple countries, a more elaborate scoring system may be helpful. A further option is to reduce the candidate pool with a simple system, then use a more complex system for final selection. Your system should provide an empirical and documentable explanation of your process to field and customer personnel. In general, the Program Office will complete this analysis.

We illustrate both a simple and a more complex system for selecting global accounts.

A simple system for selecting global accounts

Selection Criteria

This process requires you to choose a highly limited number of selection criteria. Then you determine the importance weight of each criterion. This weight represents the Program Office's assessment of the importance of each criterion in the selection process.

Assume, for example, you identified the following four criteria and assigned importance weights on a simple 1–3 scale. You will apply these criteria to each of the candidate companies.

Criterion	Importance Weight
Current revenues	3
Current profits	2
Cultural fit	1
Opinion leadership	1

Where, 1 = low importance; 2 = moderate importance; 3 = high importance

- *Nominee ratings:* Each candidate account is rated for its performance on each selection criterion. Our rating scale has the following interpretation:

    0 = does not meet the criterion at all
    1 = meets the criterion weakly
    2 = meets the criterion moderately
    3 = meets the criterion strongly.

- *Application illustration:* We show how the importance weights and nominee ratings are used to develop an attractiveness score for each of two hypothetical candidate customers (A and B). We develop the attractiveness score for each candidate by first multiplying together the importance weight and rating for each criterion. We then sum these terms to develop each customer's attractiveness score.

Criterion	Importance Weight (I)	Candidate A		Candidate B	
		Rating (R)	I*R	Rating (R)	I*R
Current revenues	3	3	9	2	6
Current profits	2	2	4	1	2
Cultural fit	1	2	2	2	2
Opinion leadership	1	1	1	2	2
		Attractiveness Score	16		12

The summed totals, Attractiveness Scores, are index numbers of attractiveness. In this illustration, Candidate A-16 scores better than candidate B-12. (A *perfect* candidate would score 21.)

A more complex system for global account selection[3]

The simple system may be too blunt an instrument to give you sufficient discrimination among candidate accounts. A more complex system has three major differences:

- It includes a greater number of criteria.
- Instead of a simple 3-point scale for the importance rating, it uses a constant-sum weighting system. (In a constant-sum scale, the weightings given to each criterion are made to sum to an agreed-on number; we use 100.)
- Candidate ratings for each criterion are on a 10-point scale, where:
    1 = meets the criterion very weakly
    5 = meets the criterion moderately
    10 = meets the criterion very strongly.

Intermediate scores represent intermediate positions. We revisit the previous illustration in the following table.

Note that for both methods we used subjective assessments for candidate ratings. In principle, we could develop more objective criteria. For example, in this illustration, for current revenues (and current profits), we could associate ratings with specific dollar values—1 = $1 million; 2 = $2.5 million; and so forth. Similarly, we could develop scales for the other criteria.

---

[3] Both of these methods are termed *compensatory* approaches since high performance on one criterion can balance out poor performance on another.

Criterion	Importance Weight (I)	Candidate A		Candidate B	
		Rating (R)	I*R	Rating (R)	I*R
Current revenues	30	9	270	7	210
Current profits	20	7	140	3	60
Opinion leadership	15	2	30	5	75
Cultural fit	10	5	50	6	60
Future growth potential	15	5	75	4	60
Technological sophistication	10	8	80	8	80
	100	Attractiveness Score	645		545

Again, candidate A scores better than candidate B.

Portfolio issues

In using the selection criteria we just outlined, the firm typically seeks to optimize the potential return and risk for each individual global account. But, in addition to focusing on individual global accounts, the firm should also consider the entire set of customers in the global account portfolio. In selecting individual accounts for the global account program, the firm must consider the return and risk of the entire portfolio of global accounts.

The portfolio return is a weighted function of all the global accounts. The portfolio risk considers not only the risk on individual global accounts, but also how these different risks interact or correlate. The firm must be concerned that some future environmental event does not impact on a large portion of the global accounts and send the firm's profitability diving. In other words, during global account selection, the firm must be concerned about the relationship of each prospective global account to all of the others. The firm may reject individual accounts for portfolio reasons, even though they may appear perfectly acceptable when considered individually because the firm would be placing "too many eggs in one basket."

Completing the Selection and Nomination Package

Over and above the quantitative analysis, at least two other documents should be included in the nomination and selection package:

Strategic account business plan

Each account being nominated should already have a strategic account business plan. If this is not available, you should reasonably ask—Where has this candidate customer been? How can this account move from undeserving of a strategic plan to a nomination for the global account program? Lack of a strategic plan should immediately send up red flags.

One-page narrative

This narrative provides the opportunity for subjective input into the selection process. The person responsible for the nomination—Program Office personnel or someone in the field—should complete it. The narrative should complement the candidate analysis—it should answer two important questions:

- Why does the customer want to be in the global program?
- Why do you want the customer to join?

The answer to the second question should address such questions as:

- Specifically, how will our worldwide account relationship improve because of program membership?
- Specifically, how and where will our account revenues improve because of program membership? What countries will experience growth?
- What new business opportunities will develop because of program membership?
- Will our share of the account's wallet increase?
- What operational efficiencies shall we gain by adding the account to the global program?

If there are not good answers to these questions, you should seriously question whether to add this account to your global program. Far too often, nominations are knee-jerk reactions to customers' casual requests. No one has thought through the requirements, implications, costs, and benefits of joining the program.

The nomination package, along with others, should go to the steering committee for approval. If selection criteria are agreed and well understood, and the Program Office provides ongoing advice and counsel, few inappropriate candidates will reach the committee. A well-designed and well-executed nomination and selection process ensures you will accept into your global program only truly deserving customers.

Managing Global Account Program Size

If you execute the nomination and selection process properly, only qualified candidates will be approved for membership in the global account program. Unfortunately, lack of funds and/or human resource assets may limit the scope of your program and the number of accounts you can accept. Nominated candidates may successfully meet all criteria yet may be unable to enter the program. For this reason, we do not recommend informing candidate customers until the process is complete.

Many firms budget their global account programs for a given number of accounts, for example 100. These decisions may pose difficulties. For example, if the globalization trend continues and your business prospers, an increasing proportion of customers will become eligible for program membership. We recommend flexibility on the number of accounts in your global account program. Nonetheless, if your roster size is rigidly fixed at the top 100 global customers, you have two main options:

- *Use a stack-ranking process and remove the bottom accounts:* Keeping strict criteria and periodically culling out under-performing accounts is a viable option. It can delay problematic situations posed by fixed roster size. Removed accounts are returned to regional/local management.
- *Develop a two-tier structure for global accounts:* Two tiers is a viable option as it differentiates the resources provided to global accounts; after all, not all global accounts are equal! Several firms differentiate global accounts based on current and potential revenues. For example, for Tier-one account GAMs may be senior executives with single account responsibility. GAMs for Tier-two accounts may be less senior managers responsible for two or more accounts.

Decisions at the margin—which accounts go out and which accounts are added—are always difficult. Ultimately, you must align the number of accounts in your global program with your process capability and available human assets. We address these issues in Chapter 6.

Communicating about the Global Account Program

When the necessary processes and tools for global account nomination and selection are in place, you must inform all relevant parties. These include all those who touch the customer—field personnel such as sales, customer service, and technical service—and those in more internal functions such as brand management, operations, and R&D.

Simply put, you cannot over communicate the details of your nomination, selection and management process for your global accounts—especially selection criteria. We suggest that you:

- Send a broadly circulated internal announcement letter from the Program Executive or, preferably, the CEO.
- Post details on your field-sales website.
- Place articles in company newsletters and magazines.
- Include announcement and discussion of the global account program on the agenda of all sales meetings around the world.
- Ensure reference to the global program is made in senior executive speeches.
- Brief all executives in your Executive Partnership Program so they may properly respond to questions from the field and customers.

This communication program has two key objectives:

- Inform as many internal people as possible about the global account program and the process for becoming a member.
- Clarify the benefits customers will receive from being members. This avoids misunderstandings and unrealistic expectations, especially in the sales force.

You should not limit communication about the global account program to the time of the launch. Global account management has the potential to become *just another corporate initiative* that, if not carefully managed, will go by the wayside. Further, when the program is introduced, there are bound to be internal critics—it will be viewed as a *waste* of resources or, worse, personally threatening to their own careers. When times get tough and resources are short, some will call for eliminating this "costly overhead."

The Program Office must anticipate these difficulties and be proactive in dealing with them. It should not concentrate solely on program launch and then on operational details. It should consider several initiatives:

- Brand marketing techniques are typically focused on customers and other external constituents. Use these techniques to brand the global account program for internal consumption.
- Identify program successes. These are results you would not have achieved without the global program—for example, global contracts and global R&D partnerships. Do this on an ongoing basis.
- Communicate the overall status and performance of the global program on a regular basis—at a minimum, semi-annually.

Monitoring Customer Performance in the Global Account Program

Customer acceptance into the global program roster is not guaranteed for life. Typically, customers are selected as global accounts for the long run. The firm anticipates that the relationship will grow and strengthen over time. Yet, things change. Perhaps the global account's once enthusiastic agreement to a global account relationship has waned and the firm can no longer gain access to the account's senior management. Some factors that may affect your global account program include:

- Market demand conditions
- Competitive inroads
- Mergers, acquisitions and divestitures
- Managerial changes at the firm and the global account
- Strategy changes at the firm and global account
- Reformulation of global account criteria
- Shifts in the global account portfolio balance based on differential global account success and strategic direction.

Any and all of these changes may affect a particular customer's suitability for program membership and, possibly, lead to deselection. You must, on a periodic basis, monitor and reevaluate program members. Some commonly employed evaluation methods are:

At the field level

- Ongoing internal performance reviews—conducted by field operations management and the Program Office
- Management visits to accounts, discussions with field teams
- Discussions among account and supplier executives at business meetings and social events
- Account satisfaction surveys completed annually
- Global account manager input to executives and the Program Office—especially the annual *roster rationalization* review.

At headquarters level

- Program Office activity monitoring—contract volume, revenue growth, account plan quality, GAM travel
- Semi-annual inspection of performance against targets, including revision as necessary—conducted by the Program Office for the Executive Sponsor

- Steering committee review of top 10/bottom 10 performing accounts, at least annually
- *Ad hoc* reviews resulting of major account changes—leadership/management changes, account economic performance, mergers, and acquisitions
- Random inspections by senior management—for example, reviewing account status at monthly staff meetings, seeking account input during a business call.

If your program is working well and there is open and ongoing customer dialogue at multiple levels, there should be no surprises. Regardless, undertaking a formal annual review process can help to keep your global account program on-track.

Key Messages

- Selecting the *right* global accounts is a critical management challenge.

- Funding and other resources applied to the *wrong* accounts in your global program are wasted. More deserving accounts not receiving these resources are opportunity losses.

- An effective nomination and selection process will help ensure you choose the appropriate accounts for your global account program.

- The process should be formal, tough-minded, and well communicated within the firm. Nomination functions as a rough screen. Selection is more fine-grained—you may use either a simple or a more complex system.

- Your global account roster should be monitored on an ongoing basis—you should make additions and deletions as appropriate.

- Communication is critical—both at launch and on an ongoing basis.

CHAPTER 6

DESIGNING THE LINE ORGANIZATION FOR MANAGING GLOBAL ACCOUNTS

PROLOGUE

At the restaurant

Constance was worried about her firm's global account program. The conversations with fellow travelers convinced her that she needed to learn more. She had taken George's business card and called him to have dinner. "I want to spend some more time picking your brain on global account programs. If you can spare the time, the dinner's on me," she told him. Constance was pleased George had accepted.

George was glad Constance had called. After his cab-ride with Jace, he realized he might need some professional help. He had also been wondering how he might help Constance. He told Constance, "I'd like to bounce some ideas off you also, maybe it's time for some group therapy."

Constance was already at the bar when George arrived. "So, Constance how was your day?" he asked. "My meetings went fine, but I couldn't get this whole subject of managing global accounts out of my head. I guess I really came to understand how little I really know. I spoke with Jack Simpson, our global program lead. Jack is concerned our customers don't see us as very global. That is consistent with a customer phone call I received as I was leaving Boston. Our global accounts want the global account managers to have decision-making authority, but my current organization doesn't seem to let that happen.

George took a drink—this was going to be a long dinner. "I have some of the same concerns about our level of globality. Before we got on the plane, I had a conversation with my top global account manager. He's getting so frustrated about the lack of cooperation from country and regional managers that he almost threatened to quit. Todd overheard my conversation and said he was facing similar problems in his firm. It's not as though we've been idle. We now have better people and we've made a lot of process changes—what with intranets and extranets—and all our global account managers write pretty good global account plans. But you know what; our basic line organization hasn't really changed. We layered the global account program on top of our original organization, so life is much the same for most of the company."

> *Constance thought, this is what Jack Simpson has been trying to tell me, but I guess I wasn't really listening. She exclaimed loudly, "It's the organization, stupid!" George looked puzzled. Constance went on, "Before I became CEO, I was involved in a critical project that required we make some organizational changes. These were very painful and I still carry some of the scars. Maybe I've been avoiding the organizational issue because of the potential for more pain if I make serious changes in the way we do business globally." She picked up her glass. "OK George, let's go have dinner and see if we can explore our organization structures and learn something from each other." "Sounds like a plan," said George, "but let's hope we won't be the blind leading the blind!"*

Managing global accounts is difficult at best and impossible without an organizational model that supports your efforts to serve global customers. Line organization is one of the more difficult issues to address when you establish your global account program. Indeed, global cooperation between the many business units that touch your global accounts is critical for a successful global account program. Leading thinkers on global strategy suggest that organization is the "Achilles Heel" for global firms. They also argue that no single organizational structure is the "silver bullet." "Coordination is crucial to success. Reporting lines and structures should change as the nature of the international business becomes global."[1]

Influential writers on organizational culture reach the same conclusion. For example, "Rather than there being one best way of organizing there are several ways, some very much more culturally appropriate and effective than others."[2] The nature of managing global accounts requires that many ingrained corporate and individual cultures must work together to support a given customer. Without a culturally sensitive organization, your global accounts will be less than satisfied.

Regardless of the specific organizational design, placement of the global program within the corporate hierarchy communicates a significant message about the importance of managing global accounts. A global account program hidden deep in the organization, far from the centers of power, will have

---

[1] Thomas Hout, Michael E. Porter and Eileen Rudden, in *Global Strategies Insights from the World's Leading Thinkers*, Boston, MA: Harvard Business School, 1998.

[2] Fons Trompenaars and Charles Hampden-Turner, *Riding the Waves of Culture*, New York: McGraw Hill, 1998.

little organizational clout. Global account managers will find it difficult to secure required resources. Indeed, as we discussed in Chapter 4, every effort should be made to appoint a high-level executive to *own* the global account program. This executive should report as closely as possible to the CEO so there is no ambiguity regarding the importance of managing global accounts to the organization.

Typically, the firm introduces global account management in the context of a pre-existing organization. The structure you adopt will have a major impact on many other parts of your firm. The journey from a pre-existing line organization to one encompassing global account management (or from one global account organization to another) will doubtless meet with resistance. Typically, many executives are committed to the current organization, often for reasons of power and prestige. They may be unwilling to accept the changes required for effectively managing global accounts.

> Battery manufacturer, Exide, had a conventional geographic structure based on 10 separate country organizations. Exide set profit targets for country managers—when successful, they earned large bonuses. The compensation system often led these managers to take actions detrimental to their colleagues—for example, exporting to each other's countries, and cutting prices. For example, the British subsidiary sold batteries in Austria at prices 10–15 percent lower than the German subsidiary. The geographic focus also encouraged local plant construction that was sub-optimal on a system-wide basis. In 1999, Exide introduced a global business unit structure focused around six product groups. This action solved the internal competition problem. But, demoted to local coordinators, half of Exide's top European managers resigned.
>
> Later, Exide acquired international battery maker, GNB Technologies, in an attempt to regain a significant presence in the North American battery market. Concerned that GNB's CEO might resign, Exide tilted back to the geographic model and gave the CEO significant geographic responsibility.[3]

Firms conducting business in many countries typically manage their geographically diverse operations via some form of geographic area structure—for example, North America, EMEA, Asia Pacific, and Latin America.[4] In these firms, country managers typically report directly to geographic region

---

[3] *The Wall Street Journal*, June 27, 2001.

[4] The global firm may also operate global product divisions. These are frequently matrixed with a geographic structure. See Noel Capon, John U. Farley and James Hulbert, *Corporate Strategic Planning*, New York: Columbia University Press, 1988. For simplicity, we base our discussion on the geographic organization.

directors. These regional executives have top-line and, sometimes, bottom-line responsibility. For an appreciation of how difficult it can be to make serious organizational changes, let us look at IBM.

In, *Who Says Elephants Can't Dance*,[5] former IBM CEO Lou Gerstner gives us a glimpse of the difficulties posed by organizational fiefdoms when he attempted to implement a new structure for managing global accounts: "Although we implemented the new industry structure in mid-1995, it was never fully accepted until at least three years later." (Personally, we think Gerstner was probably being optimistic.) "Regional heads clung to the old system, sometimes out of mutiny, but more often out of tradition. IBM needed to do a massive shift of resources, systems and processes to make the new system work. Building an organizational plan was easy. It took three years of hard work to implement the plan." (We provide more depth on IBM's global organizational evolution later in this chapter.)

Selecting your organization structure is a very serious challenge. It must be carefully thought through and tested using various scenarios. If it takes three years for a CEO of Gerstner's stature and savvy to drive organizational change in a failing corporation (IBM experienced a $14 billion profit switch, from +$6 billion to −$8 billion in just a few years, in the early 1990s), you know you cannot be arbitrary in your selection. Further, you cannot expect a global account program to fit nicely into the current organization. Superficially, this may seem like a straightforward matter, but trust us, you must evolve your global account organization for it to work effectively and efficiently.

Organization for managing global accounts comes in several forms. We discuss three approaches—the matrix organization, the market-integrated organization, and the new region structure. These are alternative ways to organize for managing global accounts. Serving global customers should be the firm's top priority—you must choose the line organization for your global account program with this priority in mind.

The Matrix Organization

When firms seriously embark on global account management, they frequently incorporate the global account program into the existing organization. This leads to matrix management. In the matrix organization, global account management shares space with the geographic-area structure.

---

[5] Louis V. Gerstner, *Who Says Elephants Can't Dance*, New York: HarperCollins, 2002.

To fulfill his responsibilities, the GAM must cut across the firm's geographic region organization. This challenge is similar to a NAM dealing with a geographically organized sales force. However, the global challenge is much more complex. First, regional geographic heads typically control many functions in addition to sales, and they often have bottom-line responsibility. Second, compared to NAMs, GAMs must deal with many globalization challenges such as time, distance, and cultural differences.

Reporting relationships

The GAM is responsible for global account planning, strategy making, action-program development, implementation, and high-level relationship building. Local sales and support personnel, for example technical service and logistics analysts, generally conduct day-to-day interaction at dispersed account locations around the world. Local personnel, including NAMs, report "solid line" through to country managers. They may also report "dotted line" to the GAM.

The GAM operates *horizontally in a vertical world*. Typically, GAMs report (solid line) through their own geographic and/or functional organizations. Of course, if a major multinational firm is located in a small country, the GAM's revenue responsibilities may be greater than his/her country manager. In addition, GAMs may also report to a senior global manager with customer responsibilities. This second manager may be the executive owner or, perhaps, a global industry (market sector) director with planning/strategy responsibility for one or more market arenas. In the firms we studied, geographic and customer-focused reporting relationships ranged from a strong solid line to a weak dotted line.

In most global account programs, GAMs reside at the global account's headquarters. For example, your GAM for Deutsche Telecom would be stationed in Germany and report up through the head of the EMEA region. Figure 6.1 shows there are multiple combinations of direct and dotted-line reporting using the matrix organization structure. Firm size, breadth, and scope of the global account program, and the current management system each influence the particular chosen structure.

Suppose the pre-existing geographic-area structure comprised powerful geographic-region managers. The initial global account manager–geographic manager (GAM/GM) relationship is likely to be a strong solid line; conversely, the global account manager—customer-focused manager (GAM/CM) relationship is likely to be a dotted line. Over time, as the global account program earns credibility, these relationships are likely to change. The GAM/CM relationship becomes stronger as the GAM/GM relationship

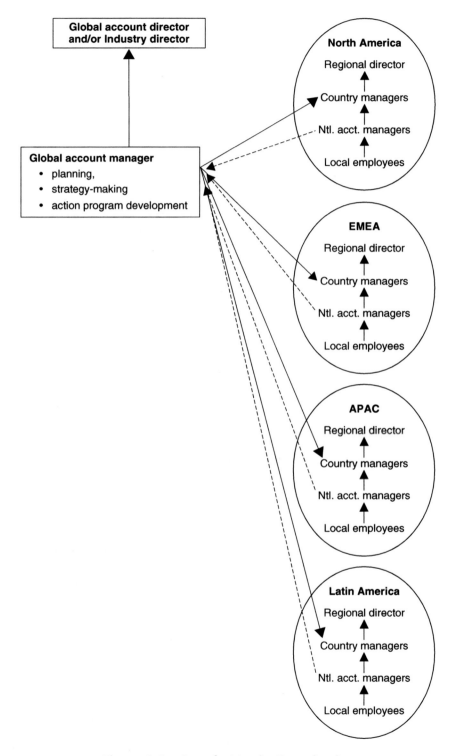

Figure 6.1   Sample Matrix Organization

weakens. In some firms, the GAM/CM relationship transitions to solid line and the GAM/GM relationship is little more than *care and feeding*. Put another way, as the GAM becomes an *integral part* of the firm's organization, local management becomes progressively more *in-tune* and customer-focused.

To offset the conflict inherent in the matrix organization, some firms have supplemented their matrix organizations by introducing new roles. For example:

Headquarters account managers

In its original matrix organization, HP identified a role for headquarters account managers (HAMs), later called account program managers (APMs). At HP, GAMs typically resided in the headquarters cities of their global accounts. The APMs were their representatives at corporate headquarters. The APM's mission was to "champion the critical needs and significant opportunities of the global account within HP headquarters, and to establish HP as a strategic vendor through long-term sales, growth and customer satisfaction."[6]

APMs worked with GAMs on developing new business opportunities. They were involved with technical, pricing, and strategy issues to support global customer relationships. APMs also served as a focused channel for product divisions into global account management—they developed a network of resources across customer industries. APMs also shared best practices in managing global accounts, and so aided their GAMs.

Regional account managers (RAMs)

Because of span-of-control issues, RAMs are often a critical element in fully functioning global account programs.[7]

> In Unilever's structure, country-based KAMs report to that country's national account director. The KAM for a specific account, for example Wal-Mart in Argentina, also reports (dotted line) to Wal-Mart's Latin American RAM. This RAM, in turn, reports to the Wal-Mart GAM.[8]

---

[6] Tammy Masden and George Yip, "HP: Global Account Management, A, B," Los Angeles: Graduate School of Management, UCLA, 1994. When first introduced, reaction to the HAM program within HP was mixed. After a couple of years, 57 percent of GAMs funded half a HAM, 31 percent funded a full HAM.

[7] For more insight on this intermediate level of account management, see Christoph Senn, "Operating Globally: Not Without the Regional and Local Level," *Velocity*, 2 (1st Quarter 2000), 6–8, 43, and Tony Millman, "Regional Account Manager (Europe): Interesting Job Title, but What Does it Mean?," *Velocity*, 2 (1st Quarter 2000), 33–36.

[8] Package delivery firm DHL operates a similar RAM structure, Edmund Bradford and Francis Rome, "Applying Total Customer Management at DHL: How One Leading Company Has Proved the Payoff," *The Journal of Selling and Major Account Management*, 2 (Autumn 1999), 117–123.

Cisco Systems has regionally based Gateway Global Account Managers (GGAMs). These GGAMs ease communications between GAMs and locally based NAMs responsible for their global accounts. Global systems engineers (GSEs) and global service managers (GSMs) also support GAMs.[9]

Each of these roles helps firms to transition from a *status quo* organization to a new matrix organization.

Pros and cons of the matrix structure

The matrix organization has one major benefit—it gives attention to both geographic and customer dimensions. Further, if the pre-existing organization was based on geography, the matrix is an organizational evolution. Implementing a matrix organization is less disruptive than full-scale organizational change.

The major problem with the matrix organization is potential conflict. The GAM must deal with two different, yet often very strong, local and global pressures:

- *Local pressure:* The GAM's leadership comes from the geographic regional director and/or the country head. This individual is primarily concerned with optimizing performance in his region or country.
- *Global pressure:* The GAM is responsible for optimizing account performance globally. Necessarily, effort and accountability cut across geography.

The conflict arises because decisions to optimize global performance may cause sub-optimal local performance (and vice versa), at least in the short run. Said another way, when your firm views customers globally, performance in individual geographic regions/countries may be compromised. This conflict takes many forms. For example:

- *Misaligned account importance:* The subsidiary of a global account may be relatively unimportant to the local country, but very important to the global account and hence to the GAM. Conversely, the subsidiary may be important to the local country, but much less important to the global account and GAM.
- *Travel:* To fulfill global responsibilities, the GAM must travel to a different region/country. These trips are wasteful from a narrowly

[9] Jay Parr, Director of Operations, Worldwide Strategic Accounts, Cisco Systems, SAMA Annual Conference, Orlando, FL: May 6–9, 2001.

construed geographic perspective. Unless other arrangements are made, the GAM's geographic superior must finance the trip; he also suffers the opportunity cost of the GAM's time spent in other countries.

- *Global Contracts:* To secure a global contract (previously awarded regionally/nationally), the GAM may have to agree to lower than normal prices. The supplier gains overall from additional revenues in the global contract. But, the agreement may negatively influence revenues and profits in the geography that previously won the regional contract. Further, the geographic manager may face pricing problems with other customers, if prices are set lower for the global customer.
- *Potential Business:* Potential future global business requires that the firm expend resources in a specific geographic region. But, the likely major beneficiary of future sales revenues may be a sister region.

Resolving matrix issues

Ideally, these potential conflicts should be dealt with preemptively. You should develop a customer-focused, global account management culture, driven from the top of the organization. The entire firm should strive to do what is best for the customer. You should work hard at bringing geographic executives *on board* by having them accept global account management as a positive organizational innovation. Of course, regional executives likely experienced customer-related problems in the pre-global account management era. You should specifically address these and other potential problems by developing appropriate systems and processes. Possible actions include:

- Funding international travel and other global-type GAM expenses as a corporate budget item. These expenses fall outside the regional structure and are separate from the GAM's regional/local responsibilities.
- Giving country managers performance targets that comprise sub-targets for local customers and for the local operations of global customers.
- Developing shadow earnings systems such that:
  - Geographic regional/local managers secure credit for global revenues earned outside their geographies by GAMs located within their geographies. Revenues earned within their geographies, from global accounts headquartered outside, are counted fractionally greater (for example 1.5 times) than revenues secured from both local customers and global accounts headquartered in their geographies.

- In each case, the firm must make appropriate adjustments in revenue/profit objectives and/or quotas. An alternative approach requires changes in revenue/profit objectives:
  - The firm develops global P&Ls for each global account. These accounts are removed from local P&Ls. Global account performance locally is measured on customer service levels.
- The Executive Owner plays a significant role in evaluating GAMs. He is also active in evaluating other executives responsible for local dealing with global accounts. In particular, in concert with country managers, he may develop local goals for NAMs.
- Global account issues are discussed at regular top-level biannual meetings. Attendees include senior geographic managers, GAMs, and PEs. Other high-level managers such as the Executive Sponsor and Executive Owner also attend.
- Executives senior to the GAM negotiate global/geographic conflicts. Two important roles are the Executive Owner and the global account's PE. The biannual meeting mechanism (noted above) should reduce the number of conflicts raised to these organizational levels.
- Senior executives have both geographic and global account responsibilities. They understand the local/global trade-offs firsthand and are less likely to act parochially.

Notwithstanding the various approaches to avoiding conflict in the matrix structure, conflict will certainly arise. The firm should put in place well-defined and minimum-step escalation procedures that provide resolutions in a timely manner.

Kuhn Inc. was organized as a conventional geographic area structure with several regional directors. Kuhn developed ten global planning units, each based on industry. Each GAM reported (solid line) into one of these planning units. In addition to his geographic responsibilities, each geographic regional director had global responsibility for two or three industries.

In the final analysis, the number and difficulty of issues you encounter with a matrix structure depend upon your company culture. For example, IBM had a strong country management culture for most of its history. It also had a strong culture of assigning responsibility to self-contained vertical silos. These silos were expected to be self-reliant and manage their responsibilities without outside assistance or interference. The introduction of a matrix structure was very difficult to accept and delayed execution of a fully functioning global account organization.

The Market-Integrated Global Account Organization

We noted above that geographic-area/global-account matrix organizations evolve over time.[10] Frequently, the geographic reporting relationship becomes weaker and the global reporting relationship becomes stronger. Some firms take this evolution to its logical conclusion by essentially eliminating their geographic area organizations. Regardless of the apparent superiority of line organizations other than the matrix system, we should not underestimate the political will needed to make a switch away from an organization in which geography is a major design element.

In 1995, IBM scrapped its geographic organization and introduced a global sales force. IBM's goal was to serve customers across the globe and avoid turf battles between regional sales managers. Initially, GAMs reported into 11 industrial sectors, later reduced to 6.

Asea Brown Boveri was traditionally organized as a matrix of global product segments/business areas and countries/regions. By 1999, ABB's global key account management (GKAM) system (started 1993) was responsible for about 20 customers in various industries—for example, fine chemicals/pharmaceuticals, automobiles, and utilities. More recently, ABB eliminated country budgets—only product segments/business areas would set budgets.[11]

At textile giant Milliken & Co., global account management operates within high-level market segmentation, for example industry. Within each industry (for example, distribution, health-care, and education) Milliken & Co targets individual accounts.

In these firms, geography is no longer the critical organizational dimension. The key organizational dimension is market, typically industry. What may have been planning organizations in a geographic-area structure

---

[10] For one company's experience in merging different approaches to global account management resulting from a joint venture, specifically Concert, formed by British Telecom (BT) and MCI, see Peter Naude and Donald McLean, "Watching the Concert: How Global Account Management Developed within the Concert Alliance," *The Journal of Selling and Major Account Management*, 2 (Autumn 1999), 13–30.

[11] Fritschi, *op. cit.*

become line organizations—the geographic dimension essentially disappears. GAMs have strong relationships with local personnel responsible for global account operations in their territories. The GAMs, in turn, now report directly to their respective industry groups.

> In the global business unit of a major U.S. bank, each KAM has two roles. First, each is the GAM for one or more accounts based in his home country; second, each is a local NAM for a global account headquartered elsewhere, for example, Europe or the U.S. For example, one executive might be the GAM for SONY, based in Japan. He might also be the NAM, in Japan, for Kodak. Market (industry) executives are exclusively responsible for revenues and profits, and the bank budgets global account management by industry.

In reality, market-integrated organizations often retain residual elements of the matrix structure. For example, global companies must retain some amount of country-level presence because of legal definitions of the corporation. They need a country structure to speak with a single country voice, for example taxes, legal protection, corporate image-making, and *care and feeding* of locally based personnel. But revenue, cost, and profit responsibility no longer reside in the geographies—expense budgets by geography no longer exist. Spending in a particular geography is essentially the summed expenses of individual industry activities in that geography. In essence, the firm views its business first and foremost by industry, rather than by region/country.

The major advantage of the market-integrated global account organization is a complete alignment of the firm with its major customers. By focusing the organization on customer industry, GAMs secure superior information on industry trends—they add significant value in conversations with executives at the global account. This organization clarifies authority and accountability. There is no longer discussion of solid-line and dotted-line reporting relationships, and there is no need for shadow revenue and expense systems to mitigate global/local conflicts.[12]

Sometimes the line organization can become quite complex.

> A senior Citibank executive described the organization of Citibank's Global Relationship Bank. "(It is a) country organization with a matrix to an industry organization that transcends . . . The key marketing responsibility is the industry organization. The country organization

---

[12] Of course, this market-based organization may still be matrixed with a product-division organization.

exists primarily for administrative purposes." Citibank's Parent Account Managers (PAMs) report to two industry heads. One head oversees all Citibank's accounts in a particular industry. The other head oversees all Citibank's *global* accounts in a particular industry. Within a particular country, Citibank's Subsidiary Account Managers report both to the geography in which they operate and to their PAMs.

Notwithstanding CEO Lou Gerstner's initiative, IBM found it difficult to articulate its new industry alignment to those executives responsible for modifying reporting structures, measurements, work direction, and other factors involved in growing and supporting global accounts. Many believed the IBM structure just added another factor to the matrix organization and that it was not a pure market-integrated organization. Despite the original conception, country managers did not totally disappear and the geographies remained very strong. The global accounts were moved out of the country measurement and into the industry organization. As a backlash, the countries preferentially put support resources into local customers bringing in country-based revenues.

Pros and cons of the market-integrated structure

The major benefit of the market-integrated structure is minimizing geography as an organizational design element. More specifically the structure attempts to align the organization with global customers. Management has a global perspective and is measured globally—yens, euros, dollars all go in the same bucket. Solutions developed in a particular geography, and installed in another, receive fair attention, and resources are more easily moved to the point of need. The firm removes geography as a barrier to serving global customers.

Notwithstanding these benefits, global account management is now fragmented among different industries and global account management may develop different operating modes in these industries. The challenge then becomes to maintain a single community of practice in managing global accounts.

Depending on your business, the market-integrated model may create redundancy. Industry units may create segment solutions that would have value in other segments. The problem is that the new *industry silos* may not encourage cross-industry cooperation. IBM addressed this issue by creating a cross-industry unit. This unit was responsible for identifying solutions that had multiple industry applicability (Figure 6.2).

Figure 6.2   Market-Integrated Organization

The New Region

In the *new region* approach, global customers are pulled out of the regular geographic-area structure and managed in a new *region*. This approach is less traumatic than developing the Market-Integrated Global Account Organization. The geographic-area structure remains intact, albeit with less power and responsibility than previously. We discuss two ways of implementing the new region concept.

Full separation

Global accounts are completely removed from the existing geographic regions and placed in a new *global-accounts* region. Managers in the new *global-accounts* region have complete authority and responsibility for developing and managing these global accounts. GAMs no longer work through local personnel reporting in the geographic structure. The firm develops totally new structures for local sales, servicing, and technical support—these report into the *global-accounts* region.

These new local structures operate side-by-side with the remaining geographic structures that retain all accounts not selected as global accounts. Many individuals, previously working for the former geographic regions, transfer to the new *global-accounts* region. In smaller countries, the global region may share sales, service, and technical support personnel with the local country organization (Figure 6.3).

GAMs no longer have to persuade their geographies to provide resources for serving global accounts. The firm decides key resource allocation issues at a much higher level—between the *global-account region* head and the

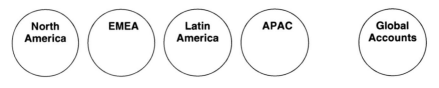

Figure 6.3   New Region Organization

geographic heads. Resources required to serve global accounts now rest exclusively within the *global-accounts* region.[13]

In 2000, HP conducted a major organizational realignment of its global account program. In the new organization, global accounts were placed in a region with its own funding and own resources. Previously, GAMs reported to country managers. Because country managers/regional heads were relatively unconcerned about global performance, there were many conflicts. HP hoped to remedy this problem by placing global accounts into their own distinct and separate region.

The major problem that HP encountered was resistance from the geographies. To form the global-accounts region, each geographic region and individual countries "lost" important customers. After a few months of attempting to work with the new structure, HP reverted to a matrix organization with significant support delivered through industry groups.

As another example, in 1998, Lubrizol, an additive supplier for petroleum-based products, formed a global organization for its major global accounts, mostly the major oil companies.

Partial separation

The geographic region structure remains intact but the firm adds a new *global-accounts* region. The firm places selected global accounts and the global account organization in the new region. Local implementation still occurs through the geographic regions. Compared to full separation, geographic region heads retain responsibility for global accounts, but with a difference.

For non-global accounts, the geographic head continues to exert full authority and responsibility, as already discussed. The geographic head is measured and rewarded based on his performance in his geography. For global accounts, the geographic head is directly responsible for revenues secured

---

[13] This type of organization is a global version of the self-contained key account unit, Capon, *op. cit.*, Chapter 3.

within his region, *but is only measured and rewarded based on the global perform-ance of these accounts.* The geographic head is thus highly motivated to work with GAMs to help them secure increased performance from global accounts.

As we saw in Chapter 4, in October 1995, Van Leer Packaging, a sup-plier of steel drums to the oil and chemical industry lost a major contract, in France, with the French oil company, Total. This loss occurred largely because Van Leer's British subsidiary refused to offer price concessions for a Europe-wide agreement. After a management shake-up, Van Leer introduced the partial separation system as a way of securing less provincial thinking by its country heads.

Pros and cons of the new region structure

Because this organization separates out global accounts, customer responsive-ness and execution can be faster and more consistent. Accountability up and down the line is clear, and the structure sends a clear customer message about the importance of global accounts. Once the systems are developed, the firm can more easily develop profit and loss statements by account. Finally, the geographic regions may have a deeper focus on local markets, now they can no longer fall back on revenues from global accounts. Potential negatives are unhappiness in the geographic regions, additional costs, and a need for elab-orate internal cost transfers for purchased services. These factors could lead to problems with working relationships between GAMs and locals.

In reality, as with the other organizational models, you may need to incorporate variations. Firms with heavy revenue streams in services need country personnel to deliver service. It is not always practical to separate these local personnel into country and global units. Perhaps service is best delivered by a combination of headquarters-based service personnel report-ing to the global region and outlying service people reporting to another structure. For example, a specialist in a particular solution would be part of the GAM team in a GAM region. The services people delivering the solu-tion would be part of a geographic structure.

Evolving the Global Account Organization

Earlier, we indicated that the firm has many options for organizing to address global accounts. In previous sections, we identified a variety of ways to organize. We also suggested that change may not come easily and that internal resistance is highly likely. Even corporate leaders with such stature as Lou Gerstner at IBM may find the going difficult. To get a sense of the journey on which you may be embarking, consider global account organization development at IBM.

- *Stage 1:* In 1990, IBM's organization was based on a traditional country and geographic region structure. An overlay of selected international accounts was named, primarily for tracking. Then a program with "Top 100 international accounts" was put in place, informally asking country management to cooperate with their local sales representatives.
- *Stage 2:* In 1993, IBM implemented a Global Customer Management program (GCM). This initiative singled out 150 accounts as a special group of global customers requiring additional support. This GCM program had limited success because the country/geographic region structure remained in place. The countries were still in charge and the remaining infrastructure changed very little.
- *Stage 3:* By 1995, IBM realized that the country organization was getting in the way of serving global customers. These customers were demanding global consistency—in technology and service levels. To begin to answer these requirements, IBM adopted an *Industry* model, focusing on key industry needs worldwide.

    Industry leaders were responsible for IBM's business worldwide. IBM also changed the reporting lines of senior global account personnel located in local country organizations. Rather than report through the country structure, these personnel now reported above the geographies, through the industry sectors into the world-wide industry executive. This innovation enhanced the focus on global accounts and eased the process of providing resources locally. Country managers still executed on a local basis.

    With this new organization, customer's global needs now had a powerful voice inside IBM. Previously viewed on a country-by-country model, global customers were now considered in the context of a global industry model. Total revenues and projects were recognized at a global level. Special attention from each product and service group ensured that IBM met these customers' global requirements.
- *Stage 4:* Whereas the industry structure breathed new life into its global program, IBM continued to struggle to meet the GAM's needs for addressing global opportunities. Around 1997, additional support was secured by locating opportunity managers in major countries. Opportunity management's responsibility was to secure resources for complex deals crossing country and product manager lines. This

program had some positive impact on complex opportunities, but GAMs continued to struggle on opportunities that did not make the cut.

• *Stage 5:* In 2001, IBM introduced another program to support the larger, more complex, global accounts, and segregate support required to close and execute large global deals. For global accounts meeting the new criteria, IBM elevated the GAM position to an executive level. These "super" GAMs report directly to industry leaders and have a staff reporting directly to them.[14] Their greater reporting authority and executive connections within IBM are helpful for getting things done.

The journey from Stage 1 to Stage 5 took Eleven years. Throughout this period, the international staff organization working closely with IBM's GAMs believed they knew the requirements for executing a successful GAM program. Unfortunately, they had insufficient power to effect the needed changes. IBM's global account program continues to evolve.

Of course, the general problem is that organizational change to support global accounts runs directly counter to the current corporate power base, typically focused on geography. Most executives think they know what is necessary for their particular area of control. Change management is a very painful process, and without a power position most global programs will have to work through a long process of incremental steps to reach an effectively functioning program. Further, we may expect to seek pendulum-like activity where firm's position on a global customer-to-geographic axis fluctuates through time.

Key Messages

• The line organization for global accounts has an important impact on the way in which GAMs do their jobs, and on the day-to-day activities of local account managers serving global accounts.

• Firms introducing global account programs frequently put in place a matrix organization.

• The difficult global/local tradeoffs in matrix organizations can be eliminated with more advanced organizational forms.

---

[14] In Chapter 3, we noted that IBM had backed off this reporting relationship in Europe.

Chapter 7

Securing Effective Global Account Managers

PROLOGUE

Constance back home

Constance *learned a great deal on her New York trip. By the time she and* **George** *finished dinner, she was convinced she should take action on her global account program. She called Jack Simpson to her office to discuss ramping up the program.* "**Constance***, your enthusiasm is terrific and I'm so glad you want to move forward, but . . . " said Jack. The "but" took some of the wind out of* **Constance***'s sails. Jack continued, "The problem is that qualified global account managers (GAMs) don't grow on trees." Constance hadn't really considered that GAM skills were in short supply. She decided to call* **George***.*

"**George, Constance***. Do you have a minute to discuss global account management with me?"* **George** *wasn't surprised by the call. Their dinner conversation left a lot of unanswered questions, and they had promised to circle back on these. "Sure* **Constance***, I have some time, and a few questions of my own. What's on your mind today?"*

"**George***, I remember you saying you did a pretty good job of securing high quality GAMs for your global program. I just met with my global account executive. He told me we couldn't really move forward aggressively because we lack talent for the GAM position. How do you fill openings as you grow your program?"*

"Well, I may have said that, but the fact is we have the same problem. These guys have to be so well rounded that it is difficult to find, develop and keep them. They really have to understand our business model—where the profit comes from—account planning, and have detailed knowledge of their customer, competition, and our firm. They have to identify new opportunities and build relationships with executives from the customer and within our organization. They need skills in business acumen, strategic vision, execution and leadership, and they must understand the impact of culture in getting things done globally. Your executive is right, GAMs are rare birds." **George** *waited for a response. Silence!*

Constance *was not sure* **George** *had answered her question. "OK,* **George***, you've convinced me, they are rare. But how do you fill your positions?" She was hoping* **George** *had a formula or at least an approach she* could steal. "Well, we're still working that issue. We're building a recruiting strategy, looking outside as well as inside the company. I have introduced a selection process involving some of our key executives. A consultant helps us with training. Also, I'm implementing a certification process that puts some discipline in the way we bring people along." **George** paused for a moment, "Am I getting to your question **Constance?**"

Constance was taking all of this in. Clearly, her firm's informal approach was not adequate. She was impressed that **George** had thought through the issues and developed what appeared to be a formal process. "**George**, you spent some time with **Jace**, do you think she could help me with this issue?" **George** recalled his conversation with **Jace** on the plane. "Yes, we spoke briefly about the problem of finding talented GAMs—she was pretty familiar with the issue. I think she might be able to help."

"OK, I think I'll give her a call. Now what did you want to discuss." **Constance** was anxious to get off the phone and work with Jack on GAM recruiting. "Well, I was actually going to discuss how your firm builds business acumen skills, but it doesn't sound like you can help me much." **George** hoped he hadn't offended **Constance**, but there wasn't much point of prolonging the call. "You're right on the money **George**, but maybe in a couple of months. Thanks for your help."

Constance was not encouraged by her conversation with **George**. Finding good GAMs was going to be harder than she thought. "I hope Jack has a plan for addressing this issue," she thought aloud. **Constance** noticed a message from **Todd Jenkins**, the GAM she met on the New York trip. "Looking to expand my career, please call if you're recruiting GAMs." **Constance** thought, maybe things are looking up.

The GAM is the heart and soul of any global account program. Do not make the mistake of underestimating the talent required to effectively serve a global customer and manage a global account team. The GAM must be able to manage complex business relationships across a multitude of cultural dimensions. They must understand their customer's far-flung business model and possess a deep understanding of their own organization. They must identify opportunities to engage their global accounts and bring firm resources to bear on global account problems, and deliver them value. To be successful, GAMs must have a passion for travel, new places and new environments. The GAM position is not for job-hoppers. The successful GAM commits to working with the global account for an extended time period.

To state it very precisely, the GAM is the single point of accountability for the global customer in your company. He is responsible for driving the supplier–global account relationship and creating value both for the customer and for your firm. In creating value, the GAM is the focal point for driving innovation between his global account and all business units and functions within your company.

Without effective GAMs, your entire global account program will fail. For this reason, it is critically important that you attract and retain highly effective men and women in these positions. This chapter focuses exclusively on GAMs. It explores their roles and responsibilities and the competencies required to execute them. We also provide insight into the entire process of recruiting, selecting, training and developing, compensating, and retaining GAMs.

Roles and Responsibilities of Global Account Managers

Clarity in defining roles and responsibilities of the GAM is a necessary first step to securing effective GAMs. Anything less would be like erecting the walls before laying the foundation. Based on previous discussion, we can expect the GAM's roles and responsibilities to be complex. We shall provide examples from several firms that are addressing these issues. These will provide you with a good starting point but, of course, generalized prescriptions must be tailored to your industry or business model.

The GAM's core objective is to earn revenues and profits for your firm. NAMs are focused on business within a single nation-state. GAMs must orchestrate many people's actions around the world to optimize global revenues and global profits. The GAM occupies a boundary role between the global account and your firm. At the global account, the GAM must sustain and grow current revenue sources and identify new opportunities. Inside your firm, the GAM must secure needed company resources to enable revenue and profit growth.

In a very real sense, the GAM is a "political entrepreneur." GAMs frequently operate without line authority and get things done largely through personal influence. First, they need political skills to reconcile different agendas, identify and influence those who impact decision-making processes. They must learn which bells to push and which strings to pull both in the customer organization and in their own. Second, their role is essentially entrepreneurial. GAMs coordinate operational capabilities of their own organizations, coordinate, and realize synergies between individuals, the global team, and organizational competencies, resolve problems that create cost savings, and develop innovative ways of managing the value creation process.[1]

To earn profitable business for the firm, the GAM must engage in many activities with the global account. Essentially, we have boiled down these activities to a few roles and responsibilities—develop and implement a global account plan that delivers value, develop and maintain global customer relationships, manage global customer satisfaction and loyalty, and build and manage the global account team.

Develop and implement a global account plan that delivers value[2]

At a macro level, the global account plan comprises three major elements— **situation analysis, bridge to strategy**, and **framework for account action**. The *situation analysis* comprises a deep understanding of the global customer, competition, and the firm's position at the account. The *bridge to strategy* includes planning assumptions, and identification of opportunities and threats for the firm. The *framework for account action* embraces the global account strategy and related action programs that provide a road map for addressing the opportunities and threats. Historically, planning was conducted on a rigid timetable and the plan reworked annually. Today, change occurs so fast that the global account plan must be a living document. The plan must be updated continuously in the context of a periodic overall re-evaluation. The importance of the global account plan is less the final document, but the learning process in which the entire team collaborates to successfully develop a meaningful plan. Only by completing the process can value-added opportunities be recognized, assessed, prioritized, and developed. We dedicate Chapter 8 to the Global Account Plan.

Develop and maintain global customer relationships

To develop and execute the global account plan, the GAM must identify high-level global-account decision-makers, then develop and maintain close working and personal relationships with them. These individuals typically have such titles as CEO, COO, division president, and other policy-level executives. In addition, the GAM must be sure to cultivate future high-level

---

[1] Our colleague Kevin Wilson initially coined the term "political entrepreneur." For more on Wilson's perspective, see Kevin Wilson and Nick Speare, *Successful Global Account*, London: Kogan Page, 2002.

[2] Some of the material in this section is discussed in greater detail in Chapters 5, 6, and 7 of Noel Capon, *Key Account Management and Planning*, New York: Free Press, 2001.

executives. GAMs must be able to interface seamlessly with customer executives around the world, and be able to zero in on those executives that may truly have an impact on the firm's business, now and in the future.

Manage global customer satisfaction and loyalty

The GAM must ensure that processes are in place to measure global account satisfaction and loyalty. GAMs should identify areas of customer satisfaction and dissatisfaction by analyzing and evaluating customer feedback. They should develop action plans to reduce gaps between customer expectations and perceptions regarding the firm's products, services, and relationships.

Build and manage the global account team

Rarely do GAMs work alone—the GAM's global team performs much of the actual work. This is particularly important, for the GAM may have to address global account concerns anywhere in the world. Because of time and distance constraints, GAMs must have team members they can trust to work effectively with the global account on a day-by-day basis. The GAM must build and manage the global account team. Depending on the organization, the GAM may have some direct reports, but the majority of support is typically provided by a virtual team.

A virtual team is a collection of full-time and part-time individuals with different skill sets. The use of dedicated and shared resources allows the GAM to address the global account's requirements, while containing costs. The virtual-team concept allows individuals from different functions and geographies to be more directly connected to global customers. A virtual team stands in opposition to a "the next available expert," system, and builds relationships between the supplier's personnel and the global account. In many cases, the GAM reserves a fraction of the expert's time, but sometimes full-time team members are called for. Even so, a virtual team may be the best solution, to relieve the GAM of the otherwise "care and feeding" burden.

Summary

GAMs have an impressive list of roles and responsibilities. The skill sets required to fulfill these roles and responsibilities are impressive also. Before we turn to that topic, let us see how two major companies think about GAMs. Citibank's perspective on its PAMs (GAMs in Citibank's terminology) is elegant in its simplicity.

Citibank: The PAM's job is to identify the needs of the customer, and then connect the customer to the capabilities that are available internally. Being a team player, as opposed to being a star, is critical for PAMs.

IBM: Today, Managing Directors (MDs) own the global account relationships, even though many other individuals touch the client in some way. (MDs are GAMs in IBM's current terminology.) IBM expects the MD to have business relationships at the highest levels in the global account. The MD is the single individual held accountable for global revenues. The MD is responsible for developing and maintaining the global account plan. Also, he is responsible for inspiring the global account team to identify substantial global opportunities. The MD is responsible for managing those team members that spend significant (greater than 50 percent) time supporting the global client.

What Level of Authority Should the Firm Grant Global Account Managers?

What authority should the firm be willing to grant GAMs to carry out their roles and responsibilities? Many firms sidestep assigning authority, but this is not a trivial issue. The degree of decision-making authority granted to GAMs has a major influence on the candidate set for GAM positions. Further, if you set expectations that GAMs will have a great deal of authority, then run them through the ringer on each decision, you will cause a great deal of frustration. GAMs will be dissatisfied and management will have serious morale issues. You must be seriously concerned that the actual levels of empowerment that GAMs enjoy correspond to those that the firm specifies in defining the GAM position.

During the formative years of IBM's global account program, Client Executives (CEs) were led to believe they had some degree of pricing authority. (At the time, Client Executive [CE] was the IBM terminology for Global Account Manager [GAM]; this has now evolved to Managing Director [MD].) Based on this belief, several CEs developed and presented customers with global proposals. At the last minute, these CEs were forced to negotiate pricing approval with IBM management in several individual countries. Not only were these CEs made to look foolish in front of their customers, on some occasions a deal was lost because of slow reaction time. Why did such a problem occur? IBM finance executives told CEs they had pricing authority, but financial operations staffers were adamant that CEs should not control profit-level decisions. This internal battle continues even today, regardless of the fact that IBM has granted "pricing authority" to a limited number of MDs.

As a second illustration, a multinational manufacturing firm's global account was a European-based bank. This bank acquired several Latin American banks. The GAM promised to extend headquarters pricing to the new acquisitions. He was severely embarrassed, and the global account very upset, when Latin American countries refused to honor the deep discounts provided in Europe.

Delegating authority is tricky to execute. In the global context it can also be extremely risky. Properly delegated, decision-making authority can be an important element in building account relationships. In our research, we identified a broad range of attitudes relating to authority that firms delegate to GAMs. They tend to fall into three camps:

- *Skeptics:* To skeptics, GAMs are elevated salespeople. Skeptics believe that giving GAMs the ability to commit resources and/or set prices is a sure recipe for over-committing resources and/or pricing low. They acknowledge that GAMs may "get the deal," but are horrified over the potential profitability implications.
- *Enlightened:* Enlightened executives populate the other end of the spectrum. They recognize that GAMs are high-level strategic thinkers. They believe GAMs will make responsible judgments in the firm's best interests. They take the necessary actions to ensure the firm stands behind decisions made by the GAMs.
- *Fence sitters:* Fence sitters are willing to give GAMs some level of authority. But they require check and balance systems before executing on GAM decisions.

In any global firm, reasonable people may disagree on the appropriate type and level of delegation for GAMs. Regardless of whether you are a skeptic, enlightened, or fence sitter, you must have a delegation process. You must be very specific regarding what authority you are delegating. You must clearly document and communicate your policy to the entire organization. And you must follow through on whatever authority you have delegated. We clarify with a few examples of the types of authority sometimes delegated to GAMs.

Pricing

Most firms do not delegate full pricing authority to GAMs. Setting global prices is typically a complex exercise often involving country-specific issues and legal requirements. Some companies allow GAMs negotiating room, for example, by allowing them a range of discounts off-list, that does not require approval from local pricing managers. In these cases, the GAM negotiates the country price based on market conditions and corporate-profit-margin requirements. In other firms, GAMs have the *authority* to quote a discount, but must secure final approval from local pricing managers. Considerations concerning price-authority delegation to GAMs are product complexity, need for speed, competitive situation, current process efficiency, and regulatory situations.

Resource commitments

If your market offer combines product and service elements, the ability to commit resources can be a powerful tool for GAMs. But, it can be a nightmare for the business unit delivering the service. When your GAM can commit to global implementation, it can make the difference between winning and losing a deal. Winning is one thing, but the task of getting those service resources to the required countries at a specific point in time can be daunting.

Hiring and firing

Many firms allow GAMs to select global-team members. The logical extension is to give GAMs authority to remove people from their teams—for unsatisfactory performance or to satisfy a customer request. Also, country management should secure GAM approval before removing a team member from a global account. Delegation to the GAM can be a cultural stretch. For example, suppose the firm has a French GAM assigned to a global account based in France. Giving that GAM the ability to select local team members in the U.S. or Germany would likely test the cultural maturity of most corporations, country managements, and individual team members.

Base pay and incentive compensation

Generally speaking, firms do not implement single global compensation plans. Rather, individual countries build compensation practices that fit their own cultural and economic environments. This reality can be extremely challenging for a GAM attempting to effectively manage a global compensation program. When a representative with responsibilities for other accounts conducts much of the local coverage of a global account, it is even more complex. Delegating to GAMs the authority to determine and administer base pay and incentive compensation is very difficult.

> At IBM, a global sales plan team develops sales plan templates. It expects all countries to follow corporate guidelines. Countries can modify templates, but only after gaining approval from the corporate overseer of the global account program. If a remote resource on a global account spends at least 50 percent of their time selling to the global client, the IBM MDs can set targets and determine if the team member met those targets. This is still a challenge but, at least, reduces the complexity.

Spending and budgets

As we discussed in Chapter 4, one of the key indicators demonstrating senior management commitment to the global program is a visible international budget covering GAM expenses. An important consideration in delegating authority to GAMs is their ability to make spending decisions without having to seek approval on individual expenditures.

Summary

Although our bias is toward delegating more (rather than less) authority for GAMs, we do not take a strong position. We believe the appropriate delegation level is a matter of circumstance—company background, GAM competence, and environmental requirements. The important issue is that management understands that this is an important tension that must be managed.

Management must decide the delegation level it is prepared to accept across the various potential areas of delegation. It should communicate its decisions widely, and then stick to its decisions. The level of authority granted is an important driver for recruiting and selecting GAMs. Certainly management should only delegate authority to executives it believes are competent to exercise that authority.

Skill Sets for GAMs

To fulfill their roles and responsibilities, GAMs must possess a complex inventory of knowledge, skills, and abilities (KSAs). GAMs must make difficult decisions across several difficult dimensions, for example, global versus local, strategic versus tactical, long-term versus short-term, and growth versus profit. A few years ago, a well-known assessment organization conducted a study for a major U.S.-based high technology company with a 10-year history of global account management. The GAM role was judged the second most complex job the firm had ever assessed—the most complex was CEO. We classify these KSAs for GAMs into business management; boundary spanning and relationship building; leadership, communications, and team building; and global.

Although the skill set inventory is little different in type from that required by any strategic account manager, the global dimension significantly *ups the ante*, right across the board. GAMs must employ their skills in multiple cultures, in multiple languages, across immense geographic distances (physical and time zone). Further, because the organization structure (for example, geographic-area) may be inhospitable to global initiatives, the GAM must have an additional degree of sensitivity, perspective, and experience. GAMs must be globally savvy, have an international frame of mind, a global outlook, and an awareness of, and a tolerance for, cultural diversity.

Business management

The GAM is really a results-oriented, market-focused business manager, where the market is the global account. Such a global business may represent hundreds of millions of dollars in revenues and significant profits. Not only are GAMs responsible for these revenues, in some global account programs they may also be responsible for profits. To manage such a business successfully, the GAM must be able to develop and implement the global account plan. We highlight KSAs needed to fulfill this responsibility.

Business and financial acumen

The GAM must have a solid understanding of the global business environment, especially as it impacts the global account's industry and the markets addressed by the global account. He should be able to have an intelligent conversation about the world economy and those global political and economic institutions that impact firms operating globally. He should be able to take apart company financial statements so as to gain deep insight into his global account's performance.

Strategic vision and planning capabilities

The GAM must be able to craft the global account plan and keep it updated on a day-by-day basis. He must have the information gathering and analytic abilities to keep abreast of developments in the global account's industry, actions at the account, actions by competitors, and actions at his own firm. He must be fully cognizant of his firm's capabilities and display superior knowledge of its market offerings. He must be able to identify opportunities and draw on the firm's resources to develop innovative-targeted solutions. He must also have the skills to develop a coherent strategy and action programs that guide the firm's actions to exploit those opportunities.

Portfolio management

The GAM has global responsibility for the account, but operates with limited resources. He must manage current business, expand current business, and develop new business. In other words, he must manage a portfolio of opportunities and threats. Balancing many different balls requires a high degree of skill in portfolio management.

Implementation Skills

Planning and strategy development may be critical, but the GAM must also possess a different set of *hard* business-oriented skills. He must make things happen—be able to execute—around the world, with a documented and traceable plan. Culturally acceptable global negotiation skills are critical for the GAM, at the very least, when contracts are up for bid. Consultative selling skills are important for working with the account in a collaborative way—understanding its global business issues and strategies, and making global sales—often for very large contracts. Finally, the GAM must possess effective problem-solving skills for resolving difficult global issues—for example, imports, exports and international law—in a loosely constructed environment with little supervision. Significant skill is required to clearly define the problem or situation, logically diagnose causes, identify solutions and create action plans—all the while taking risks, but balancing those risks against the impact on the global business. The GAM must also be able to monitor the situation at the global account and anticipate problems so they may be avoided or, at least, have their impact mitigated. When executing in a global model, there are so many places the ball can be dropped—a well-trained GAM minimizes dropped balls.

Boundary spanning and relationship building

The GAM must work across many organizational boundaries. These include functional and hierarchical barriers at both the global account and his firm. These are global boundaries (not just domestic). They include the extra dimensions of nationality, culture, time, and distance that are much attenuated (or do not exist) domestically.

GAMs must possess a set of personal and political skills. They must manage a complex set of relationships. They must navigate both within and between the global account and the firm. They must also interface with third-party organizations that may be instrumental in enhancing important relationships. In particular, the GAM must possess top-flight communication skills, including presenting and listening abilities, in a milieu where participants may embrace multiple native languages.

The GAM must possess qualities that enable him to build credibility and trust with key executives—both in the global account and his firm—on a worldwide basis. GAMs must display heightened cultural awareness so they are equally at home in multiple American, European, Asian, and African settings. These settings include business meetings and also social occasions. All these settings are necessary to building deep and productive relationships—with executives from the global account and also among the GAM's own colleagues.

Leadership, communication and team building

In most cases, GAMs are not successful by doing things around the world themselves. Rather, they must exercise leadership and team-building skills. Again, these skills are not unlike those required of KAMs, but for GAMs we are painting on a global (not domestic) canvas.

Leaders must set direction, extract promises of behavior, communicate, provide feedback, learn, and model effective leadership behaviors for individuals and global team members. They must understand cultural differences among their own team members, and display significant cultural understanding while exercising their own particular leadership styles. The GAM must understand the language of organizational currencies for encouraging people to act as required around the world—inspiration, satisfaction at completing the task, enhancing organizational position, strengthening a relationship, and improving self concept. Getting things done by team members is one thing—getting things done by other personnel within the firm is a precious skill that relatively few GAMs possess. Being able to get things done by global customer personnel is even more rare.

The GAM must possess extraordinary communication skills. First, not only does he need to communicate effectively, in general he must communicate with a large and varied audience. Perhaps most important is the ability to communicate effectively in general with personnel at the global account. These individuals include the customer's global executive team and may also include employees deep in the organization, perhaps upwards of 100 different individuals.

Second, the GAM must communicate effectively within his own organization. In particular, communication with the global account team is critical for developing the global account plan and executing the various action plans. Additionally, he must communicate effectively with a broad variety of organizational units to secure resources for his global account and otherwise secure their cooperation. Finally, he has to communicate with his firm's executive team and the global account program.

In contrast to domestic KAMs, GAMs must communicate effectively with multiple cultures. Although most firms use English for global team communications, language skills are still an asset. More particularly, language sensitivity is important, regardless of firm or account country location. When GAMs communicate in a language other than their native tongues, they must be very precise with language, directly or for translators. For example, they should avoid colloquialisms such as domestic sports references.

Finally, the GAM must be able to build and manage the global account team. GAMs must inspire a diverse cadre of organizational members to join their teams. Once joined, they must pull together to build the global account plan, then to execute the strategy. GAMs should possess mentoring skills to develop team members—the next generation of GAMs may be drawn from this pool. They must be able to manage individuals from many different nationalities and cultures, operating in different functions, based in many countries around the world. And, they must inspire effective communication among these team members. Significant skills are required to assemble such a team, and then turn it into an effective machine that marches to a single drummer.

Of course, global team membership varies from firm to firm. At Saatchi & Saatchi, for example, critical personnel on a client account team include those with responsibility for client service, creative development, media, and production. The GAM is responsible for the client relationship, client loyalty, client revenues, and strategic leadership with that client.

The global team working with a typical IBM global account manager includes personnel focused on:

- **Financial offerings**—crafts opportunities into global contracts and proposals.
- **Sales operations**—tracks progress and reports to the firm on all the metrics. Also handles sales operations issues.

- **Relationship sales people**—remotely based and assigned to the global account's specific country organizations.
- **Brand specialists**—for example, software, hardware, services and personal computers, assigned at the headquarters location.

When IBM wins a major outsourcing contract, the responsible IBM executive is also assigned. Team size is roughly related to customer size, diversity of the global account's various divisions, and its organizational structure for global operations.

Global

Many requirements for GAMs are fundamental skills with a significant global overlay. A domestically focused GAM will just not cut it—truly successful GAMs must consider themselves global citizens. We are talking about understanding global business drivers and world economies, global industry knowledge, global product knowledge, unique country considerations, strategic vision, and planning capabilities that consider global markets. GAMs must be able to solve complex problems that involve imports, exports and international legal and regulatory systems.

The successful GAM's relationship management skills must encompass the account's global environment, consultative selling skills for global sales, cultural empathy, cross-cultural and ethnic communication skills, global team leadership across cultures, time, and distance, and persuasive skills to convince product support teams that the needs of the GAM's account are critically important.

We, the authors, have roots in Africa, Asia, Europe, Latin America and the U.S. We have a passion for international travel that makes us restless if we stay in one spot for very long. But when we arrive, we take time to see the country and dive into its culture. We believe the drive for multiple cultural experiences is the *sine qua non* for effective GAMs.

Summary

Required competencies for an effective GAM are impressive, even daunting. We offer a top-level summary of skills required by GAMs versus those of domestically based KAMs (Table 7.1). Unless the firm identifies individuals who possess (or can quickly learn) the required skills, the best-laid plans for managing global accounts can wither on the vine. That is why the firm must introduce a robust system for identifying promising human resources to fill these positions.

Table 7.1   Skill Sets for GAMs

Skills for KAMs	Headlines for Expanded Skills for GAMs
Business Management	
Business and financial acumen	Global industry and business drivers and world economies
Strategic vision and planning capabilities	Focus on global markets and opportunities
Portfolio management skills	Balance global opportunities and threats
Implementation skills	Make things happen around the world
Boundary Spanning and Relationship-Building	
Internal functions, virtual team, and customer relationship management	Global relationship management skills that encompass the client's global environment and culture
Leadership and Communications Team Building	
Leadership skills Communications skills	Must display leadership, communication abilities and cultural empathy for individuals and team members around the world by understanding motivational and communication tools
Team-Building skills	Must construct and develop a diverse global team from multiple cultures across multiple time zones and global distances

Securing Effective GAMs

Effective GAMs with the necessary competencies are extremely hard to find. Further, potential GAMs are difficult to develop. As a result, the investment to build a competent GAM force can be substantial in monetary cost and length of development time. What may be even more serious is the opportunity cost of appointing an ineffective GAM. The lost opportunity may severely impact on the firm/global account relationship—an ineffective GAM may lose sales revenues far into the future and destroy teamwork that will take years to repair.

Your global strategic customers expect your best people. If you provide less than your best, you will endure weaker relationships and lost revenue opportunities. In addition, your competitors want your best GAMs— investing in a person that switches sides benefits your competitors and hurts you. So, it is not just a question of getting the best people to be GAMs. The

GAM position must be sufficiently attractive that the *right* people not only aspire to be GAMs, they want to stay with you once they earn the position. At some firms, GAMs are overall perceived as having extraordinary status because they represent the customer. Can you say at your firm: "People are breaking down doors to get GAM positions?"

Here are questions to ask of your firm as a checklist regarding your GAMs:

- Do we have the talent pool for filling our GAM positions?
- Do we have a system in place to attract talented candidates?
- Do we have a process to identify, recruit and select GAMs?
- Do we have a process to develop and train GAMs?
- Can we build the skills we need while implementing a GAM program?
- Can we outsource some of the skill-building, training, and development tasks to external providers?
- Can we build a compensation plan that will sufficiently motivate GAMs to deliver the growth and profit we require from our global accounts?
- Do we have a process for minimizing losses of our most talented GAMs?

Your approach to securing GAMs must closely relate to the roles and responsibilities you wish them to fulfill. We noted earlier that key issues are the degree of authority delegated and the organizational level the GAM position represents. Because of the GAM role's importance, we believe the process should be rigorous. The higher the level you position your GAMs, the more rigorous the process must be. Today, most firms have structured methods, and invest considerable money, time, and effort in developing candidates for executive-level positions such as country manager, factory manager, human resource director, industry or productline VPs. These individuals are often given cross-functional or international-development assignments, attend prestigious Executive Development programs, or participate in fully funded Executive MBA programs. And most firms have standardized selection methods for winnowing down a set of candidates.

When seeking GAMs, you should seriously consider building in some of the tested methods you use to fill these executive roles. After all, at the end of the day, the revenue and profit responsibilities of these senior executives often pale in comparison to the financial contribution from a single GAM. Just do the math and consider whether you should invest significantly more in your GAMs.

GAMs are incredibly important to the future of your corporations. You cannot afford not to implement a first-rate system for recruiting, selecting, training and developing, measuring and compensating, and retaining GAMs. Unless you take this very seriously, you will not appoint and retain persons capable of fulfilling the critical roles and responsibilities we have discussed.

Recruiting

You must be very clear about the organizational level for which you are recruiting GAMs. The position definition plays a major role in determining the quality of your GAM candidates. If the GAM position is seen as super salesperson with little decision-making authority, reporting at a low organizational level, you will get one type of candidate. If the GAM position is seen as a NAM with a little extra responsibility, you will get another type of candidate. If the position has significant delegated responsibility and reports at a high organizational level, you will get quite another.

The organizational level is also critical for access at the global account. If the GAM reports at a low organizational level, access at the customer will also be at a low level. But, if the firm requires that global account access be at a high level—even with the CEO—then the GAM must be of a much higher caliber, and report at a correspondingly higher level.

Basically, you have two GAM sources—inside and outside the firm. Regardless, you should consider developing systems to produce a talent-pool inventory. As global account programs grow in importance and expand in scope, the requirements placed on GAMs will expand concurrently. Because of the role's importance, you cannot afford to have GAM positions go unfilled—or to fill them with inappropriate personnel.

For internal candidates, you need systems for identifying potential GAMs. You must also ensure they have opportunities to gain the relevant skills and experience via training programs and job assignments. Among approaches that we have seen used successfully are:

- Domestic sales and sales management
- Positions that require interfacing with multiple firm divisions, such as marketing/sales coordinator
- International assignments to broaden global perspective
- General manager positions
- Executive assistant to the global account program executive provides an invaluable view from the top.

For external candidates, the firm should implement a continual process of recruiting/interviewing potential candidates for future available positions.

Inside candidates bring with them knowledge of the firm. That expertise should enhance their ability to work on the organization to secure the internal resources they need to develop and implement their global account plans. This knowledge should also help them resolve conflicts between divisions, countries, functions, and internal power bases such as finance.

An obvious source for GAMs is NAMs. In effect, the firm elevates the customer-relationship position by territory expansion—from a single nation-state to the entire world. The major benefit of this candidate source is knowledge of the global account—typically based on experience in the account's most important market. The major negative of generalized job expansion, from national to global, is that individual account managers may not be currently functioning at a high level—even nationally. Even high functioning NAMs may not possess the broader and deeper skill set needed to be successful at the global level. Certainly, wholesale promotion of NAMs to GAMs, without the appropriate training, development, and weeding-out mechanisms, is ill-conceived. Not only will individual GAMs fail, significant human resource costs may follow.

A major U.S. industrial company with a successful national account program introduced global account management. One KAM, born and raised in Dayton, Ohio, had been very successful with his Cincinnati-based key account. However, this individual rarely traveled outside Ohio and, when appointed to be a GAM, did not have a passport. Six months into his tenure as GAM he had to be removed from the position. Shortly thereafter he left the company.

Of course, successful NAMs may meet your enhanced global criteria. If so, you secure the benefits of ensuring that the basics of business management; boundary-spanning and relationship-building; and leadership, communication and team-building skills; are already in place. Of course, global-oriented training may be necessary.

The firm may also draw GAMs from many other internal positions. In one major U.S. manufacturing firm, corporate account managers (CAMs) are secured from four major areas—sales, marketing, technical, and manufacturing. This firm also focuses heavily on direct international experience or, at least, working in an international environment. For example, several

CAMs were previously country general managers—Ireland, Portugal, and Ecuador. In many cases, successful candidates start from scratch in building global account relationships. This firm balances global teams by, for example, supporting a CAM drawn from sales and marketing with a colleague whose background may be R&D or manufacturing.

IBM formed a developmental-GAM position for some of its larger clients—this position focuses on international sales issues and closing global deals. Many projects within organizations have a global element that must be managed—these may also be used developmentally. Although these global project managers may not have sales responsibility, many of the needed skills and attributes parallel those required by GAMs.

Some firms believe GAMs can be a significant source of competitive advantage. They make significant human resource investments to staff this role.

> When Citibank hires for its PAM track, it anticipates that successful candidates will achieve these positions in about seven years. In those seven years, Citibank makes sure that its PAMs possess the critical skill requirements and types of behaviors that are critical to success. Ninety percent of Citibank's PAMs are appointed from within the organization.

One useful process for identifying, assessing, and developing promising GAM candidates is to develop a skills database. Earlier we introduced some critical skills for effective GAMs. Your firm needs a system for assessing the current skill base of potential GAMs on those critical dimensions. For example, consider four important skills for assessing GAM candidates— developing and maintaining client relationships, knowing the global account's business strategies, knowing our firm's technologies, and knowing our firm's international operations (Table 7.2).

The global Program Office should maintain an inventory of potential GAMs. Periodically, the Program Office should assess each potential GAM on tables such as these. It should develop clear verbal descriptions for each score and ensure these are thoroughly understood by potential candidates and their managers. The potential candidate's manager should review initial self-assessments for accuracy using appropriate processes to resolve disagreements.

Depending on the particular criterion, you may require a GAM candidate to score "4" or "5" to be acceptable for a position. Candidates would have to demonstrate they had reached the appropriate level in a previous or

Table 7.2   Simple Assessment Tool for Critical GAM Skills

Knowledge, Skills and Abilities	Level of Competency				
	Minimal 1	Low 2	Moderate 3	High 4	Very High 5
Developing and Maintaining Global account relationships					
Knowing the global account's business strategies					
Knowing our firm's technologies					
Knowing our firm's international operations					

1 = minimal competency level; 5 = very high competency level.

current job. Suppose, for example, you appoint corporate-level GAMs to manage the firm's entire relationship with your global accounts. You are evaluating two candidates A and B.

- *Candidate A:* Candidate A is a highly successful KAM in one of your four business units. This candidate scores "4" or "5" on the first two criteria—*global account relationships* and *global accounts business strategies*. *Knowing our firm's technologies* is "2" or "3" because his experience is with a single business unit. Since the candidate has had no global exposure, *knowing our firm's international operations* scores a "1." This assessment could lead directly to career development actions. For example, you could place the candidate in a corporate-wide position with significant international exposure where he would secure experience with all firm technologies.
- *Candidate B:* Candidate B is a successful manager in an important corporate R&D department. He is keen to advance to a GAM position. He scores "3" level on *global account relationships* based on experience with R&D partnerships, and "2" on *global account's business strategies*. On the other hand, *knowing our firm's technology* is "5"—*knowing our firm's international operations* is "2." This candidate needs very different career development options perhaps, by moving into a domestic KAM role.

Using this system, the firm should populate KSAs tables with accurate assessments of all potential candidates for GAM positions. These tables contribute to the process of identifying and developing candidates. They do not replace the judgment of responsible executives or other company programs designed to bring high potential individuals to management's attention.

There are powerful arguments for internal GAM appointments. But, if top quality internal candidates are not available, you should seek outside candidates. What you should not do is appoint unqualified internal candidates. Most firms are reluctant to appoint GAMs from outside the firm. When they do, the primary factor is the candidate's knowledge of the global account and/or its industry. If your business model requires GAMs to possess a great deal of specialized industry knowledge, hiring outside candidates maybe the way to go. Three possible sources are:

- Global account managers with competitor companies also targeting the global account
- Other executives with significant knowledge of the account's industry
- Executives working for the global account.

Over and above significant industry knowledge, these candidates may have relationships with senior executives at the global account. The downside is that they typically lack intimate knowledge of your firm. This deficit is balanced by powerful industry- and/or account-related credentials. These candidates may also have a complete set of global account management skills that internal candidates do not possess. Finally, some candidates may have no meaningful relationship with your firm or the global client—superior global account management skills may make them viable candidates.

In many cases, global account management is geared to enhancing internal efficiencies by resolving internal conflicts. Outsiders have to navigate the internal company maze without the benefit of experience. A *maze-bright* GAM only develops firm insights and executive contacts from years of working inside the firm. The outsider may always be viewed as an outsider and therefore be less effective.

Selecting

We assume that the firm has developed a recruitment pool of available GAM candidates.

The Selection Process

Selecting GAMs is a complex job. By developing and effectively managing a rigorous selection process, you can avoid some of the pitfalls of sloppy systems.

For example, you should not allow a single manager to appoint individuals to the GAM position. Management needs a rigorous process that offers a slate of candidates, each of whom has been pre-approved as meeting the GAM criteria.

The *process owner* should be a member of the Program Office who is critical to managing the recruiting and selecting process. This individual maintains the set of selection criteria and the skills database. He also manages the process by which potential candidates are screened against these criteria. In the most successful programs, this person is also qualified to be, or has been, a GAM. Hence, he brings to the process a level of credibility that is absent if the *process owner* is viewed as just a *process staffer.* Appearances are important; when managed by a *staffer,* candidates may view the process as ineffective and bureaucratic, even when it is not. The process owner should be highly involved in the appointment decision and should be measured on how successful GAMs are selected.

The selection process should be formal and rigorous to ensure the firm selects the best possible candidate(s). Remember you are entrusting your most important global clients to this individual(s). We strongly believe that formally and consistently applying screening criteria improves the likelihood of securing predictable results. Process formality also signals the importance of the role, both to your internal organization and to your global accounts. Also, it imparts to your candidates the level of importance you place on the KSAs you identify as critical to the success of your global account program.

Finally, the selection process should conform to the same rigorous standards you employ for other critical managerial positions. Typically, these systems involve two core elements: first, structured methods to assess competencies; second, multiple interviews with senior executives experienced in managing global accounts. These interviews focus on the roles and responsibilities of the GAM position and the required skill sets.

Selection criteria

We noted earlier that only the CEO position is more complex than that of the GAM. As global team leader, the GAM manages many complex issues for a complex customer. The GAM must build credibility at account headquarters and also with the global account's executive team. The GAM is also at the center of resolving multiple internal cross-functional and cross-divisional conflicts. The GAM must build credibility with your firm's key operating executives so as to manage these issues. The GAM must demonstrate value both within your firm and with the account. The pressures can be enormous and the pain of resolving global issues can be severe. Clearly, it takes a special kind of person to be an effective GAM. Working hand in hand, the Program Office and Human Resources (HR) staff should hammer out clear selection criteria and ensure the recruitment and selection process is well understood by field management. As part of this process, HR works with the set of GAM roles and responsibilities developed by the Program Office, and turns these into GAM position descriptions. These descriptions play a key role in ensuring that senior managers have has clear guidance on managing the GAMs. The selection infrastructure combines HR practices, Global Account Program Office involvement, and field management execution.

Many companies employ assessment tools to screen GAM candidates. For example, Personnel Decisions International (PDI) suggests the following:

- *Cognitive testing* to measure the candidate's propensity for inductive and deductive reasoning. These tests focus on the ability to recognize patterns, handle complex problems, and draw appropriate conclusions.
- *Personality and work style inventories* can help determine a candidate's personality traits and motivations, and how they relate to people. They can assess flexibility, adaptability, and openness to new ideas, and may assess leadership potential.
- *Inventory of relevant experiences* can ensure a candidate's complete background is available to relate past experiences with GAM requirements. For example, suppose a candidate's own ingenuity developed a global brand program without executive support. Further, suppose a candidate traveled extensively, acquired a deep understanding of multiple cultures, and was successful in cross-geography team building. She would satisfy several GAM skill requirements.

Competencies can be assessed through computer-based (formerly paper and pencil) methods and through structured interviews. Structured questions help to gauge the candidate's depth in critical competencies. Simulations can also help form an opinion of how a candidate may respond in typical GAM situations—they provide an opportunity for demonstration of critical skills that may be unobservable in current positions.

Global skills are important criteria for effective GAMs. The sorts of experiences that may be acceptable as qualifiers include international assignments, project management, extensive international travel, assignments in a global account environment, and living abroad as a family member.

Consider the following example of a GAM candidate with whom we are familiar. He traveled extensively with his family attending schools in Europe and Israel before joining the firm. He served a tour of duty with the Israeli army. He lived in ten different countries before settling in the U.S. where he earned an MBA. He speaks five languages and understands several more. For most of us, he would be a dream candidate.

We know several firms that have invested significantly in identifying criteria for the *ideal* GAM.

> Oracle Corporation conducted research with GAMs, senior management and global accounts. The resulting profile was used to develop criteria for GAM selection and performance evaluation. The profile is also used to create personal development programs for each GAM.[3]

Decision time

So, you defined GAM roles and responsibilities, you settled the authority delegation issue, you identified required skill sets, and implemented a formal selection process. You have identified ten strong candidates for four GAM positions. How to proceed?

The appropriate process depends on the GAM organizational level and on your global management structure. We have observed several effective approaches:

- *GAM is a high-level executive position:* The selection team comprises the CEO, COO, and Global Vice President of Sales. This team of executives reviews the situation at each open global account. It selects the candidate believed to be the most qualified. This approach works well if the *process owner* has done a good job of prescreening the candidates and provides the selection team with all relevant factors. GAMs selected through this process have excellent credibility—they have been *handpicked* by top management.
- *GAM has significant authority but is not a high-level executive position:* The selection team comprises senior executives and current GAMs. It reviews candidates put forward by the *process owner.* This team reviews

---

requirements for the global account and selects the candidate by majority vote. A more senior executive may ratify team decisions. This method works well with mature programs where experienced GAMs are available to act as jurors. Of course, similar boards can function well without GAM jurors.

When the Marriott Corporation introduced its global account program, it selected 11 GAMs to serve its 30 *Alliance Accounts*. Each candidate completed a battery of psychological tests and was interviewed sequentially by two VPs, to a standard format. The selection committee comprised the executive VP and the five VPs who conducted the interviews. J.W. Marriott Jr, Chairman and CEO, approved the final recommendations.[4]

Role of the global customer

The firm uses either of the two methods just discussed but the process generates not a single choice, but two or three candidates. These candidates are offered to the global customer—*the global customer* makes the final choice. This method is appealing if the customer wants to build a high-level relationship and welcomes your firm's involvement in its strategy development. Giving the account final choice can be a very positive step in relationship building. To illustrate, a few years ago, IBM provided Coca Cola with a short list of GAM candidates—Coke executives made the selection.

In selecting GAMs, management must seriously consider the inside/outside question. We discussed the core issues. Further, selecting internal candidates may provide a positive morale boost by providing exciting opportunities to firm employees. Conversely, if sufficient GAM expertise (or potential) is not available inside, outside hires may be the only reasonable approach, at least in the short run.

Training and development

Training and development play two critical roles in securing future-high-performing GAMs. (We discuss the specifics of developing GAMs in Chapter 9, in the context of training infrastructure.) First, training and development impacts on the caliber of your recruiting pool—the type of

---

[4] David Townshend, VP Alliance Accounts, Marriott Lodging at Strategic Account Management Annual Conference, Orlando, FL, May 2–5, 1999.

individual you are seeking will be reluctant to "join up" if you do not provide well-designed training and development. In this day and age, professionals entering a challenging new assignment expect to be trained— it is that simple! Second, if you do not invest in your existing GAMs, you are sending them the wrong message. We observe that many firms are not sending the right message!

Earlier, we laid out the primary skill set for GAMs. A skills assessment is one vehicle for assuring that GAM candidates possess these primary skills. The firm may develop these skills through a combination of job experience, education, training, coaching, and mentoring.

Regardless of how ready a candidate is for a GAM position, some training is probably valuable, if only to establish commonality in systems, processes, and language. Further, even a high-functioning NAM will need help broadening his planning expertise from national to global. Training to manage a far-flung network of team members, operating a global Intranet system, selling to international customers, managing international projects, and multi-cultural and foreign language study may also be appropriate.[5]

Training requirements are influenced by organizational placement of the GAM position and the recruiting pool. Further, training required for new GAMs is likely to differ from training for seasoned veterans. Regardless, the firm should base all training programs on a formal skills assessment. For example, a recruitment process that promoted NAMs to GAMs would benefit from a standardized approach as training requirements are likely to be common across many candidates. By contrast, if you recruit GAMs from many different backgrounds and experience, tailored training may be more effective. There are many potential areas for training—for example, high-level selling, negotiations, planning, relationship development, and cultural sensitivity.

Essentially, the firm can devise external and/or internal educational experiences. In general, a well-designed mix of internal and external programs is most beneficial.

Although less available than key/strategic account programs *per se*, educational opportunities in global account management are publicly available from such organizations as the Strategic Account Management Association (SAMA), Columbia Business School, William Patterson

---

[5] Ensuring that GAMs understand cultural taboos around the world is particularly important. See, for example, Roger E. Axtell, *Do's and Taboos around the World*, 3rd. edition, New York: Wiley, 1993.

University (New Jersey), and the University of St. Gallen (Switzerland). In these programs, participants learn, for example, how global account programs and GAMs operate in other organizations, what global accounts expect, and various global business issues.

These options are many. For example, consultants offer specially designed global account planning workshops where novitiate GAMs learn how to develop global account plans. Other courses focus on specific areas of required expertise such as contracting, business practices, global product management issues, and account procedures and programs for GAMs.

A more serious approach is to develop GAM certification programs, combining internal and external educational experiences, such as with leading Schools of Business. These programs are an excellent vehicle to ensure your GAMs possess the KSAs you require for your global account programs.

At IBM, certification candidates must complete a business school program. They meet skill requirements, write a client project paper, prepare a package containing certification-relevant information (i.e., resume, accomplishments, and knowledge of client), go before a board of their peers and relevant executives and are recertified every three years. The mandatory client project paper is particularly important. It provides candidates the opportunity to apply what they learned during the formal educational program—they write a paper analyzing their account's industry, its strategies and organization. When candidates believe they have completed the requirements, they have three personal interviews with board members. These interviews validate the certification package and the candidate is brought before the entire board for certification.

Citibank has a two-year training program for PAMs. This program combines formal training at Citibank institutes in London and Tokyo with rotational job experiences. Program length depends on the individual PAM, but lasts a minimum of two years (maximum three years). Citibank makes a substantial training investment in global account management and believes that PAMs form a common bond by being trained together. Citibank requires PAM trainees to go to their training programs with a current client problem.

The firm should also put in place processes for continual GAM upgrading.

Feedback mechanisms

Feedback mechanisms are essential for continually upgrading GAM expertise and performance. The feedback program should include fellow global team members, firm executives and customer personnel. The process can be as straightforward as a 360-degree feedback program. Of course, the ability of 360-degree feedback programs to operate effectively may be limited by culture but, nonetheless, can be highly valuable developmentally.

Access to senior management

Providing GAMs with access to an Executive Oversight Committee is a valuable way to provide leadership development. Not only do GAMs have an opportunity to see how executives interact, they are exposed to problem solving at an executive level.

Global account panels

Customer panels/Advisory Boards have many purposes. In the context of continually upgrading GAM expertise, GAMs gain experience in how their firm executives interact with executives from various customer firms. Such experience can be invaluable.

> At Schneider Electric, global competencies are built through mentoring and on-the-job training. Schneider holds annual week-long meetings—experts are brought in to train managers on specific topics. At annual *muscle-building* training, Schneider selects special topics, for example communicating soft costs to customers.

Measuring performance and compensating

The implications of Measuring and Compensating for securing future-high-performing GAMs are similar to those for Training and Development. How you measure and compensate GAMs has a direct impact on your ability to recruit and retain highly qualified and successful individuals. High-performing GAMs want to be measured appropriately and accurately, and compensated accordingly. If your measurements do not recognize both results and effort, and you do not reward GAMs commensurate with their overall revenue/profit contribution, recruitment and retention is much more difficult.

Having said that, measuring and rewarding GAMs solely on current financial results is inappropriate. Of course, the GAM role is highly important for securing revenues in the current year, but the GAM should also be building a long-term inter-organizational relationship. Focusing solely on this year's financial results sends GAMs the wrong message, and displays a lack of clear understanding of the GAM role. It also sends the wrong message to customers for whom the GAM is supposed to be a "trusted advisor!"

Because the GAM role has critical short-term and long-term elements, measurement and compensation should incorporate both results– ("R" measures) and process– ("P" measures).

Regarding "R" measures, it should go without saying, but we emphasize the fact that, when totaling the GAM's performance against quota, "a dollar of revenue is a dollar of revenue." We have seen many firms that give greater weight to "home-based" revenue versus foreign revenue. We have also seen firms treating *product* revenue as more important than *service* revenue. And some firms focus more heavily on *new revenue sources* versus *increased revenue from existing sources*. Measurement and compensation systems based on these principles are excellent examples of misalignment, misdirection, and mistaken policy. Nonetheless, in the early stages of managing global accounts in a geographic-based line organization, the firm may need to count non-domestic revenues as some multiple of domestic revenues—for recognition purposes, and to guarantee that country management allows locally based GAMs to place appropriate attention on non-domestic opportunities.

Unless the GAM places proper effort and emphasis on managing the global account, results are likely to be unpredictable and contain surprises. For this reason, the firm should build a manageable number of "P" measures (3–5) into the GAM's Performance Appraisal and Compensation, by means of a Management by Objectives or Balanced Scorecard system. Examples of candidate "P" measures are:

- Quality of the global account planning process and strategy development
- Implementation of strategic initiatives at the account
- Delivery of agreed services to the account
- Depth and breadth of executive relationships at the global account
- Global account willingness to beta-test new products
- Effective use of the partnership executive (PE)
- Usefulness of the firm's website for the global account
- Quality of GAM's strategic communication plan

- Customer satisfaction score and improvement
- Feedback from country management regarding GAM support of local business
- Progress against objectives for account action plans.

The underlying rationale for measurement and the compensation plan should be to drive behaviors that are generally consistent with the objectives of the global account program. These objectives typically include protection of base business, growth in base business, penetration of new business opportunities, improved customer satisfaction, and achievement of partnership status. The Program Office is responsible for designing appropriate measurement and compensation systems. Of course, because the firm's strategic position and objectives differ from global account to global account, measurement systems for individual GAMs will necessarily differ from one another.

In general, because the GAM role typically has a large element of long-run relationship development, we recommend target compensation based on 80–90 percent salary and a 10–20 percent bonus, where the bonus is highly leveraged. The high salary component emphasizes the long-run strategic nature of the job—the highly leveraged bonus rewards the GAM for exceptional sales results in the short term. We firmly believe that the bonus should not be capped.

The absolute compensation level is critically important in attracting the right individuals to be GAMs. Candidate GAMs are often country managers, product-line managers, and regional sales VPs—they will not take pay-cuts to become GAMs. Absolute compensation is also related to the value the global account delivers to the firm. In our experience, in many cases, global account manager compensation ranges between that of first-line and second-line domestic sales managers. If senior executives assume GAM roles, they must be compensated appropriately. In the final analysis, what the firm is prepared to pay to individuals managing one of its most important assets says a lot about senior management commitment to managing global accounts.

Developing the "right" compensation system is a laudable objective to which the firm should pay significant attention. Further, because of general environmental instability and changing firm strategy, we expect the compensation system to evolve over time. The key word is "evolve," for sharp swings in compensation system can demotivate GAMs.

Not only should the firm focus on GAM measurement and compensation, it must also be concerned about global account team members. Many team members are locally based and essentially paid by a domestic country organization. But, their compensation should include recognition for their role in working with the global account. In many cases, working on the global account is just one of many responsibilities for a global team member. Unless the firm builds in provision for recognizing their role at the global account, domestic concerns may overwhelm them.

Consider, for example, the following situation. The global account decides to test a complex product in a small country. The local account manager would have to spend significant effort "baby sitting" the test, but may only have marginal revenue potential that would count toward his regular compensation. Yet, this test is critical for the global account and the GAM. The firm must develop a compensation system to reward this local account manager. First, a popular method of addressing this issue is to provide the GAM with a bonus pool that can be used to reward such team members. Typically, the Program Office has a budget that is available for allocation among individual GAMs. On average a GAM might have $10,000–$15,000 to allocate, the specific amount being related to the global account's share of overall revenue growth. This budget is allocated to individual team members based on performance against activity targets related to the account plan, or for some specific extraordinary achievement. A second way of rewarding local personnel for special perform- ance related to global accounts is to designate some portion of an individual country bonus for local members of global account teams, in consultation with the country managers.

At Square D/Schneider Electric many GAMs are paid more than other directors or management level employees—their job is consid- ered very difficult.

A major industrial company compensates GAMs with both salary and bonus. Salary adjustments are based on such factors as customer satisfaction, revenue growth, quality of account planning, and exe- cution. Bonus is based on specific targeted revenue opportunities, teamwork, product line balance, and a measure of personal growth.

At Citibank, a large percent of PAM compensation is given in the form of a bonus to reward good work.

Retaining

GAMs are extremely important to the global account relationship. A sig- nificant amount of time must pass before a newly appointed GAM can fully understand the challenge and develop a basic set of functioning relationships. Resultantly, the GAM should not turn over every couple of years. Rather, a minimum time on the job is at least 3–5 years—indeed, many GAMs may spend an entire career in this position.

If you have a serious global account program, your overall investment in an individual GAM is highly significant. The value of your GAM human resources is high, and unplanned attrition can be very serious. You should think seriously about retention strategies. Since your well-performing GAMs are typically highly sought after by competitors, you should continually monitor job satisfaction and make appropriate responses.

Of course, financial remuneration is an important factor in GAM retention, but other factors may also be critical. In particular, if you want to attract high-fliers to the GAM position, they will want to have some sense of their future with the organization when it is time to move on— career-path planning is essential for these individuals. Indeed, many GAMs move into such positions as VP of sales, VP of marketing, or into general management. In addition, the ability to retain high-performing GAMs may be directly related to corporate support for the global account program.

> International package delivery firm, DHL, has a well-developed global account program. Relatively few GAMs leave DHL—those that do leave frequently wish to return. Former DHL GAMs discover that their new companies do not provide global account program support equivalent to that at DHL.[6]

Recognition is also important. Elevating the GAM position publicly can be an important retention device. Citibank makes its PAMs visible within the bank by giving Global Banking awards. Citibank also nominates PAMs to be members of its *Chairman's Club*—here they meet and interact with very high-level Citibank executives.

Retaining GAMs is a critical firm issue. As one senior Citibank executive famously put it—"Our critical assets walk in the door at 9 o'clock and leave at 5 o'clock." That is how you must view your GAMs. When you have them performing at a high level, you must be assured that they will, indeed, come back the next morning.

---

[6] Edmund Bradford and Francis Rome, "Applying Total Customer Management at DHL: How One Leading Company Has Proved the Payoff," *The Journal of Selling and Major Account Management*, 2 (Autumn 1999), pp. 117–123.

Key Messages

- GAMs are the heart and soul of any global account program.

- The roles and responsibilities for GAMs must be well-defined and the firm must be clear about delegation of authority.

- KSAs for GAMs should flow directly from these roles and responsibilities.

- You must develop a formal and rigorous process for recruiting, selecting, training, developing, measuring, rewarding, and retaining GAMs.

CHAPTER 8

DEVELOPING EFFECTIVE GLOBAL ACCOUNT PLANS

PROLOGUE

Todd has itchy feet

Todd was at the end of his rope. He tried reaching **Constance** to see if she was looking for global account manager talent. **Constance** impressed **Todd** with her focus on managing global accounts. She had given him what sounded like solid advice when he discussed senior management commitment. She said, "Put your concerns into a presentation and work them up the line."

That's what **Todd** set out to do. He worked hard to build a global account planning process for producing a global account plan for his customer. But he needed senior management commitment to execute the process. In particular, he needed budget money to run a planning session. He also wanted to do some traveling to secure better customer intelligence. He wanted the customer involved and planned on including his Partnership Executive in customer meetings. **Todd** was excited about the process he was developing. He even touched base with **Jace** to get some consulting advice.

"**Todd**, you seem to have done your homework, but you may have overlooked some details," **Jace** said when they spoke. "You have included all the proper sections in your planning document, but you seem to have left out some planning tools." Well, thought **Todd**, I wanted to include all the tools, but my boss pointed out we don't have a CRM system or budget money to get the tools to support a few global customers. Further, we have limited market research capabilities. "Well, **Jace**, let's just say I thought of more tools, but was overruled by management." **Todd** continued, "What else have I overlooked?"

Jace didn't want to leave **Todd** with the impression he could do this on his own. Global account planning took resources, money and a lot of global savvy to do it right. **Jace** knew from earlier exposure to **Todd**'s company that senior management wasn't fully behind the global program. This would make it very difficult to do the planning right. "There are quite a few issues requiring special attention. Cross-cultural issues, communication problems because of your infrastructure weaknesses, language barriers that delay timelines, and the time and energy it takes to overcome these impediments." **Jace** didn't sugar-coat it for **Todd**.

*"Thanks for the advice. I may give you another call after I do some more homework." After **Jace** hung up, **Todd** felt a little overwhelmed. He completed his presentation and began to "work it up the line." He proposed a planning meeting in Paris where some key customer executives lived. Senior executives made him feel as though he'd asked for a vacation in Monte Carlo. They turned him down. He requested additional travel money to bring team members to Boston from Europe and Asia. Again, he couldn't convince them of the value. They said, "You're the only global account manager making these kind of requests."*

*   **Todd** mused, Maybe **Constance** needs an experienced global account manager with good ideas on how to make global account planning fit into the fabric of the business. Hope she returns my call.*

We noted earlier that the planning document marking the conclusion of the planning process is not the most important element in the planning arena. The greatest value in planning emerges from the process of creating the global account plan. The adventure lies in discovering information about the global customer, the industry, competition, and the company itself. The excitement resonates from engaging the global team in discussions with various customer executives to gain insight into the deepest account needs. The fulfillment derives from the debates that link customer requirements with the company's ability to deliver value. And personal, team, and organization learning occurs throughout the process as old ideas are swept away and both company and global account executives gain new insights.

Notwithstanding the discovery, excitement, fulfillment, and learning that can derive from the global account planning process, securing corporate support to build a global account plan is not easy. Overall, experience in building global account plans is very limited. For example, in a recent Internet search for "account planning," we secured 58,500 hits. A similar search for "global account planning" delivered us 56 hits. This has also been our collective experience. Increasingly, companies are developing account plans for customers based within a single country. But, a far smaller number of firms and account managers are willing to invest the time and energy it takes for global account planning. Developing a global account plan is more difficult by an order of magnitude than developing a domestic account plan.

We divide this chapter into five parts. First and second we lay out the basics for any account plan and the account planning process. Third, we suggest the impediments companies can expect to encounter in transitioning from domestic-based account planning to global account planning. Fourth, we develop the groundwork for successful global account planning. Fifth, we discuss criteria for knowing whether or not your global account planning is working.

Basics of the Account Plan

We baseline our perspective on the account plan to enable discussion of the *global* account plan. Of course, there are as many ways of putting together an account plan as there are innovative people that focus on the matter. Most organizations follow similar macro-level structures for the account plan. We conveniently label these as *situation analysis, bridge to strategy,* and *framework for account action.* We show the headlines on three approaches in Table 8.1.

The purpose of developing any account plan is to identify opportunities and threats at the account, and then prepare an action framework for working with the account and developing the inter-firm relationship. The action steps that result from the account planning process typically focus

Table 8.1 Alternative Approaches to Account Planning

	Capon	IBM	Xerox
	Learning in Action (LIA)[1]	Account Planning Process	Account Management Process
Situation Analysis	Key Account Analysis: Account Fundamentals Analysis of Strategic Coherence Buying Analysis Customer Value Analysis	Understand Customer's Industry: Build solutions for customer's industry Research Customer's Business Environment: Review and document the Business Drivers by customer buyer groups Understand strategic customer's direction Study Customer's Environment for Your Product/Services including Spending Analysis	Understanding the Customer's Industry & Business: Go-To-Market Strategy Financial Results Business Drivers Initiatives Critical Success Factors Decision Process and Financial Criteria Organization Charts

[1] Adapted from Noel Capon, *Key Account Management and Planning*, New York: Free Press, 2001.

	Capon	IBM	Xerox
	Competitor Analysis		
	Company Analysis	Determine Current Relationship and Coverage Strategy Identify Gaps & Strengths	Xerox Business Position Customer Satisfaction Business History Account P&L Major Achievements
	Relationship Assessment		Relationship Assessment
Bridge to Strategy	Planning assumptions	Develop Current Opportunity Portfolio	Customer Business Requirements Core Business Processes
	Opportunities and Threats	Research New Opportunities	Problems and Opportunities
		Align With Customer Business Initiatives	
		Prioritize Opportunities	
Framework for Account Action	Vision Mission (opportunity execution)	Develop Customer Validation Plan	
	Strategy including expected results	Gain Agreement on Actions	Overall Account Strategy Account Opportunity Map Retention Plan Resource Identification Executive Involvement
	Relationship Strategy		Relationship Strategy
	Action Steps		Competitive Countermeasures Customer Satisfaction Strategy Product Opportunity Prioritization Value-Added Opportunity Prioritization Business Outlook
	Resource Commitments to execute the strategy		Action Plan & Team Roles & Responsibilities
	Budgets and Forecasts		

on the upcoming year, but should be developed in the context of a Three-year view of the relationship. After all, strategic accounts are the firm's core assets—strategic thinking should extend beyond the upcoming calendar year.

Of course, some plans are more sophisticated than others. Nonetheless, regardless of the specific plan headings, all account plans contain certain fundamental building blocks. Conducting these analyses is mandatory—the strategy and action programs flowing from these building blocks are only as strong as the building blocks themselves.

Situation analysis

The situation analysis comprises several building blocks.

Understanding the industry

Any account planning process must commence with a solid understanding of the customer's industry. Critical to achieving "Trusted Advisor" status is the account manager's ability to provide insight and foresight on industry dynamics and processes, as well as advice and counsel to the account's executives.

Understanding the customer

Account managers must secure deep understanding of account requirements. Failure to fully understand customer needs is the main reason for failure of global account plans. Account managers should know the external environment and challenges the customer faces, its current and future competitors, past performance, and strengths and weaknesses. In particular, account managers should develop a deep understanding of their account's customers; after all, these customers are a driving force in determining account needs. They should understand future customer potential, customer strategies, primary initiatives, and the likelihood of success.

Understanding your competition

All account plan methodologies should contain an element of understanding competition. Account managers should analyze the competitor presence at their accounts, know their wallet shares, and the reasons why. They should have a clear grasp of competitor strengths and weaknesses compared to the company, and understand competitor relationships with their key contacts. Finally, they should be very aware of competitor strategies and initiatives.

Understanding your company

Account managers are often focused externally and have less than a deep understanding of their own company. To secure positive account decisions in the face of competitors attempting the same thing, account managers must clearly understand what their firm brings to the party. Account managers must be very clear about their firm's strengths and weaknesses at the account, its products and services, solutions, and the various resource constraints that affect doing business with the account.

Understand company/account relationships

Separate from the product/market focus of the previous item, account managers should analyze their company's presence at the account. They should clearly define the current relationships team members have with account personnel and compare these with those of competitors. They should clearly understand the individual strengths and weaknesses of team members and have a precise sense of their time availability to spend with customers?

Bridge to strategy

The account manager bridges between foregoing elements in the situation analysis, and the framework for account action. Based on these elements, account managers develop planning assumptions. They also identify threats to the firm's current business at the account, and opportunities for increased business.

Framework for account action

The bridge to strategy morphs into the framework for account action. The firm develops a vision and mission for doing business with the account, and then decides which threats and opportunities to address. The firm develops a strategy for the account by allocating resources as appropriate. Within this strategic framework, the firm lays out action plans to secure its objectives. In better-developed planning systems, the firm identifies opportunities, and works out action plans, jointly with executives from the strategic account.

Basics of Account Planning

Although the end product of the account planning process is an account plan, as noted above, most learning comes through the planning process. The better planning processes are directed by the account manager but are conducted in teams. In addition to individuals with selling responsibilities, the team should include personnel from such functions as sales operations, product units, finance, information technology, marketing research, together with senior executives. In the better planning processes, personnel from the account play a major role.

The planning process often commences with an offsite meeting. In the better processes, personnel from the account conduct a briefing early in the process, laying out the account's challenges, objectives, strategies, and initiatives. Of course, there is always an issue of inter-firm sharing of sensitive data, for both supplier and customer firms. As supplier and customer firms learn to trust each other and move toward a partner-type relationship, impediments to data sharing should diminish.

Regardless, data from customers form a significant part of the raw material for the situation analysis. The account team goes to work with these and such other data as analyst reports, competitive data, detailed profiles of industry trends, and technology forecasts. The team conducts a series of analyses as it drives toward *the bridge to strategy* and *framework for account action.*

The planning process is about educating, collaborating, communicating, and developing an account strategy and action programs. Oftentimes, team members meet with specialist functional areas such as finance, service, brand organizations, marketing research analysts, and competitor intelligence groups. In the better planning systems, when the team has completed the process, account personnel return. Together, company and account personnel discuss the strategy and action programs so as to secure account buy-in and, perhaps, agreement to spend resources for mutual gain.

The plan document morphs into several operating action plans. Here account managers use the plan as the guiding strategic imperative in addressing the account. They use it to track the progress of action programs and assess their success relative to action program objectives. In addition to these direct functions, the account plan has multiple other uses.

For example, management should use the individual account plan, in combination with sister plans for other accounts, to drive business and allocate resources across products/services and accounts. The plan should also form the basis for evaluating the account manager and account team members. Account plan outputs should also prove valuable to operations—for forecasting and to finance—for budgeting. In many account programs, PEs support account managers (Chapter 4)—the planning document is a valuable briefing document for these and other executives. Finally, the planning process *per se* and follow-ups during the operating period are often valuable opportunities for enhancing the company/account relationship.

Impediments to Planning for Global Accounts

In broad strokes, global account plans and the global account planning process do not differ greatly from "regular" account plans and planning. Unfortunately, at a finer-grained level, things are not that simple. Many factors can interfere with the effectiveness of the global account planning process. The major difference is the size and complexity of the canvas. We address several critical issues.

Who is the global account?

Global accounts are much more complex than regular domestic accounts. Some global accounts operate under different names in different countries and may be very difficult to identify. Some accounts are very large but essentially focus on a single industry—for example, General Motors or Ford. Other global accounts have businesses that span multiple industries—for example, General Electric or Tyco. The combination of geographic complexity and product/market complexity makes planning for these sorts of accounts very difficult. What makes life even more complicated is when the global account uses an intermediary, such as a value-added reseller (VAR). Then, it may be difficult to identify the ultimate destination of the firm's products.

The problem of culture

There is much written about culture and business.[2] To start with, individual companies have internal cultures—working for Citibank is very different from working for Cisco. Then there are cross-cultural differences. Executives brought up in different geographies have different beliefs and patterns of behavior—for example, consider differences among U.S., European, Latin American, and Japanese executives. These beliefs and behaviors are often very deep-seated. When we interview senior corporate executives they mostly affirm their cultural awareness, but few know how to harness cultural differences to drive customer success. All too frequently, we see executives making one cultural *faux pas* after another.

---

[2] See, for example, Fons Trompenaars and Charles Hampden-Turner, *Riding the Waves of Culture*, New York: McGraw Hill, 1998.

The company arranged a two-day joint planning session with a Japanese global account. During a cocktail reception at the end of the first day, a South American GAM literally backed a Japanese client into the corner of a room. The GAM's lack of awareness of "personal space" parameters caused the client great discomfort. The following day the client cut short his participation in the planning session.

The local French and German managers for a global account had never met nor even spoken on the phone! At a global account-planning workshop with the client in London, they almost came to blows over a cross-border selling issue. The German accused the Frenchman of unethical practices, implying these were standard practices for most Frenchmen.

Cross-cultural issues are particularly evident in the global account planning process. First, different cultures place different values on planning. Some cultures place a higher value on thinking through issues relating to the future, other cultures want to "just do it," and wait for the consequences. Second, some cultures focus on generalities, whereas others are concerned about the myriad of details. For example, the Xerox GAM (Japanese) for a major Japanese automaker continually complained that U.S. representatives would not provide him the level of detail his account required. The U.S. team members did not understand what the fuss was about. Third, different cultures put different values on time and sticking to schedules. For example, we have seen many occasions when a U.S.-based GAM complained about the timeliness of responses from European and Latin American personnel. In our experience, meeting start times are important to U.S. and German cultures, but of little consequence in Latin America, or even Italy.

Unfortunately, we have seen many cases where the team leader attempts to impose his cultural values on the global account planning process, with little or no consideration for cultural differences. Certainly, we believe that a U.S.-based executive working for a Japanese multinational company should conform to their employer's norms. But Japanese head-office personnel should attempt to understand the U.S. culture as well. The key is to seek levels of compromise that respect each other's culture but do not jeopardize the planning process. We believe strongly that in managing any global project, and specifically global account planning, you should start from the premise that cultural differences will manifest themselves. Being aware of, and sensitive to, these differences goes a long way to mitigating any negative impact.

You must respect the culture of the individuals on the global team. Where culture gets in the way of accomplishing objectives, you must make customer and company requirements central to your process, and learn to reconcile differences in a creative manner. Cross-cultural issues have complex roots and may require complex solutions. Training, experience, and mentoring are three complementary approaches to ensure that global team members work together in agreeing how to address your global accounts. Read, study, and take advantage of alternative forums to broaden your sense of becoming a global citizen.

The problem of language

Like it or not, English is becoming the universal business language. English may be the native language for Great Britain and the former British Empire, but for executives in many other parts of the world it is at best a second language. But, even if English is the international business language of your company, some team members may need instructions in their native tongue. There are some serious issues here:

Common terminology

A major communication problem in many organizations is lack of a common terminology. The same term means different things to different people; and/or the same idea is captured with different terminology. This problem is bad enough within a single domestic firm; it is magnified when firms and/or business units are acquired. Now shift to a global firm, especially one that has grown through acquisition. And consider not only the supplier, but also its global customers. Although terminology can be a very difficult issue, it is not insoluble. The Program Office should play a major role in addressing this problem.

Translations

Interpreters can get some of it right, but not always. In one situation, the GAM sent a global account plan draft to various countries requesting several responses by specific deadlines. Many countries met their deadlines, but the relevant Japanese executives did not respond at all. After many written follow-up requests, the GAM finally discovered his Japanese team members were deficient in English. They could not understand the document well enough to respond, and had sent it outside the company for interpretation. Further, the document contained so many acronyms; the interpreter had considerable difficulty with the translation. Consider some other well-documented foreign language problems:

> Original: "Come Alive With the Pepsi Generation," *Pepsi*
> Translation (Chinese): "Pepsi Brings Your Ancestors Back From the Grave!"
> Original: "It takes a strong man to make a tender chicken,"
> *Frank Perdue*
> Translation (Spanish): "It takes an aroused man to make a chicken affectionate!"
> Original: "It won't leak in your pocket and embarrass you,"
> *Parker Pens*
> Translation (Spanish): "It won't leak in your pocket and make you pregnant!"
> Original: Chevy Nova, *Chevrolet*
> Translation (Spanish): Chevy Nova—(No va—it doesn't go!)[3]

Vernacular

When communicating with the global team, the GAM should keep things clear and simple. In particular, avoid the vernacular. For example, in many countries, especially the U.S., sports analogies play a major role in the language of business. These make no sense to someone who is not part of the culture. To illustrate, a GAM was dealing with team members in Argentina. The GAM received a report on the company/customer relationship and asked the Argentinean team to "employ a full court press" (give the task top priority and address with extra energy) in working with the account. The Argentineans were not familiar with this basketball expression, and were also timid in conveying their ignorance to the GAM—they did not respond to the request.[4]

Infrastructure weaknesses

We cover infrastructure issues in more detail in Chapter 9 but focus here on specific planning issues. To manage development of an effective global account plan, the GAM must secure significant external data—on

---

[3] From various sources on the Internet.
[4] A full court press is a defensive move that applies full court pressure on opponents, while protecting against an easy basket.

markets, competition, and the global account. First, a frequent problem for the global account planning process is that this environmental analysis is insufficiently broad. It does not include accurate information on situations in local markets, especially those that are distant and different from the company's home market. It is not unusual for the GAM to think he knows much more about overseas markets than he actually knows.[5] As a result, significant opportunities may "slip through the cracks."

A second problem concerns internal company data. To develop a solid global account plan, the GAM needs account sales and profit data from the various countries in the world where the account operates. Regrettably, many company's systems do not allow this type of "roll up." Rather the typical roll-up is within countries, across customers, for that is the way most companies budget and report results. Assiduous GAMs may spend many hours with in-country personnel trying to construct a global revenue and profit picture. Less responsible GAMs enter the planning cycle with little understanding of global revenues, and even less sense of profits. The particular data problem is not just a concern for preparing global account plans— it has major implications for the ability to track company success at the global account, with attendant implications for measurement and control (and reward) systems.

Clearly, one solution to these infrastructure issues is to employ comprehensive CRM software tailored to managing global accounts. Unfortunately, many companies implement these infrastructure elements on a country-by-country basis. Further, individual countries may be unable to accommodate CRM software selected in the headquarters country.

Resources for global account planning

Planning at the corporate, business unit, and product line levels is well developed in many companies. Strategic planning sets the broad direction, and operational planning drives day-to-day activities. A characteristic of most planning systems is geographic localization, even for global companies. When plans do come together on a regional or global basis, senior managers are typically involved.

---

[5] Ernest Gundling, "Going Global, What How and with Whom," *Velocity*, Fourth Quarter, 2002, p. 43.

A problem for global account planning is the interaction required among many less senior people. For an individual global account plan, a conscientious GAM should meet with a significant number of colleagues all over the world, many of whom should also meet with each other. All too frequently, travel budgets are insufficient. We have come across many cases where travel budgets were frozen and GAMs were unable to visit customer locations or team members. More insidious is the inability of team members to attend global account planning sessions. If the company's global infrastructure is based on geographic regions, team members typically must secure funding from their countries. Often, country managers are reluctant to pay for international travel for planning activities where they see little direct benefit.

Travel budgets for planning are just the most visible resource shortfalls. As indicated earlier, good global account planning requires other resources that team members cannot be expected to provide individually. For example, a corporate or industry group should provide market and competitor analysis—often this is not available. Has your company purchased the necessary software to put global account planning on line with differential access and ability to update in real time?—Or are you still working with hard copy and faxes? Relevant executives may have a good understanding of how global planning should be done, but insufficient resources can be major showstoppers.

Data interpretation and analysis

Typically, financial data from around the world must be consolidated in the currency of your company's headquarters country. This requirement presents a set of issues that distinguish global account management from regular account management. Of course, the company must convert all currencies into a single unit to which management can relate. But a simple conversion is not simple! The first issue is "as of when?" When considering last year's revenues, what date should we use? End of year? End of each quarter? In budgeting next year's revenues, should we use forecast start of year, mid-year, or what? It is one thing to deal with exchange rate issues if individual countries are experiencing moderate inflation rates. It is quite another when inflation rates are many hundreds of percent p.a. One of us worked with global accounts in Latin America when daily inflation rates ranged between 5 and 10 percent. Menu prices were in pencil, salaries rose daily, and small errors in price quotations could spell disaster. Global account planning was very challenging.

Successful Global Account Planning

The previous section suggests that global account planning is a daunting task. You may be asking yourself if it is realistic to conduct global account planning, given all the barriers. Of course, we believe it is essential; that is why we wrote the previous section. We are convinced that, by being aware of the critical issues, you will be better able to craft a successful global account planning process. In this section, we provide some tips on making your planning process the best it can be.

The global account manager's responsibility

The GAM is the focal person for developing the global account plan—situation analysis, bridge to strategy, and framework for account action—a road map for addressing the global account. A seasoned GAM brings significant information into the planning process, but other global account team members also provide important input. Typically GAMs have less than perfect information, but they must integrate the various strands of data from various sources to develop planning assumptions, and then surface and prioritize opportunities and threats, and develop the strategy. The GAM is ultimately responsible for the entire process and outputs.

One hands-on area for the GAM is working with the global account at the corporate level. The GAM should be fully apprised of the global account's big picture objectives, strategies, initiatives—especially global procurement initiatives and action programs. The GAM should also be familiar with other corporate-level account initiatives such as reorganizations and infrastructure changes. Further, the GAM should figure out the impact of these changes on the global account's various organizational entities—business units, major product lines, geographic regions, and individual countries. The GAM must pull together these data and assess the impact on the company overall and on such individual sub-units as regions and countries. Stated another way, the GAM develops the top-down perspective. In addition, the GAM must integrate the various country- and business-level plans at the global account.

Other responsibility arenas

The GAM needs data from the global account's corporate headquarters. A well-developed global account plan for customers providing significant current (and potential) international revenues also requires information from the periphery. Typically, global companies have local personnel responsible for the global account, either as a full-time or as a part-time responsibility.

These local NAMs provide the bottom–up perspective. Full-time NAMs have local knowledge and should understand the account's objectives, strategies, initiatives, and action programs within their countries, and the impact on their firm. They should also understand the implications of country-level activities for countries where they have no direct responsibility. In some companies, RAMs with responsibility for several countries perform the cross-country integration. For smaller country operations, part-time NAMs may not possess detailed customer knowledge but may, nonetheless, possess industry insight that is helpful for planning purposes.[6]

We do not expect GAMs, NAMs and RAMs to secure all relevant information direct from their contacts with the global account. Of course, such information should carry great weight, but they should also tap internal company sources. These sources include, but are not limited to, global account team members and senior company executives with global account contacts. Technology experts may have global account contacts, and marketing, finance, accounting, and product management personnel may also be able to provide valuable insight. For example, at a typical IBM global account, around 160 IBM employees touch the global account worldwide—about 20 full-time equivalent employees.

Getting started on the global account plan

Typically, companies have well-defined planning timetables. Frequently, there are significant organizational pressures for these timetables to be driven by the firm's annual planning and budgeting cycles. We urge that the timetable driver be the global account's buying process. It is far more important for the global account plan to synchronize with the account, than with internal budgetary requirements. Regardless, a kick-off event to focus attention on the global account planning process has much to recommend it.

IBM's experience in the late 1990s provides a good illustration of the starting point for an effective global account planning process:

> The International Sales Operation (ISO) helped GAMs get started on preparing global account plans. The ISO hosted meetings at key locations in the U.S., Europe, and Asia. Senior executives from various

---

[6] The local account manager can range from being a fully dedicated national account manager for the global client's local operation, to being part of a salesperson in a geographically organized local sales force.

IBM divisions and key geographic-based sales executives briefed GAMs and global team members on the latest product advances, global economic views, market trends in various industries relating to information technology, and points of interest about IBM that might impact on customers. The ISO presented IBM's international support capabilities to customers and global account teams; a senior IBM executive reported the latest industry news. In another portion of the meeting, individual GAMs and team members worked to kick off the global account planning process. Customers were encouraged to present their strategic outlook to inform the entire global team. Typically, various team members were responsible for portions of these breakout meetings and managing the process.

Information requirements for global account planning

As with any planning process, the starting point for developing the global account plan is collecting and analyzing information. We highlight a few procedures that can improve the efficiency and effectiveness of this process.

Develop an ongoing process

Information requests from the GAM to NAMs and RAMs should not be one-time events just for the annual planning cycle. The GAM should develop an ongoing process for two-way communication from the center to the periphery, and vice versa. When this process is running well, the GAM may not need a data dump—much required information will already have flowed through the company. Further, the data will be of higher quality. After all, nobody likes to get 11th hour "urgent need now" requests. Techniques such as regularly scheduled conference calls, interactive web sites for team members, and a disciplined process of newsletters and electronic communication such as Lotus Notes or Docushare ameliorate these problems.

Establish consistency in requests

GAM's requests for information from countries/regions and other organizational units should be as consistent as possible. When countries learn to expect the GAM's requests for similar data updated on a regular basis they have some confidence in setting their own information-gathering priorities. They also gain confidence in the GAM. The alternative of continual requests for wildly different types of information leaves countries with the impression the GAM does not know what he wants. Of course, circumstances change and new information will be required. Then the GAM can explain the deviation. Rather than the request seeming like a useless activity, it can convey useful strategic information to NAMs and RAMs. If the firm develops a process and documents requirements that all GAMs use, the likelihood of consistent requests rises.

> The general manager for Southeast Asia for a *Fortune* 100 company was constantly plagued by emergency information requests from GAMs to satisfy bid submissions, client inquiries, management reviews, and planning needs. In general, these requirements were not "overnight surprises" to the GAMs. Unfortunately, GAMs tended to wait until the last minute, then expected an immediate response. Such behavior reduced credibility of the entire global account program with important internal constituencies

Conduct face-to-face meeting(s)

Regardless of whether the annual planning cycle commences with a kickoff meeting, as in the IBM example, somewhere during the planning process, the GAM should conduct a 2/3-day meeting with planning team members. It may not be realistic, on cost grounds, to include all team members, so those attending should be carefully chosen. In general, full-time NAMs and RAMs should attend. For the rest, the choice depends largely on the situation and the anticipated opportunities. Opportunities and the evolving global account strategy help determine other potential attendees. They include the PE, technology experts, outsourcing experts, product marketing, contracting specialists, and financial experts.

Including key customer personnel is also important. In our experience, the GAM learns a great deal from customer executives by providing a forum for talking about their company's strategic direction. A good approach is to turn a half-day over to customer personnel, but the GAM should work hard to ensure that the right account personnel attend. The GAM should negotiate presentation content with account personnel, leaving significant time for Q&A. Inviting customers to such a meeting allows team members to interact with customer personnel they might otherwise not meet. An international meeting is always a good place to mix social and professional contacts.

What follows is a typical agenda for a planning session, based on the IBM planning format (Table 8.2). Much baseline work should be completed prior to the meeting. Meeting time is too valuable to spend *creating* market and customer information. Rather, the meeting should focus on *validating* and *modifying* that information.

The frequency and length of these meetings depend on many factors including product cycle length, global account buying process, size and

Table 8.2   Typical Agenda for a Planning Session

DAY 1

Topic	Leader	Objectives	Activity
*Opening/ Introductions	Global account manager	Team Building	Each person introduces themselves— responsibilities
*Customer business environment	Customer or global account manager	Build team knowledge for planning	Review Industry Review customer drivers and strategies
*Strategic direction	Company Industry Strategist	Your company's strategic direction	Review your company's business initiatives
Customer relationship	GAM plus any relationship managers from remote locations/ divisions	Ensure team understands current relationships and linkages	Each leader presents team then identifies gaps and potential new relationships
Buying profile	GAM with assistance from global operations	Understand current buying preferences and future plans	Current revenue stream, wallet share, buyer groups, competitive buying
Coverage plans	GAM with global team	Develop coverage plan for the future	Review previous session output and identify coverage and skill gaps
Opportunity review	GAM	Ensure all feasible opportunities are identified	Review pre-work on initial opportunity assessment in light of today's discussions
Initial opportunity prioritization	Global Team	Select best chance wins	Debate and discuss with global team

*Customer attends these sessions.

Table 8.2—continued

Day 2

Topic	Leader	Objectives	Activity
Opportunity sessions	Dependent on opportunities and relationship owners	Assess each opportunity for fit based on customer, resources, competition	Sessions with the most knowledge able resource based on objectives
Map opportunities	All	Align opportunities	Align high-priority opportunities with buyers, relation-ships, countries
Strategy and action plans	GAM	To ensure execution of opportunities	Assignment of individuals, work to be done, reporting, and deadlines
Customer areas not covered	GAM	Identify need for new relationships based on opportunities	Review current coverage based on new planning information. Assign responsibility for each area
Final prioritization	All team members	Ensure all new news is in plan	Review pipeline, relationships, resources
Customer validation plan	GAM	Strategy to get customer agreement to your plan	Review opportunities with key customer contacts to gain agreement
Team operations	GAM	Set operating parameters to execute plan	Review team responsibilities, project plan operations, reporting responsi-bilities, tools

complexity of the global account team, account globality, and travel budget. In some cases, these meetings should be global in nature; in other cases (as in the IBM example) regional meetings may be appropriate. Regional meetings imply greater stress on the GAM, but they may be worthwhile for focusing on regional issues, and allow overall greater team member participation.

Resolving information disconnects

We expect strict agreement between the GAM's understanding of the global account's corporate perspective, and information from the global account's periphery in individual countries/regions. It is not unusual that, far from head office, corporate initiatives do not get implemented. This is as true for the global account as for your own company. For example, your global account may be pursuing a corporate-driven global procurement initiative. But, individual countries and regions may offer considerable resistance to such an initiative. The GAM must have a good understanding of any disconnects between the global account's corporate perspective and the perspectives in individual countries and regions.

Planning documentation

Planning documents are part of a system. The Global Account Program Office can have a major impact by strongly enforcing a standard table of contents for the plan. It should also develop templates for account, competition and company information gathering, planning assumptions, opportunities and threats, strategies, action programs, and resource requirements. Until a few years ago, these would have been in hard-copy format. Nowadays they should be stored in an electronic library for easy access. Messaging software, such as Lotus Notes, should allow for personnel at remote locations to communicate with the GAM. Notwithstanding the importance of standardization, individual accounts may require some level of idiosyncratic treatment.

The ability to compare is one reason for imposing some degree of order on the planning process by using a standardized set of templates. The global account plan sets out the rationale for, and actions at, the individual global account, but it is not a stand-alone document. This year's plan should be compared with other plans—for example, this year's plan with last year's plan. Did last year's assumptions hold? Did the opportunities and threats identified last year actually materialize? Did the firm achieve its objectives at the global account? Did the firm implement last year's strategy at the global account?

One particularly important planning document is the global account relationship map. *The global account does not make decisions to buy/not buy your products/services. Individuals within the global account make these decisions.* The GAM needs a lot of information about global account personnel. At each account location around the world, global account team members must know the decision-makers, influencers, gatekeepers, champions, spoilers (opponents and detractors), and information providers. The GAM must develop elements of the global account relationship map with an underlying governing philosophy, prepared to a standard format. The relationship map is an important device for managing current business—it is also highly valuable when the company is expanding its scope at the account.

IBM expanded the range of contacts within global accounts beyond a traditional focus centered on the chief information officer (CIO). It reaches out to other global account buyer groups. IBM uses the global account relationship map to examine relationships around the world consistently and to extend business globally.

Setting time lines

Document standardization places one form of discipline on the planning process. Timelines provide a second type of discipline. All planning activities should take place in a calendar format. This discipline is critical for any form of planning. It is especially important in global account planning because of time to complete plans, and geography. Planning-team members may have to travel halfway around the world to attend meetings. The GAM should develop and agree to the planning timetable with customers, team members, and organizations that rely on global account plan output, as early as practicable.

The calendar affects the planning process. Suppose the company's planning cycle is January through December. The GAM could develop a planning schedule by estimating the lapsed time for different activities, considering all interrelated plans, and working back from January 1. There should not be a standard planning schedule across global accounts. A sensible schedule depends on so many factors relating to your firm as well as the global customer. It bears repeating that—the planning cycle should be linked to the global account's business cycle—not to your firm's internal operations. Of course, if the plan is continually incremented forward, the annual planning cycle is much less significant in managing the global customer.

Sign Offs on the Global Account Plan

As with any plan, the GAM will have to get various sign-offs internally. The nature of these sign-offs depends on the organization for managing global accounts, the GAM's reporting relationships, and the nature of the resources required to implement the plan. One sign-off is critical above all—customer executives from the global account. The global account plan should be a joint undertaking between the firm and its global customer executives. Quite likely, the global account will have to provide resources to implement the plan. Unless the global customer agrees to the plan, the various actions laid out in the plan are less action plan items and more the GAM's wish list. We cannot overstate this issue—to be worthwhile, critical global customer executives must be on board.

Communicating the global account plan

The perfect account plan will never be implemented if it is not effectively communicated. The GAM is responsible for explaining the plan to a variety of constituencies. These include internal firm management and global account executives for approval; the account team for education and direction; internal company functions for awareness, understanding, and potential support; local operations to clarify their role in strategy implementation; and the PE, especially if this person was not deeply involved in developing the global plan.

Ease of access

The completed global account plan should sit on a *groupware* site with varying degrees of password access linked to organizational position. Much data and analysis in the global account plan is confidential. The GAM should be very selective regarding security issues—who gets to see what parts of the plan needs to be a well-thought-out strategy. Many times the plan documents personal information about team members or customer personnel. The GAM should control information inflow and outflow.

In addition to the global account plan *per se*, the GAM should manage several additional sections on the global account website—best practices, success stories, and a place to post messages and ask questions. Messaging software allows personnel at remote locations to interface with the global account plan, subject to access and modification rules. These sections help ensure the global account is not a sterile document—rather, it is a living entity. The plan functions as an information-sharing device. It provides a bird's-eye view of the current state of play at the global account.

Global account planning and performance reviews

To keep the firm focused on the global account plan, the Program Office must institute a formal review process. In addition to the GAM's superior, senior executives should also be part of the review process. Depending on the particular circumstances, representatives from product (brand) groups and geographic regions should also be present. Much of the review process can be electronic with selected GAMs asked to make formal presentations.

The Program Office should standardize templates for these reviews. At a minimum, they should contain the following:

- General customer information to bring reviewers up to speed on the customer's business
- Significant supplier wins and losses from the previous year to give reviewers perspective on the current situation

- Customer's market challenges to demonstrate the GAM's understanding of the customer
- Customer's business initiatives to ensure that the GAM has been communicating at the right levels and understands where the customer is heading
- Customer's preferences for suppliers
- Current use of your products/services to show the GAM's understanding of your firm's presence in the account
- Customer satisfaction history, pointing out any significant situations—positive or negative—that may influence future business
- Supplier coverage strategy at the customer, pointing out any areas of weaknesses and/or needs for additional coverage
- Global account team strategies for new opportunities (forecast data) and current issues that need resolution
- Other major supplier initiatives at the account.

At IBM, the Global Industry Executives require that GAMs for all "super" global accounts (top 60) conduct formal reviews with them personally, and with key industry specialists. The GAM for each global account in the second tier (next 400–600) conducts an electronic review with their management team. A minimum requirement is an annual review. Specific opportunities are reviewed on a regular basis until the business is closed. Some GAMs find this process excessively bureaucratic, but the firm must maintain a cadence throughout the entire planning process.

These reviews also allow GAMs to demonstrate that opportunities do not fit neatly into the firm's current operating periods; revenues may not be earned until several quarters have passed. This information informs executive management of anticipated revenues in subsequent quarters.

In addition to internal reviews of the "state of the global account," the GAM should also conduct periodic reviews with customer executives, in concert with the PE. After all, well-formulated action plans flowing from the global account plan often require action by the global account, as well as by the supplier. These reviews may be especially important in pursuing opportunities. For example, when a major global chemical firm introduced regular global customer reviews, it found that some accounts were not pursuing agreed-upon projects. They had simply lost interest. More projects were in place than either supplier or global accounts had appetite for. Under the mantra that *less is more*, the chemical firm and its customers agreed to rationalize the numbers of projects. Further, these meetings may also generate more ideas for new opportunities.

Aggregating global account plans

We emphasized that the planning process should be systematic. We highlighted the benefits of year-by-year comparisons for individual global accounts. But, contemporary comparisons across global accounts may also be valuable. For example, the executive owner may wish to compare one global account plan with another. This comparison allows testing of opportunities, strategies, and action programs for one global account against a closely related global account—for example, a competitor. Further, the executive owner will need to aggregate across global accounts for resource allocation purposes. This executive must confirm that total requested resources of various types conform to availability. And the financial office will need its own type of aggregation.

Unfortunately, few companies have in-place systems to synchronize global account plans. For example, as late as 2003, at IBM, budgets were not aligned with the account planning process. By contrast, before the HP merger, Compaq rolled up individual global account plans so that individual GAMs could pool resources.

To recap, a successful global account planning system should roll up forecast product demand, financial budgets, and HR budgets. If global accounts are a major part of the company's business, a simple and easily accessible integrated system has enormous benefits in organizational efficiency. Another important roll-up area is the company's overall position with global accounts. Many companies build their situation analyses around (in part) a SWOT (strengths/weaknesses/opportunities/threats) analysis. Aggregating these analyses across global accounts may offer significant insight into the company's overall market position. For example, is there a pattern to the threats you face?

How Do You Know When the Global Account Planning System is Working?

Most companies invest a lot of money and effort in their planning processes overall. However, when we ask companies about the effectiveness of these processes, typically, we find that most have little idea about the relationship between planning effort and company results. Those relatively few companies conducting global account planning (versus other types of planning) have even less idea. This is not because executives are irresponsible. It is just that measuring planning performance does not seem high on the priority list. Is this a problem?

We believe that failure to understand the value of global account planning is a significant problem. Unless there is a good idea of cause and effect, when budget cuts arrive, resource uses that cannot justify their existence are the first to go—and they should be! If this means that global account planning gets the axe, that is a problem. The IBM regional meetings for global account planning (discussed earlier) that initiated the annual cycle did not pass the relevance test and fell victim to budget cuts. GAMs found the meetings extremely worthwhile, but no one within IBM had gathered evidence to demonstrate meeting effectiveness, nor the cost savings from having several regional events.

Please do not misunderstand us. We firmly believe that each and every company activity should justify its committed resources. Yet, we also believe global account planning is critical. To assess whether global account planning is valuable in your organization, you should address the topic from several perspectives. For each perspective, you should ask some critical questions:

From the perspective of a global customer

- How is your global planning process received by your global accounts? Is your process enthusiastically endorsed across the board, or is the acceptance lukewarm?
- Do your global accounts welcome review meetings as a means of building the company/account relationship?
- Can you link global account satisfaction and loyalty to the planning process?
- Do global accounts wish to develop and/or continue partnership status? Does this result from the additional value your planning process identified and your firm subsequently delivered?

From the perspective of a global team member

- Do global team members for your accounts take ownership of the plan resulting from their inclusion in your planning process?
- Do team members believe the planning process adds to their knowledge of the global account and its industry?
- Do team members believe the planning process adds to their understanding of individual roles and responsibilities in successfully managing the account?
- Has your planning process led to team members closing more business in less time than previously?
- Is there a greater feeling of team unity and successful cooperation, best practices sharing, and learning as the result of your planning process?

From the perspective of a global account manager

- Does the planning process improve GAMs' ability to perform their jobs?
- Has the global planning process enabled GAMs to develop and achieve their goals at the account more effectively and efficiently?
- Does the planning process assist GAMs in developing, motivating, and managing their global teams?

From the perspective of your company (across global accounts)

- Has the global planning process delivered account plans that produced profitable revenue growth and improved customer loyalty?
- Has business at your global accounts benefited from investment in the global planning process?
- Have you been successful in securing greater shares of global accounts' spend? Or have you reached a plateau?
- Have your GAMs identified hitherto untapped opportunities where you bring value to global accounts?
- Has the planning process taken customer relationships to a higher level?
- Has global team productivity improved and cost of sales declined?

Key Messages

- Developing a global plan is structurally similar to developing a national account plan, but is more difficult by an order of magnitude because of the vastly increased scope and complexity.

- The greatest value from developing the global account plan is the process of educating, collaborating, and communicating among the GAM, team members, and personnel at the global account.

- Dedicated GAMs can address the many impediments to global account planning. Working with customers, they can galvanize global team members into a full team effort.

- The global account plan should be an electronic living document, easily accessible and constantly modified and updated.

CHAPTER 9

ESTABLISHING THE SUPPORTING ORGANIZATIONAL INFRASTRUCTURE

PROLOGUE

George is frustrated

George was concerned about the lack of progress with his global account program. He had done some benchmarking as well as picking *Jace*'s brain. Right now his focus was infrastructure where other firms seemed well ahead. *George* believed he had many great ideas to improve his program but there seemed to be another obstacle at every turn. It was like playing his son's video games. Just when he thought he was moving forward, some sort of monster jumped out and bit him.

He had just come from a meeting with the Chief Information Officer (CIO). *"George*, I can see the value in what you want to do, but we just don't have the data you need, in the form that you need it." All *George* wanted to do was compensate his global account managers based on global revenue. "I can give you some ball park numbers, but I can't swear to their accuracy." Just what *George* needed, a compensation plan based on guesswork!

The previous week, *George* had met with the geographic heads and a couple of country managers. *"George*, I can see value in the global account management process but you have to understand that my first concern is to improve profits in Asia Pacific." And that's the way our processes are aligned.

George's meeting with the training czar wasn't much better. *"George*, you can't imagine the pressure I'm under just to get our new hires up to speed, not to speak of figuring out the best business-school executive programs for our rising middle managers. Even if I got budget approval for global account manager training, it would take me about a year to gear up. We just don't have the in-house expertise."

Next *George* met with the Chief Financial Officer (CFO). The CFO had been so effusive about global account management, *George* felt sure he could spring some additional budget. *"George*, I know the boss is in favor of global account management, but let me explain the process to you. We're a global firm and our budgets get rolled up from the country managers. We aggregate proposed country and regional budgets, match those against total resources, and make final allocations here at corporate. Whatever money *you need is in the country or regional budgets. There's no way to develop a separate budget line for global accounts and create a separate financial statement for each. There's just no way to do it. You know as well as I do that Asia Pacific is on a totally different computer system than the U.S." Then he offered more good news: "Forecasting's the same way. I rely on country-by-country forecast roll-ups—not account-by-account forecasts."*

Jace *was more sympathetic.* **George** *said, "I wish I had addressed these issues before I made the big splash about re-launching global account management."* **Jace** *knew all too well what* **George** *was facing. "Infrastructure is the last thing companies consider. Sometimes it's an inconvenience. But in most cases there are some real showstoppers.* **George***, I wish I could give you a silver bullet, but infrastructure issues are just hard dirty work you'll have to do battle over." This was not what* **George** *wanted to hear.*

The GAMs were busting his chops to get a global contracting system. **George** *could hardly wait to meet with the lawyers, I am sure they are ready to take on international law. Maybe I will go back to my son's video game. I might have more success.*

Global account infrastructure is the glue that holds the global account program together. *Infrastructure* is a broad term embracing the organizational systems and processes for getting work done. Global account infrastructure includes IT, administration, HR, business practices, global account planning, global contracting and corporate legal, education, training, communications, and financial systems. (Because global account planning is so critical, in Chapter 8, we treated global account planning as a critical success factor in its own right.)

To use a well-worn metaphor, these infrastructure systems function as links in the global account program chain. The chain is as strong as its weakest link! When account profitability systems are ineffective, when communication systems do not function effectively or when a host of other things go wrong, the firm will not achieve the global account program's goals, much less its potential.

Effectively addressing infrastructure issues related to managing global accounts is not "business-as-usual." The firm must develop creative solutions to meet growing customer expectations, competitive actions, and to establish positive marketplace differentiation. Developing the infrastructure elements that address critical global issues involves detailed and sometimes very tedious work. Management must consider the many "mechanical" details that are crucially important to an effective and efficient program. "The devil is in the details," and any individual detail can derail the train!

In general, in most firms, systems and processes grow up over time as required by various firm initiatives. These initiatives—strategies, action programs, and organizational changes—also evolve over time. Unfortunately, in many firms, the same is not true for infrastructure elements. They become obsolete and lead to mismatches between the functioning organization and its systems and processes. This was the essential message of re-engineering, and throughout the 1990s, significant numbers of firms re-engineered many infrastructure items.[1]

The problem facing global account management is that current infrastructure elements are typically based on sales initiatives of the past. Many firms launch global account programs without understanding that they are not "just another sales initiative." Rather, global account management is a totally new and innovative way of serving global customers. Clearly, managing global accounts is about more than just sales, but just to focus on this area, managing sales on a global basis is very different from directing a national sales force. Domestic systems and processes may work fine in domestic contexts; they do not begin to address the problems of managing global accounts. Firms that launch global account programs without considering the new capability requirements typically experience struggling programs or outright failure.

One simple example, built on the well-tested management saying, "if you can't measure it, you can't manage it," illustrates the problem. Put another way, when management allocates a resource to secure a business result, it must be able to measure both the resource *and* the result. Otherwise, management has no way to know whether the resource was used effectively.

Many firms launching global account programs are organized by geography. But, the financial systems are set up to aggregate sales revenues by country, and then by geographic region. The firm's infrastructure does not allow revenue aggregation *by customer* across geography. Hence, there is no way for the firm to access the financial result of resource allocations to individual global accounts—for example, global sales revenues. What is even worse, in many cases, firms are unable to measure the resource allocations to global accounts. These resources are embedded in geographic region and country budgets. The firm does not know what resources are allocated to a specific global account, and it cannot measure the result of that allocation. Such a state

---

[1] Michael Hammer and James Champy, *Reengineering the Corporation, A Manifesto for Business Revolution,* HarperBusiness, 1993.

of affairs would seem to fail the most basic principle of Management 101! Of course, required infrastructure goes far beyond measurement and control systems, but this example illustrates the nature of the problem.

Just to provide an example of the sort of basic infrastructure issues that can cause havoc, one of Xerox's global accounts conducted an internal audit. The audit showed that the customer's total of paid invoices to Xerox was $16 million higher than the Xerox report, a 25 percent difference! This discrepancy launched an acrimonious debate about current price levels and requests for retroactive discounts. By contrast, well-designed infrastructure can win the business for the firm. For example, a leading U.S. manufacturer won a substantial bid from a global customer, when the GAM provided an electronic directory of local contact information for over 100 countries. This directory was a vivid demonstration to the customer that the supplier really did have a "global presence."

Too many global account programs fail to secure their potential because the infrastructure required for implementation does not match the original vision and objectives. Unfortunately, and perhaps we are over cynical, the cause of such blunders is often senior management naivety. In our experience, far too often senior executives believe they can snap their fingers and have the "aircraft carrier" turn on a dime. They plunge headlong into projects without sufficient checking with middle management. In our context, there is insufficient foresight in planning the global account program, and a lack of in-depth understanding of what it takes to be successful. Without a broad-based shared value of the importance of managing global accounts among the supporting functions that must drive infrastructure change, the required effort and/or financial investment just does not happen. Weak executive leadership/direction compounds the problem.

In this chapter, we examine critical infrastructure needs that require executive attention and, more importantly, are critically important for successful implementation of global account management. For ease of exposition, we divide infrastructure elements into two broad categories—hard and soft.

Hard infrastructure elements are based largely on computer-driven IT, telecommunications systems, and the Internet. They embrace both hardware and software.

Soft infrastructure concerns systems and processes that are much more based on HR.

As a lead in to these infrastructure elements, we address two key elements that are critical for the infrastructure discussion—senior management and the *Global Account Program Office*. First, much infrastructure improvement, especially hard infrastructure, needs investment—often, significant investment. Ultimately, senior management makes the funding decisions, so we must discuss methods for getting senior management on board with the global account program. We covered senior management commitment in Chapter 4, but it bears repeating here as well. Second, the Global Account Program Office is responsible for much of the difficult work dealing with infrastructure issues in managing global accounts. The Program Office is a critical infrastructure element in its own right but, in addition, is heavily involved in other infrastructure elements. So, we pay particular attention to this critical infrastructure element.

Securing Senior Management Involvement and Support for Infrastructure

We have consistently made the point that the global account program will fail unless senior management is supportive and actively involved. This support and involvement is critical for getting global account management off the ground, but is even more important for continually sustaining the global program.

Of course, there is no standard process for getting senior management involved. Indeed, global account management may start from the top if an incoming CEO, such as Lou Gerstner at IBM, believes that customers are the firm's core assets, and is prepared to act on this basis. Alternatively, global account management may result from arguments brought up to the firm's executive committee, possibly driven by poor performance at individual customers. Alternatively, lower-level management may seek senior management approval for a global account "skunk-works" that it wishes to have legitimized. Regardless of the initiation process, global account management is built into the fabric of the firm by identifying various senior executive roles, filling them with "the right" senior executives, and developing a process to keep them appropriately filled over time.

In Chapter 4, we identified five specific senior management roles in global account management. We also noted that an individual executive may fill multiple roles, depending on the scope of the global account program. The emphasis in this chapter is to provide a set of systems and processes that complement the various roles that you need top management to fill. A quick review of the senior management roles follows:

- *Senior executive champion:* The senior executive champion provides leadership from the top. Not blind leadership to move forward, but informed leadership that understands the consequences of moving the global account program forward without the necessary infrastructure in place.

- *Executive sponsor:* The executive sponsor is deeply involved in the global account program process and should be heavily impacted by its results. When infrastructure systems fail to operate globally, ultimately the sponsor is held accountable.
- *Executive owner:* The purpose of this role is to manage day-to-day global account program operations. It is also the executive owner's responsibility to ensure that infrastructure issues receive the proper level of attention. When a manager who is responsible for a crucial infrastructure element is reluctant or unwilling to address the issue, the executive owner is accountable to escalate the situation to the appropriate level for resolution.
- *Executive steering committee:* This group provides additional leadership and involvement in the global account program. It should contain key executives that have responsibility for pieces of the infrastructure. This responsibility helps prevent a naïve executive team from moving forward without the appropriate infrastructure.
- *Partnership executive:* Whereas the roles discussed above operate at the overall program level, the PE is directly involved at an individual global account. One of the PE's responsibilities is to raise infrastructure issues affecting his GAM (and global account) and bring them to the attention of peer executives for resolution.

One of senior management's early roles is to appoint the executive owner—the person in charge of the global account program in general and the Global Account Program Office in particular. This person is ultimately responsible for the infrastructure needed to make the program work. He should develop a plan for systems and processes needed to implement the global account program. Program office members should do the heavy lifting to make sure that the appropriate infrastructure elements are in place.

Sometimes, particular infrastructure elements are driven by organizational failures that become highly visible to senior management. For example, soon after his appointment as IBM's CEO, Lou Gerstner asked the following question of a senior IBM executive: "Tell me, how much business do we do in a year around the world with Ford?" The answer, "Give us a couple of days and we'll get back to you," suggested a serious infrastructure weakness in measuring global revenues. Mr. Gerstner did not ask for profit. During the next few years, IBM addressed infrastructure for both global revenues and profits.

The Global Account Program Office

The Global Account Program Office, headed by a high-powered executive owner or his direct reporting personnel, is responsible for the global account program infrastructure. The Program Office directs the building and maintaining of those systems and processes that must be implemented to ensure the global account program runs smoothly on a day-to-day basis. Of course, the appropriate Program Office model will vary from company to company, but there are some fundamentals that should be followed regardless of company. For example, the Program Office should be made up of experienced sales executives, preferably with various levels of international sales experience. Members of the Program office may be located around the world, yet they work as a global team in the same way that GAMs manage their global teams. The Program Office establishes the rules of engagement, the measurement systems, compensation objectives, and GAM's roles and responsibilities. The Program Office also ensures senior management roles are filled and that scheduled meetings such as plan development, plan reviews and budget discussions occur.

The Program Office plays a critical role in many essential infrastructure elements. In fulfilling this role, the Program Office does not act in a vacuum, but rather involves many functions and business units across the firm. The Program Office also serves the global account program's operational needs and is responsible for all execution aspects. Specific responsibilities are myriad, but include developing and managing the global program's overarching operating principles and strategy, the PE program, the global bidding process, and global measurement systems—including tracking milestone progress, and securing and reporting on measures that determine the program's success or failure. The Program Office resolves program issues, provides day-to-day support to global account teams, and manages relationships with global account programs located in other business units. The Program Office's job is to ensure that the firm presents a coherent program to global customers.

At IBM, the global account program office, headed by a global account program executive, reported to International Sales Operations (ISO). The ISO managed IBM's overall international sales support, including international sales representatives—based in most major countries, an international sales call support center, and other groups such as IT and data tracking focused on international markets. The ISO head was the executive owner of the global account program. In this role, he made all ISO resources available to the global account program executive. The Program Office assisted with global bids and global sales issues, and gave direct support to GAMs on sales calls. It also dealt with IT infrastructure, GAM training and education, and other country sales operations. Making the global account program office part of the ISO ensured that resources were available for any aspect of global account management that needed attention.

Hard Infrastructure

We established that senior management must play a major role in the global account program in general, and in securing resources and making investments for the global program in particular. Further, we established that many resource and investment requests for global accounts should be managed through the Program Office. One particularly critical area is investment in *hard infrastructure*.

Information Technology is often referred to as "the new corporate infrastructure." The guts of IT deals with network bandwidth, e-structures, databases, pipelines, and computing power. Our concern, of course, is less about these (mainly hardware) issues and more about what IT can do to enhance global account management. One of the problems for managing global accounts relates to several experts' comments about IT infrastructure.

> What's difficult is aligning infrastructure with business strategy. The average life of a business strategy is less than Twelve months. IT infrastructure typically has to last from Five to Sevem years. And some database infrastructures have to last Ten years or more.[2]

So here is a major problem for managing global accounts. Although the Program Office may figure out what global account management needs in the way of IT infrastructure, it has to contend with an in-place system that may not be sympathetic to global program requirements. OK, so we just have to get resource commitment, exercise some patience, and make some changes. Right? Wrong! Just listen to another expert:

> Knowing what needs to be done is only one part of the challenge. Making the case for infrastructure improvements can be even more challenging than predicting future needs. Infrastructure is

---

[2] Peter Weill, "The Corporate Skeleton," *CIO Magazine*, January 1, 1999.

not something that demonstrates clear value to the business. It is at least two steps removed from customer interactions—it is the wire that supports the applications that support the customer representatives. There is also a general aura of bad karma around infrastructure: The stuff is invisible unless there is something wrong with it, in which case all hell breaks loose. Put simply, if infrastructure were a product, no self-respecting salesperson would want to be stuck selling it.[3]

Because of the Internet, IT infrastructure is much more visible to customers today than it was 10 years ago, but the sense of our commentator's observation still rings true. The Global Account Program Office must be engaged with the CIO to help articulate global account program requirements, and maintain oversight responsibility for meeting those requirements. For example, if the firm is developing an opportunity management system, the Program Office must ensure that opportunities can be evaluated globally, something that a domestic IT professional might overlook.

Two of the great difficulties for global account management today are that global account needs continue to evolve, and that IT is fast changing. There is a real danger that today's IT project is obsolete no sooner than approved and, worse, that IT project approval today forgoes future alternatives. The bottom line is that the Program Office must ensure close working relationships between IT personnel and GAMs. Only by continually tapping into the very real issues that GAM's face on a day-by-day basis can the firm keep up to date with IT infrastructure needed to manage the global account program.

There are many different ways to classify the systems and processes the IT infrastructure must support. A useful initial cut is between synchronous and asynchronous information:

- *Synchronous information:* Synchronous information concerns real-time communications. Here the IT system must offer various forms of voice communication (with or without video), telephone (land and mobile), video conferencing, and voice- and video-over-Internet and non-voice communications modes such as email, text messaging, groupware, and chat rooms. These methods enable communications among supplier personnel and between supplier and global account personnel. They also help ensure the team is engaged and current on

---

[3] Christopher Koch, "A Tough Sell," *CIO Magazine*, May 1, 1997.

the global account, and enable the global account personnel to be in contact with the supplier. Relevant team members are apprised of successes, problems, and opportunities at the customer, leading to quick responses and heightened customer satisfaction.

The Program Office must ensure that firm investment in new and emerging communications technologies is globally enabled. For example, a U.S. firm that standardized on a domestic cell-phone protocol would short change GAMs who need to be in contact with team members all over the world.

- *Asynchronous information:* Asynchronous information includes all forms of information storage and flow that do not have to occur in real-time. The firm may put in place systems that largely benefit the supplier, the customer, or both. These systems may be based on the Internet, intranets, and extranets, and have several different purposes.

Global account planning

Asynchronous information is needed throughout the planning process, including the situation analysis, bridge to strategy, and framework for account action—including strategy formulation, and action program development—right into the operating period.

To commence the planning process, the GAM and team members require a historical database of information on the global account. Much of this information is input into the global account planning process (Chapter 8). This information library must be appropriately organized so that the GAM, global account team members, senior management, and other organizational personnel have easy access, with appropriate safeguards for access level, and ability to input into the library.

Although, as discussed in Chapter 8, team members should physically meet during the planning process, they typically conduct much plan development remotely. They must have a process to provide input to the developing plan. Once the plan is completed and the operating period commences, they need a process for updating the plan in real time.

Managing the global account

Many suppliers' data gathering capabilities include data that is more relevant to the day-by-day business conducted between the supplier and the global account. These include, for example, data for a contact management system, information on global account RFPs (requests for proposals), and orders and deliveries around the world. This information is critical for the GAM and account management personnel in various countries, so they may keep on top of the business being done with the global account.

Successful data collection for global accounts has two basic requirements system and data. The system must be developed so the database receives information from countries around the world and can similarly be accessed from individual countries. This ability may take significant investment. You do not want to be in the position of a senior executive at a major global corporation who told us, "I am frequently embarrassed by our inability to go to a single source application or database system for information about our global customers."

But the hardware and software needed to make this happen is only one part of the issue. The other part is the data. Many of today's so-called *CRM systems* are data-impaired.

> Then consider the extent to which flawed information about customers could screw up a company's CRM initiative. In fact, it's a common problem. According to Kent Allen, a CRM specialist at Aberdeen Research Group, dirty data is the number-one cause of failure of many large-scale CRM implementations. "The reason these expensive CRM systems aren't working is garbage in, garbage out," Allen says. "What's being loaded into these systems is dirty data. So the ROI is no good."[4]

To address this problem, corporate may have to exercise a heavy hand. Business units and geographic areas often feel very proprietary about their data. This is a special problem when different business units each offer products meeting similar customer needs. Decentralized processes governing the collection and sharing of data have to change. Senior executives must make sure that all business units and geographic areas work together to put customer data, defined by rigorous specifications, into one central database.

Once this agreement is secured, the CIO should spearhead a company-wide process to clean the data and make sure incoming information stays clean. This is not easy, for individual employees change positions, change locations, change e-mail accounts, get married and divorced, and have needs for different products and services at different stages in their careers, and at different times in their lives. They also switch employers. The firm must embed such processes as training call center representatives that are helping

---

[4] Allison Bass, "Fight Dirty Data," *CIO Magazine*, June 4, 2002.

customers on other matters, to check whether the e-mail address or other pertinent information has changed, and then record those changes.

Understanding customer personnel is the core driver of a successful data mining system. If the basic hardware and software is weak, and/or if individuals from around the world provide garbage data, your global account teams will be severely disadvantaged. Your GAMs will not be able to efficiently identify new opportunities, track revenue streams, or provide customers with data on special deals based on global spending patterns, or support the global account planning process. More subtly, an underperforming data mining system for global accounts will hurt your ability to argue that you offer value to global accounts on a global scale. It will also frustrate global team members, and call into question your firm's commitment to global account management.

So, how good is your current customer database? Can it provide meaningful global information about your key global customers? Do not take the answers to these questions in faith from your CIO. Remember, it is one thing to have data availability from country to country. It is quite another to have data seamlessly integrated into a global data system—a data system that can be readily accessed by whatever software you have available.

Providing value to the global account

Over and above the benefits derived by the global account from the supplier's planning and data systems, certain types of asynchronous information can be highly valuable to the global account and play a significant role in enhancing the global account/supplier relationship. For example, the supplier can provide significant value to global account procurement personnel by tracking the account's corporate purchases around the world. The supplier may have far greater ability to make this data available than the global account itself.

> At IBM, global customers sometimes ask IBM to provide an asset management capability. They want IBM to track their own hardware, software and services purchases. The implications are considerable; the infrastructure must allow IBM to track inventory—additions and withdrawals—accurately in over a hundred and sixty countries. Difficult to do? Certainly! But, the ability to respond to this sort of request helps develop partnership relationships, and build considerable competitive barriers.

Other examples where value accrues to both supplier and global account include: providing customer satisfaction data around the world, providing prices that are unique to the global account because of special contracting arrangements, tracking responses to complaints or incidents, and special online ordering capabilities.

A well-developed IT system can also aid the global account in identifying where its order rests in the supplier's system. For example, Fed Ex's package tracking identifies package location. Similar technology can be used within the supplier's plant. Another excellent example is the status of joint projects. Projects flowing out of the global account planning system may require detailed implementation plans. If supplier and global account are working closely together, an IT system that allows each to track its own and its partner's progress can be invaluable.

Finally, the firm needs a system to track current performance against budget on a global basis. We shall discuss this topic later, but considerable IT underlies the firm's ability to make these analyses.

Financial management system

The infrastructure around handling the firm's financial management has a very direct impact on executing a global account program. The basic issue is fairly straightforward. The GAM has responsibility for an individual global account, and executes that responsibility through a worldwide team.

Most GAMs are responsible for global account revenues—the firm should have a system for accounting for those revenues. If the GAM is also responsible for global account profits or profit contribution, there should be a system for accounting for global costs and developing profits or profit contribution statements.

Most GAMs direct the worldwide teams that secure those revenues and profits; hence, a global budget is appropriate. And if the GAM is expected to make investment decisions on global account coverage, the firm should have a system for acquiring and accounting for those funds.

In our experience, in general, firms with global account programs have very limited ability to track accurately critical financial data at a customer level worldwide. Typically, the accounting systems and financial strategy for most multinational firms are built around a country metric model. Yet, most firms with global account management systems want to hold GAMs responsible for, at least, worldwide revenues at their global customers. The firm's inability to conduct this operation can be a serious frustration for GAMs. Unfortunately, this issue is often framed as investing in financial infrastructure "just so a salesperson can get paid accurately." Clearly, this is an excessively narrow perspective, but one we have seen acted out with many Global *Fortune* 500 firms. Senior management commitment comes into play here—it must take the position that global account financial tracking requirements are essential to the firm's health and growth.

Although global financial measurement systems fall into the "hard" category, many firms view building this infrastructure as an IT project paid for by IT budget funds, rather than as a financial management project. Although IT clearly has an important role to play, this perspective is unfortunate and unnecessary. In most firms, the Finance and Planning organization is very powerful—it typically controls the funding, expense budgets, investment funds, and financial measurements against which all employees, from the CEO downwards, are paid.

A global financial infrastructure helps avoid many of the problems from which geographic-based systems suffer. For example, the GAM has control over travel for himself and team members—he no longer has to negotiate travel budgets with a country manager, and/or suffer the frustration of being turned down. The GAM can set up global planning meetings less encumbered, and can invest in the global account's operations in a remote country that may otherwise go unfunded. The Global Account Program Office has an important role to play in securing commitments from the financial organization, so that the capability for global data is put in place.

The financial infrastructure for managing global accounts typically runs as an adjunct to the firm's geographic financial system. For a variety of reasons, not the least of which is the concerns of local tax authorities, the global firm's P&L system is typically measured at the individual country level. Individual country performance is aggregated across countries to develop a global view of the firm's performance. The global account P&L operates as a shadow system for measuring firm performance at individual global accounts, and is aggregated across global accounts to assess financial performance of the global account program *per se*. This global P&L should also be sufficiently flexible to handle investments in individual global accounts, and in the global account program.

> Schneider Electric uses a special funding mechanism for global account management. Total uses of these (MAP) funds aim for 70 percent seed money and 30 percent for more general purposes. These funds can be used for customer-specific activities and also for broader global account management. Schneider finds these funds especially useful for developing business in remote countries and in start-up situations.

A secondary issue concerns "who gets what financial information?" As far as GAMs are concerned, this issue relates to the empowerment discussion in Chapter 7. Highly empowered GAMs should receive full P&L data for their global accounts. Firms typically provide less empowered GAMs with revenue data, but not profit or profit contribution data. In general, we advocate providing GAMs with full financial disclosure on their global accounts. If senior management is unhappy with this level of disclosure, it should question whether it is appointing the "right" people to the GAM position.

Soft Infrastructure

The second major category of infrastructure elements we chose to call "soft." Not because it is easier to address, but because it deals more with people, skills, and processes, than with machines and bits and bytes. In some respects, "soft" elements are actually more difficult to address than some of the "hard" infrastructure elements. Of course, some "soft" infrastructure elements also require hard infrastructure, but the drivers are procedures and people.

Global pricing and global contracts[5]

Global customers want consistent worldwide pricing. Global customers do not necessarily expect a single global price, but they do expect a rational pricing method. Instant global communications has reduced a firm's ability to price based on local conditions. We have seen examples where prices for the identical product were 300% higher in a remote country than in the home country. The "remote" market had little competition and, historically, the supplier was able to secure that price from local customers. Today, such profit margins are unsustainable. The global customer will view such price disparities (and less) as price gouging. Continued price disparity will motivate your global account to introduce new competitors to your "local" market with globally priced contracts.

Today, most suppliers secure business at a country level, and write country-specific contracts. But, when major customers become part of a global account program, they expect to sign a single global contract. The global account expects overall worldwide consistency, and may require that your firm contractually agree to a particular level of performance, product quality, and/or availability,

---

[5] For a thoughtful discussion of global pricing and global contracts, see Das Narayandas, John Quelch and Gordon Swartz, "Prepare Your Company for Global Pricing," *Sloan Management Review*, (Fall 2000), pp. 61–70.

regardless of location. For the global account, your performance in Kazakhstan may be as (or even more) important as your performance in France. Further, your global accounts are developing global procurement organizations to improve overall procurement effectiveness. They do not want to make a global deal, and then revert to country-by-country contracts. Without a global contracting infrastructure and an organization that can produce a global contract, you will be viewed as unresponsive. Unresponsiveness to customer requirements reduces your chances of winning the business.

You must build a pricing and contracting infrastructure comprising expert and knowledgeable executives on global pricing, global contracts, and global contract negotiations. These executives must have sufficient power to resolve conflicts between the GAM striving to pull off a complex deal, and the vested interests of such internal organizations as business units and geographic regions and countries. Global pricing and contracts are very complicated issues. The Program Office should play a role to assist in developing negotiation guidelines with the relevant internal organizational units, so that GAMs understand corporate standards and processes regarding delegated discount levels and other concessions to the global account. This should be completed before engaging any customer on a complex global deal. Without the professional support of knowledgeable negotiators, global account team members will waste their own and their customers' time chasing issues that should not arise.

One way to deal with the global account's pricing concerns is to develop a Competitive Pricing Index that states the average price globally for various products and services. A global account does not necessarily receive the best price from this historical data, but the GAM may uses these data as starting points from which to discuss pricing issues. Of course, global accounts expect to receive global pricing, but actual prices may vary from country to country, with variations handled very carefully with significant coordination through local account managers.

We do not pretend that global contracting is easy to accomplish—there are a myriad of country-focused issues that must be resolved. But these difficulties open the way for the firm to secure competitive advantage. Consider the perspective of the International Association of Contract and Commercial Managers (IACCM):

> In a recent survey on international contracting, buyers rated the performance of vendors as 'poor' or 'very poor.' They were unhappy with their ability to make and execute on global

commitments. Some corporations are addressing the challenge of global contracting and gaining significant competitive advantage. Others remain imbedded in 'ownership tussles' and revenue disputes that frustrate sales initiatives and guarantee implementation problems."[6]

IBM built the financial infrastructure into its customer relationship model. A special unit in the Finance organization focuses exclusively on global bids. This group helps develop global contracts by providing pricing methodologies that make contracting easier. For example, prices are always set locally, but special bids for global account business are based on percent discount matrices by country or geographic region. IBM does not change list prices; list prices are modified prices by various discount percentages.

The Program Office provides these delegated pricing discounts to GAMs so they can reduce response time to special bid requests. The GAM needs only to refer to his delegated matrix. For bids requiring deeper discounts, the GAM makes the financial business case to the special bids group—it can secure quick approval or disapproval from its senior executive. This process avoids waiting several weeks for a response from each affected country. It reduces the average response time to global bids from over a month to a matter of days.

When IBM wins a bid, the bid unit works to ensure it is executed under the terms and conditions of the contract. Pricers are assigned in each country to ensure local systems and billing is accomplished with the prices negotiated by the GAM.

IBM's success with global pricing and contracting has important spillover effects for other functions within IBM. The customer-centric focus led many other executives to consider the customer in their part of the firm, for example, legal and administration, even though they were not, typically, directly involved with customers.

---

[6] Tim Cummins, *Global Pricing and Contracts, Velocity*, January 2, 2002. According to Cummins, IACCM director, IACCM's objective is to raise the status, profile, and professionalism of commercial contracting. Its membership is drawn from the sales contracting and procurement communities, and spans more than 300 corporations in over 70 countries. In a recent benchmark study IACCM concluded that, "Overall, respondents told us that 'Managing Business Risk' is the unchallenged leader in terms of primary role of the contracts organization (with either 'Reducing Costs' [Procurement] or 'Supporting Sales' [Sales Contracts] in second place). This has been accompanied by a marked—though not dramatic—shift of reporting line to either Finance or Legal. Over 70% of participants now have resources consolidated globally, regionally or by major business division, against less than 50% when we started these surveys 7 years ago."

Opportunity management

If your GAMs are doing a good job, they are generating more opportunities than you have the resources to fund. Further, since global opportunities are implemented in many countries around the world, you must make sure that required resources are available in specific countries when needed. A critical infrastructure element is a formal global review process for opportunities. Only when the firm has clarity on its ability to execute on a global opportunity can it minimize the probability of derailing customer satisfaction and putting the entire project in jeopardy.

The global opportunity system comprises two separated but related elements. The primary element focuses on an individual global account, the GAM, and members of the global account team. The GAM is responsible for fleshing out individual global opportunities. These steps are essentially an extended part of the global account planning process. Once an individual opportunity has been worked through these steps the second element kicks in. That is an opportunity management system that evaluates and prioritizes the entire set of opportunities from all global accounts.

The opportunity from an individual global account

The key to success in global opportunity management is deep understanding of the global customer. For GAMs doing a good job, this process is ongoing. Nonetheless, it finds focus in the global account planning system. The system we describe may seem bureaucratic, but it is the only way we know of forcing the discipline to win globally. Further, only with a formal process can the firm weed out ill-formed or ill-advised and/or impossible-to-win opportunities.

- *Step 1:* Develop a description of the global opportunity including the value to the global account, value to the firm, and the competitive situation for this specific opportunity.
- *Step 2:* Document detailed opportunity elements. The popularity of "solution selling" has led to the bundling of many sub-opportunities—these must be clearly identified. Of course, you may face various competitors for the overall opportunity and for individual opportunity elements that can be disaggregated.
- *Step 3:* Conduct opportunity analysis by focusing on the global account's ability to fund its initiative, decision-makers for differing funding elements, and the degree of urgency for completing the project. Identify what firm resources will be needed if the

opportunity is secured, including location and timing, and the long-term financial impact, including the customer's future (growing, stable, declining market).

- *Step 4*: Make a serious analysis of the firm's chances of winning the opportunity and the various economic and political threats. This entails assessing the competition and its likely actions.
- *Step 5*: Develop a tactical plan on how the global account team plans to win this global business.

As early as feasible, individuals in each country (or teams according to customer size and complexity of the opportunity) should review and comment on the oppotunity, preferably at Step 2. Personnel within countries should not have the power to stop the opportunities; rather, their role is to provide further intelligence on how they can, or cannot, assist in winning the opportunity. A customer orientation demands that they respond quickly.

When issues cannot be resolved, the opportunity should flow into a well-defined escalation process. The particular executive with sufficient authority to resolve such conflicts should have a global role and not just speak for an individual function. This executive should be counted on to be available, so that he can resolve issues regarding the opportunity within a few days.

The Global Account Program Office assists global account teams by advising them about the types of information the countries require. When escalations occur, it may not always be clear to the GAM why country management feels it is necessary to resist an opportunity. Since countries may have so many different legitimate issues, the Program Office can assist the decision-making executive when escalations occur. Such a knowledgeable resource can save days or weeks in resolving what may seem petty issues to a GAM, but are major issues for countries.

A French GAM for a U.S. manufacturer was very frustrated with the refusal of U.S. Operations to lower prices to the level he requested. The frustration was caused by insufficient language skills and extensive use of pricing community jargon by U.S. personnel. The Program Office stepped in to explain (in French) that the firm's single largest customer was the U.S. Government General Services Administration (GSA). Under the GSA contract, no other customer could receive a lower price. The French GAM was requesting a price below the GSA contract level. If granted, the same price would have to be offered to the GSA, causing a significant reduction in overall profits.

The set of opportunities from all global accounts

Who owns and maintains the flow of opportunities into the company's process is a function of the global account program's size and scope. If the number of opportunities is limited, the Program Office could maintain the data. When the number of opportunities grows, a special group may be required to manage the process, and should probably sit within the Finance organization when the financial implications of global opportunities become sufficiently large.

- *Step 6:* Data from Steps 1 through 5 is fed into the opportunity management data system. The system combines IT infrastructure, the human review team, and executive decision processes discussed above. The opportunity database is an important input for planning, forecasting, and generally sensing market evolution.
- *Step 7:* Opportunity management is regularized—new opportunities are fed into the system to join older opportunities that continue to be in process. Previously rejected opportunities may remain in the system if market changes might necessitate reevaluation. Periodically, weekly or monthly, the sales executive team should assess the state of the firm's opportunity portfolio.

Complaints and suggestions

Things go wrong on a day-to-day basis. Deliveries are late, invoices are incorrect, promised resources are not forthcoming, and we screw up in many other ways. Part of the GAM's skill is to avoid these occurrences, but they will happen. What matters to global accounts is not just that these failures occur but what action the firm takes when they occur. Is there infrastructure in place to address complaints and suggestions?

The first imperative is to get these global issues on the table so the GAM can start to address the problems, hopefully with the firm's help. For example, many global accounts rely on approved orders of products as input to their production processes. Late deliveries can play havoc with production schedules, even more in today's "just-in-time" world. No one likes to tell a customer bad news—but there is a world of difference between telling them as soon as you identify the problem, when they may have time to make other arrangements, and telling them late, when the problem is totally unsolvable.

Complaints and suggestions are amenable to infrastructure development. They can be categorized and expertise developed so that they can be handled efficiently and effectively. In IBM's process, 95 percent of suggestions and complaints are dealt with in 5 business days. Each goes to a complaint owner whose job is to resolve the matter within a set time period. Complaints are categorized according to the critical nature of the issue. When a problem is classified as a critical situation ("critsit"), there are set timetables for escalation to the next executive level responsible for the issue. For example, a service issue related to a broken computer has a very fast escalation path. If a manufacturing process is stopped and the IBM element causing the stoppage is not resolved in a matter of hours, escalation to get additional technical support and notify the GAM and sales executives is invoked. This is a global process—a GAM in Italy knows very quickly that there is an issue in the U.S. or China.

Human resource systems

A good example of soft infrastructure is HR systems. Perhaps the most important HR system concerns securing GAMs and global team members. We discussed this topic extensively in Chapter 7, focusing specifically on GAMs. We discussed recruiting, selecting, training and development, measuring performance and compensating, and retaining. Essentially, putting highly qualified GAMs in place should be an infrastructure process managed jointly by the Program Office and the HR organization.

A second important HR role is putting PEs in place. Here, the Program Office interfaces directly with senior management.

Xerox pioneered the Partner Executive (PE) role in the 1960s (*Focused Executive* in Xerox terminology). The primary purpose, then as now, was to develop executive-to-executive relationships so as to present Xerox as a business partner rather than as just a purveyor of individual products.

Xerox makes a significant effort to match its executives with customer executives. Criteria for matching include university attended, sports/arts interest, functional role, hobbies, charities supported, spouse/children's interests, and/or university. Xerox also attempts to match product-division executives with those customer executives whose firms are heavy-product users. Xerox Focused Executives are all volunteers, but most senior executives participate in the program.

Because of the commitment required (account planning sessions, operations reviews, regular meetings, solving account problems, rallying functional support, and following-up on commitments), the Program

Office attempts to limit the number of accounts per Focused Executive to two, but is often unsuccessful as high performers are in much demand. Xerox Focused Executives average two-to-three customers, with a range of one to six.

The Global Account Program Office developed a simple set of qualifying characteristics for Focused Executives:

- Willingness to participate in the program
- Commitment to fund related expenses, for example travel, entertainment, and client accommodations
- Agreement to be involved in the account planning process and operations reviews
- Ability to explain Xerox corporate strategy and capabilities to the customer

The Program Office manages the matching process of global account to Xerox executive by producing a list of suitable candidates for specific global accounts. Program Office managers recognize that some senior executives may not be suitable for this role. Sometimes an account manager contacts an executive directly. Regardless, the GAM makes the final selection. Focused executives receive no extra compensation, but top performers are recognized at the annual senior management meeting.

The Program Office orchestrates a half-day orientation session, including discussions with a successful account manager/Focused Executive team on working together. In those cases when the partnership was unsuccessful, the Program Office manages the "divorce" and effects replacement of the focused executive.

Enhancing your global account management program

No management process should be static, least of all a global account management process. Even if you adopted all of our suggestions, over time some of our perspectives will become obsolete, and new approaches will emerge. To state this in a very different way, right now some of your GAMs and global account team members are screwing up. And others are doing some things that are really innovative. If only you knew about each of these types of behavior and could act accordingly, think how much improvement could you make in your program for managing global accounts.

The fact of the matter is that, by and large, lateral communication systems in organizations are terrible. The left hand often does not know what the right hand is doing. That is a severe problem in domestic organizations—the problem is even greater for global firms. Nowhere is this as evident as in global account management. We discuss five distinct topics for enhancing your program:

Customer satisfaction

As competition gets tougher, high customer satisfaction does not guarantee loyalty, but the reverse is certainly true—low or moderate customer satisfaction does drive disloyalty. Measuring customer satisfaction and acting on the results is critical in enhancing performance at global accounts. Putting in place any customer satisfaction measurement system is non-trivial—putting in place a global system requires a good deal of thought and planning. A well-developed system should provide data about both your firm and the competition, and can significantly enhance your value to the global account.

- *Infrastructure:* This is the starting point for collecting and analyzing data from many countries around the world. Whether you decide to collect data independently or contract a third-party provider, web-based systems are a distinct advance over paper-and-pencil methodologies. Further, in-person and telephone interviews each have advantages and disadvantages. Your firm (or your provider) may already have multiple local systems and/or multiple business-unit systems—the global system should transcend and largely replace these individual systems. Of course, local operations may require answers to specific idiosyncratic questions. These can be either built into global measurement or handled offline.
- *The survey instrument:* The basis for the survey instrument should be measuring your performance at the global account, in areas that matter to the global account. Hence, you should develop the question set jointly with appropriate global account personnel, and share results with them.
- *Survey respondents:* Identifying the right people to survey may not be easy. Target respondents are key influencers and decision-makers. These may be difficult to identify in remote countries. Further, local employees may have perverse incentives to enter "friendly" customer personnel into the database, rather than employees that may give you good insight. Finally, individuals change positions—they are transferred or are promoted within the global account, or they leave. It is a continual struggle to keep the respondent database updated.
- *Frequency:* The firm must keep its pulse on satisfaction at the global account via systematic and regular customer satisfaction measurement.

But, too frequent measurement can lead to automatic, unthinking, responses that are of little value. Assessing the "tipping point" at your global accounts is nontrivial. This issue may be partly addressed by surveying a fraction of potential respondents each time you administer the questionnaire.

- *Change driver:* Measuring customer satisfaction is one thing, interpreting and acting on satisfaction metrics is quite another. Further, customer perceptions are not always accurate. Hence, the GAM has two quite different jobs—fix the real problems by working with global account personnel on corrective action, and communicating the reality, if customer perceptions are incorrect.

Business-momentum workshops

These are regularly held think-tank sessions where industry heads, GAMs, product-area heads, and product partners get together off-site to sit back and consider what's happening in the industry, and what opportunities might exist across all global accounts. These meetings allow leveraging of information across all GAMs. Informal meetings are held around these workshops and help create a common culture and teamwork. Citibank rotates these business-momentum workshops through different geographic regions.

Business-opportunity workshops

The purpose of these events, held periodically with both global account and supplier personnel, is to investigate the potential for new business between the firms. These events may contain a different cast of characters from those involved in the account planning process. These workshops involve "deep dives" into specific broad areas of concern to the account that the supplier may be able to address. These workshops are most fruitful if they are able to focus on ways of improving the global customer's business growth.

Best-practice sharing

Best-practice sharing has become a well-established process in many organizations. Within the global account management domain, best-practice sharing should occur at two different levels—within and across global accounts. Within global accounts, each GAM should identify best practices within their own global account teams. The GAM should give all team members the responsibility for identifying their own best practices and then disseminate them to the global account team. Across global accounts, the executive owner should give all GAMs the responsibility to share their best practices with the firm's other GAMs.

Identification is one issue; dissemination is a second. Frequently, domestic corporations share best practice in face-to-face meetings. In many cases, time and cost issues make this impractical for global account management, either within or across global accounts. Fortunately, the Internet offers options via bulletin boards, chat rooms, and e-mails. What will work for one firm may not work for another. So experiment and figure out a process that works for you.

Best-in-class benchmarking

Expertise in global account management is not firm-size-or industry-specific. Indeed, the underlying assumption of our book is that the ideas we offer are broadly applicable across industry. Your firm may have something to learn from a neighbor firm operating in a very different industry, and that firm may have much to learn from you. Indeed, this assumption underlies the work of the Global Forum and the Columbia Initiative in Global Account Management. But do not wait for us, pull together a group of non-competitive firms, identify common global account management issues and talk about them. You will be amazed at the insight you can gain from colleague executives in very different industries. If you want to start a global account benchmarking initiative, just get in touch with the authors, we will be very happy to help you out.

Getting Started on Infrastructure

So, you have just been appointed executive owner or otherwise given the responsibility for a new global account program, and you know that infrastructure is an issue. Where do you start? This is a not an unimportant issue, for poor infrastructure can hold back development of a global account program.

Perhaps the most important action it to set up a Global Account Program Office, even if you start the process with just a single member. Look around your firm for a saavy manager, experienced in the international arena. The office can grow as your global program expands, but this is a necessary first step. Much of the initial action will take place in the Program Office.

What should be the infrastructure areas that the Program Office should prioritize? In our view there are three major categories that should be addressed initially because of their importance to the success of the program.

1. Policies and systems that define the GAM and the role.
   Examples: the job description, "grade level," career path, compensation plan, professional development, selection process
2. Systems and support that directly enable the GAM's activities.
   Examples: financial reporting systems, pricing and contracting processes, budgeting process for revenue targeting and expenses, international network of country contacts ("our man in xxx"), technology tools
3. Anything that shapes the internal environment within which the GAM and the Program must operate.
   Examples: operating principles, reporting relationships, empowerment levels for GAMs and the Program Office, executive sponsorship, account ownership philosophy, account planning process, GAM's authority over the global team.

Summing up Infrastructure

As you can see from this chapter, infrastructure is essential to the success of your global account program. As a GAM, you may feel a little overwhelmed. After all, you are largely an infrastructure user rather than an infrastructure designer or builder. As a senior executive, you too may feel overwhelmed at all the infrastructure systems and processes that are required to effectively execute global account management. If you are the owner of one or more of these processes, you may be wondering how to make them happen effectively, and where you should secure the funds and resources to fuel the required activities. The answers are not easy to find.

We believe that the most critical element for infrastructure development is the Global Account Program Office, headed by a high-powered executive owner. This group is charged to focus attention on critical infrastructure elements needed for the global account program. It is here that the critical thinking on how your firm can pull the infrastructure complexity together must take place.

Key Messages

- Infrastructure is the glue that holds the global account program together.

- Senior management commitment is crucial for funding critical infrastructure elements.

- The Global Account Program Office is essential to pulling together a strategy for building global infrastructure.

- Infrastructure contains many elements that can be categorized as *hard* and *soft*.

- Infrastructure infuses the entire global account management process.

CHAPTER 10

DEMONSTRATING THE GLOBAL ACCOUNT PROGRAM'S INCREMENTAL VALUE TO THE FIRM AND TO THE GLOBAL ACCOUNT

PROLOGUE

Jace muses

Jace thought she was at the top of her game when it came to managing global accounts. Her clients generally followed her advice and her new friends, **Todd**, **Constance** and **George**, kept calling. But there was one area that continued to elude her—the answer to that ever-nagging question, PROVE IT.

Her last conversation with **George** on infrastructure was not a good one. **George** was really struggling to get his program rolling and lack of infrastructure was getting in the way. In many respects, his infrastructure struggles were a symptom of a lack of understanding by senior executives about what a global account program could produce. Stated another way, the core issue was belief in the value of the global account program.

It all went back to their first conversation at the airport bar. All three travelers had all perked up when **Jace** said, "Sounds like you need a way of demonstrating the global program's value to the company and the customer." As she was finding out, that was easier said than done. All three had called recently reminding her of what she had said, and asking the same question, "So how do we demonstrate value?"

"Well, it all depends." There it was—the catch-all consultant answer. The one you give when you can't come up with your elevator speech. Each of their questions dealt with the "who" discussion. Of course, each needed to show customers that their global account program delivered value. **Todd**'s dilemma was demonstrating value internally so his executives would pay more attention to the global program. **George** needed to convince his firm's senior leaders that infrastructure investment would improve financial returns across the board. And **Constance**'s Board of Directors and her executive team wondered if they were doing the right thing. Would investment in a global account program be good for shareholders?

Jace was not happy with her "it all depends" answer. She felt she was letting down her new friends. Each was thankful for her limited advice, but she hadn't managed to answer the "bottom-line" question. It would take more *than a phone conversation to address this issue. Each had a different position in their organizations; each of their firms had different products, different go-to-market strategies, different global program maturity, and each had different infrastructures. And, each dealt with quite different constituencies. **Jace** had to remind them that value, like beauty, is in the eye of the beholder.*

*Guess I am not as much at the top of my game as I thought, mused **Jace**. This value question seems like the search for the Holy Grail. There's not one simple way of coming at value. I'd better try to frame out an approach that can work equally well for **Todd**, **Constance** and **George**.*

The most important question to address in framing the value topic is very simple: For whom are you creating value? Unless you are rigorous in answering this question, your global account program will eventually unravel. Each business unit or function within your firm wants to know, "what's in it for me?" And, your global customers will look for you to demonstrate a "value proposition." Wall Street analysts will dig into the effect of your global program on quarterly earnings, price-earnings ratios, and other indicators of financial success, and investors will expect shareholder value to increase.

For your global account program to succeed, you must address these questions. In particular, you must show that your program delivers value to your various constituencies. Indeed, we believe it is very important to take the value creation concept to a higher level—to create clear incremental value. If you cannot demonstrate that your global account program delivers results "above and beyond" your current method of addressing major accounts, then expect continual challenges to your program's very existence.

Throughout this book we have emphasized the commitment necessary to develop a well-functioning global account program. Indeed, our second CSF focuses on senior management commitment, and each following CSF requires some form of resource commitment to aid the global account program. These commitments range from developing a new line organization—to securing effective GAMs—to action plans resulting from the global account planning process. Each CSF requires firm resources.

Right now, you probably have a process for dealing with your major accounts. Your global accounts are probably part of that process. As you start to modify the process to one that better aligns with your global accounts, you will meet internal resistance—make no mistake about it! "Here we go again—another attempt to get more resources for sales!" This is not resistance for the sake of resistance; change is hard, and many within your firm will not want "to pay the price of change." You cannot dismiss the real pain of change when individuals have to adapt their thinking and behavior to a new way of doing business that may significantly impinge on their control and day-to-day activities.

Shifting from a multi-domestic focus to a global focus is not easy. Your corporate culture will probably be disrupted. Comfortably entrenched management practices, familiar processes, and well-understood and accepted performance and recognition measures will have to change. In previous chapters, we documented the sorts of changes required and the difficulties lying in wait. Furthermore, scarce resources will have to be allocated to the global account program. If resources are going to the global account program, they are not going to Jack and Jill's favorite project. The new global account program should be worth this emotional, financial, and operational upheaval, or many colleagues will complain that the costs are too severe for whatever value the program is purporting to deliver.

And where will they complain? Right up the line to your top management. Your senior executives have many responsibilities, not the least of which is to deliver value to shareholders. If your global account program is nothing more than a resource sink, you will not deliver shareholder value. Your global account program *must deliver incremental value* to the firm, and *must be seen* to deliver that incremental value. We do not suggest that it is easy to measure that value. Indeed, it is often difficult to determine a direct relationship between any corporate initiative and increased share price. The challenge is to identify reasonable surrogates for increased shareholder value, and to ensure that your global account program delivers on these surrogates.

So let us suppose you have convinced senior management to implement a global account program. By whatever metrics, you have shown that the global account program brings value to your organization. But that is only part of the matter. So, now you go to one of your global accounts. "Congratulations, you are part of our new global account program." A possible response is the following. "So, what's in it for us?" You must have an answer to this question! If your global account program is on track, you are probably asking the global account to make some investment in the relationship. Of course, there will be extra investment in time and attention, but you may also be asking for R&D and capital investment. Further, your global account may be incurring greater risk by sharing information with you, and by betting on you rather than other suppliers. You must be sure of the value you will deliver to your global account and be convincing in your presentation.

We do not mean to suggest that securing value for global accounts and the firm is a sure thing when you introduce a global account program. Indeed, there are many risks for both the supplier and the global account. In this chapter, we provide a balanced discussion by focusing first on value for each side of the relationship, then turning to cautions in introducing a global account program.

So, where should we start? We are firmly in the camp that believes shareholder value is resultant. Shareholder value, we believe, is the reward for delivering customer value. If you deliver greater customer value than your competitors, you will secure competitive advantage. Competitive advantage brings real company rewards in terms of increased medium- and long-run sales and profits, and enhanced shareholder value. By contrast, firms that focus too much attention on shareholders are likely to get into trouble. After all, it does not take a managerial genius to increase profits in the short run— just trim back R&D, cut advertising and fire a few salespeople! The trick is to focus on the medium and the long run.

We commence our value discussion by focusing on value for the global account.

Delivering Value to the Global Account

The ultimate value a supplier delivers to a global account boils down to helping that account improve the returns it secures for its shareholders. The global account's returns will improve to the extent that it secures a better competitive position in its markets. If the global account can secure products and services from the supplier around the globe, and can secure them faster, cheaper and with greater ease than the competition, it receives significant value. How the supplier aids the global account in accomplishing this goal is a separate issue and depends on the types of the products and services offered by the supplier and the nature of the global account. Regardless, the most reasonable proxy for improving shareholder value is improving the global account's return on investment. Ultimately, there are three ways to achieve this goal—help the global account to improve its sales revenues, to reduce its costs, and to lower its investment.

Of course, it is not always easy to identify what sort of benefit a specific supplier action will deliver. For example, a supplier's new product introduced worldwide may not only reduce the global account's costs, but it may also allow it to be more competitive and hence increase its revenues. We note that the global account's costs may also decrease by reducing the sup-plier's prices. Although, suppliers often do reduce prices, there is always a trade-off between providing greater value to the global account and lesser value to the supplier. For this reason, the supplier should be very clear about the impact of its price reductions on both the global account, and the firm.

For ease of exposition, we focus on four types of value, each of which may lead to increased revenues, reduced costs, and lower investment:

- Direct value from the firm's products and services
- Value related to the global account's internal processes
- Relationship value
- Direct economic value.

Of course, these values are interrelated, but the framework offers a nice way of zeroing in on the value of the global account program for the customer.

As a related matter, the firm must understand that, in general, individu-als perceive value not as an absolute, but as a difference between actual value delivered and the expectation of that value. It is, therefore, very important, that the supplier set reasonable expectations with global account executives regarding what value will be delivered.

Direct value from the firm's products and services

In this category, we focus on the value offered by the firm's products and services as a result of the global account program.

Products that help global accounts increase revenues

Increased revenues for the global account is a highly significant value. The supplier can only deliver this sort of value by having an in-depth knowledge of the requirements of those customers the global account seeks to serve.

Some suppliers have made great progress in China by building relationships with key government personnel. A U.S. consultant was working in Korea with a U.S.-based telecommunications firm. He introduced a global account team member to a key official in China. He was able to orchestrate relationship building that led to significant business for the telecommunications firm.

Xerox redesigned and colored Citibank's monthly customer account statement. The new statement was customer-friendly—much easier to read and comprehend. The new statement helped Citibank gain bank-ing clients. It also reduced Citibank's costs because fewer customers called for explanations. This value-added solution was originally tested in two or three countries, then expanded globally. For example, Citibank's customer team from Istanbul visited Singapore to view the solution in practice before adopting it in Turkey.

IBM has helped many global account customers with market-entry consulting. Since IBM does business in 167 countries, it can quickly provide significant information on legal issues, office setup, and support. More detailed market-entry information is available through its the Global Services consulting group.

In the Print-for-Pay segment, Xerox has helped major players expand globally with a greater degree of confidence. Xerox uses market knowledge to make introductions to local "quick printers"— potential master franchisees for their countries.

Tailored products and services that are consistent worldwide

Every customer dreams of products and services tailored to its individual needs. A well-developed global account program has several features that help realize this dream. First, there is increased communication between the supplier and the global account around the world. Second, because it is part of a global account program, the global account receives special attention from the supplier. Third, customer involvement in the supplier's global account planning process should emphasize the importance of the global accounts product and service needs.

A well-executed global account program can provide the customer with the exact goods or services it requires, where and when it requires them. As a general rule, customers value consistency. Life is very difficult in a multinational firm when its various national subsidiaries buy different products and work with different systems. The ability to purchase the same standardized product, regardless of the country of delivery and manufacturing location, can be a major benefit for a large, multinational customer. Your customers will surely value your ability to supply products or services tailored to their needs in multiple locations around the globe. Of course, standardization reduces your costs; it may also reduce costs for your global account.

Citibank works hard to provide standardized financial services for its customers in many different countries around the world. Global customers place a high value on this service, in part because of the challenge of dealing with a myriad of differing banking laws and regulations.

Xerox's ability to provide a standardized product set for its global "print-for-pay" accounts, despite varying store sizes, was a major reason for securing business against its many competitors in the copier business.

In some cases, global customers may require identical functionality around the world but, for various reasons, the products have to be modified for some countries. For example, electrical specifications differ in almost every country. Because there are very few global standards, features must be specified according to the final country of use. This tailoring may affect supplier expense at the customer's location, and hence pricing. Whereas this is a product issue, the GAM can help the customer understand pricing differentials and avoid conflict at contract signing or installation.

If product standardization is carried to an extreme, some countries would receive over-built products. For example, Xerox products must meet safety standards in the various countries where they are sold. These standards tend to be the highest in the U.S., followed by Europe, then Asia Pacific. As a result, products designed for the U.S. might be too expensive in Europe, and much too expensive in Asia. What makes it even more complex for Xerox is that an Asia Pacific country, Australia, has standards that are close to the U.S. In general, this sort of issue transcends global account management and must be resolved at a country level. Nonetheless, GAMs are continually involved in explaining these issues to global customers. If communicated appropriately, they can avoid customer satisfaction issues by leveraging their relationships.

Products and services that get better and better

As the many individual relationships between supplier and global account personnel mature, broaden, and deepen, the customer gains a level of influence at the supplier that the supplier's other accounts cannot achieve. Close relationships between senior supplier management and global account personnel, orchestrated by the GAM, can lead to customized products, early access to new technology, best-practice benchmarking, and opportunities for collaboration. Also, the global account may secure early exposure to future product offerings, marketing alliances, and just plain special treatment due to its elevated status at the supplier. Across the board, the supplier will be able to provide its global account with better products and services. Indeed, the supplier's global account team can serve as a sounding board for customer ideas and can provide valuable input into the customer's decision processes.

Regardless, the GAM should be very clear about the service portfolio it offers to each global account. Because customers in different cultures have very different expectations about what services should be free, and what has to be purchased, these issues must be clearly defined and understood. In any event, when the firm provides services to the global account, it should measure the impact of these services so that it can demonstrate to the global account the value it has delivered.

Value related to the global account's internal processes

The supplier may offer value to the global account by helping to improve the manner in which the account conducts its own processes. These processes may range from manufacturing to various types of administrative issues.

Solving operational problems

By virtue of deep knowledge about its own products and processes, the supplier may have a window on addressing problems faced by the global account with its manufacturing processes. As we will see later, the supplier delivers this value episodically, when the global account has a problem. This value may be viewed as "on-demand" consulting.

IBM is a global account for 3M. 3M provides manufacturing equipment and process guidance to IBM's storage division—producers of large disk storage units. In one process, IBM Storage makes Giant Magnetic Resistive heads (GMR heads) for computer hard drives. GMR heads are extremely sensitive to electrostatic discharge (ESD) created during manufacturing. ESD product failures can result in significant product loss.

Enter the GAM from 3M. She built a strong relationship with key personnel at IBM and secured an understanding of issues facing IBM in a key manufacturing process. She brought in a core group of four people from 3M's Technology Group—this group solved the problem. IBM Storage was able to reduce GMR product loss by approximately 10 percent, a several million dollar annual saving for IBM.

IBM asked 3M to supply manufacturing system components globally, creating additional savings. When IBM Storage had other problems, it turned to 3M. The inter-company relationship, forged by 3M's GAM, delivered millions of dollars savings to IBM in improved supply chain efficiencies and increased profits. Further, 3M became a partner on which IBM could rely.[1]

Before it disposed of Rover, BMW incurred significant costs for printing the owner's manual. Historically, a standard manual covered several models and was printed in multiple languages. Xerox helped Rover redesign the manual so it only contained specific model features for "printing on demand." Each manual was unique to a specific purchased car and was printed only in the buyer's language. The Xerox printer stored all the relevant data and was connected to the manufacturing ordering system. This redesign saved BMW substantial printing costs and avoided inventory storage/obsolescence costs. Customer satisfaction improved.

Ease of doing business

Every customer places *ease of doing business* high on its wish list of supplier characteristics. Key places for the GAM to identify potential for delivering value to the global account concern those systems and processes that are fundamental to "going global." Going global is not easy, and these areas may cause the global account considerable difficulty. One such area concerns the basics of doing business globally rather than multi-domestically. Several issues are fundamental for the global account—it will want global pricing, a global contract, and be able to ensure that the supplier lives up to the terms of the contract. The supplier can make this easy or difficult for the global account. Unless you make a significant attempt, your customer may take an inordinate amount of time and resources investigating whether or not you are meeting your obligations. We have seen global accounts establishing entire departments to gather global pricing, purchasing and delivery information, and convert all currencies to a national standard. The sole goal of this activity was to ascertain whether or not a particular supplier was living up to its commitments. Quite correctly, these departments question every anomaly they discover. But, if the supplier simplified its global pricing and contracting process, it would create considerable account value by cutting these costs for the global account.

Another example is global tracking of business the supplier does with the global account. Because much of their procurement is local, most global accounts have not developed systems to track the orders they place with

---

[1] Joseph Sperry, "Strategic Account Management Association Performance Award for 2000," *Velocity*, (Quarter 3 2000), pp. 16–17.

a specific supplier on a global basis. This is important information for various reasons, including understanding the degree of partnership relationship with the supplier, and also their risk exposure. Providing global tracking is an important value for global accounts.

A global account program can go a long way toward offering this "ease-of-doing business" value. The global account team can relieve executives at the global account of much of the burden of "coordinating" projects. This value is greatly magnified during the global rollout of a particular initiative. The GAM's intimate knowledge of the global account's internal processes, policies, procedures, and politics can go a long way to ensuring that business will be conducted in a seamless manner. If the global account program is effective, the customer can sit back and relax while the supplier's global account team does its job. Further, an effective GAM can effectively address the everyday annoyances related to billing and credit for returned goods, that so often bedevil inter-firm relationships.

> Proctor & Gamble (P&G) aims to create value for itself and its global accounts by changing the traditional retailer/supplier relationship. The goal is to align key teams in P&G with key teams at the global customer. For example, P&G's shipping experts interface with its customers' shipping teams. The P&G team's goal is to understand customer cost structures globally so that P&G can develop systems and processes to reduce both the global customer's costs, as well as its own. P&G realized that its complex business practices around the world were creating problems for their customers, rather than creating value. Now, for P&G, doing business globally means simplification and standardization. To ensure that P&G creates value for both global accounts and P&G, P&G created a robust measurement system. This system measured both current operations and the impact of new initiatives on the value proposition.[2]

Relationship value

Relationship value is the value directly related to the nature of the relationship between the supplier and the global account. It includes several specific types of value. It may also concern relationships between, and among, supplier and global account executives.

---

[2] Mike Graen, "Technology in Manufacturer/Retailer Integration," Wal-Mart and Procter & Gamble, *Velocity*, Spring 1999, pp. 12–17.

A single point of contact

A single point of contact or, more importantly, a single point of accountability is a major step forward in streamlining the inter-organizational business relationship. The customer knows he can call the GAM for whatever issues that arise. As a senior 3M executive opined, "The fact that 3M is a multi-product, multi-market, multi-national company should not be the customer's problem." Making complex global coordination the supplier's problem, essentially solved by the GAM, the global team, and global account program resources, offers considerable value to global accounts.

> At Xerox, historically, it was not unusual for a customer to be "put in the middle" of competing sales forces. The copier/printer representative wanted to sell equipment for the customer's reproduction center. The Business Services group wanted the customer to outsource its work under a facilities management contract. The global account program was in part designed to prevent this inherent conflict. The GAM took the leadership role to work with the account to figure out how best to satisfy its needs

Access to higher-level executives

A critical issue for executives at the global account is having comfort that they understand their supplier's future plans and initiatives. Of course, any salesman, domestic account manager, or GAM has a view about the future, but global account executives must filter these views through their organizational levels. Smooth access to the supplier's senior management, made possible by the global account program, is a major value for the global account. The confidence that goes with securing critical data "straight from the horse's mouth" has tremendous value. Further, there is also considerable value for global account executives in understanding the supplier hierarchy and being able to take their issues to the "next level," should problems escalate.

Partnership Executive programs fulfill this need. Related executive involvement initiatives are Customer Councils. Typically, these councils comprise a specific group of customers. For example, before sale of its personal computer (PC) division to Lenovo, IBM secured a better feel for customer issues by creating an advisory council of customers conducting global rollouts. IBM personal computer executives addressed this group and secured first-hand feedback on how customers perceived IBM's strategy and support.

Fewer risks

Increased collaboration and greater partnership potential from membership in a global account program may reduce risk for the global account. Perhaps the supplier will take some of the financial-risk burden in joint ventures and other expansionary moves. Having "skin in the game" should lead to best efforts by the supplier to make sure the venture is a success. Of course, such arrangements may also benefit the supplier.

> At Xerox, a global account's desire to have "the latest" technology in remote locations was the impetus for Xerox to enter those geographies early. Through innovative approaches to account "spares stocking" and internal "key operator" training, products were launched before the local Xerox operation was really ready.

Value to global account executives

We noted earlier that organizations do not make decisions; people in organizations make decisions. Thus, not only may the supplier deliver value to the global account, the supplier may also deliver value to global account executives *per se*. These "executive" values are typically related to global account objectives, but they may also be related to an executive's personal objectives. For example, a close personal relationship between a global account executive and the GAM may enable the global account to receive such benefits as better and faster service. The global account receives value directly, but the global account executive may gain stature, respect, and career advancement within his company.

> At one firm with which we are familiar, a U.S.-based customer was entering new geographic markets around the world where it did not previously have a presence. One such country was France where, at the time, smart cards were in heavy use. (Smart cards were then not used in the U.S.) The GAM alerted the key customer executive to this cultural/technical anomaly. Armed with this insight, the customer firm was able to enter France with the proper equipment, and the customer executive avoided a serious "black eye." He was extremely grateful.

In addition, of course, the supplier can deliver value to global account executives via hospitality and special activities such as sporting events, concerts, and the like.

Direct economic value

We noted earlier that supplier initiatives may offer revenue enhancement, cost reduction, and/or lowered investment, and possibly more than one of these values. But there are some aspects of a global management program that deliver economic benefits to global accounts as a result of the program *per se*.

Lower cost of doing business

When the supplier implements a global account management process, global accounts frequently attempt to reduce purchasing costs. Global agreements usually allow global accounts to negotiate reduced-price contracts by leveraging enterprise-wide volume. Related to the ease of doing business noted above, an umbrella agreement covering worldwide terms and conditions can achieve significant savings in administration, management, and legal expenses. A global contract eliminates the "shopping" expense for each new facility and streamlines the credit approval process. These savings can be particularly impressive when you negotiate an *evergreen* agreement, and product, service, and pricing schedules need only be changed periodically. In general, smoother and faster worldwide implementation processes also create cost savings for the customer.

To the extent that the customer is sufficiently comfortable with its global supplier, it may reduce its supplier base. Indeed, an effective global account program may be the driver for a supplier-reduction program. By concentrating procurement with fewer suppliers, each remaining supplier achieves economies of scale that may, in part, be shared with the global account.

A Bird's-eye view and a local focus simultaneously

A global supplier works with the customer on many levels, for example country-by-country, regionally, and globally. If the global account consolidates purchasing at a single supplier, that supplier can provide the global account with all the information it needs to develop and manage the interfirm relationship. By contrast, if the global account has several suppliers, its information needs must be aggregated across multiple suppliers. Since this coordination task may be costly to perform, an effective global account program leading to sole sourcing may bring the global account significant cost savings. Said another way, sole sourcing with an effective global account supplier provides the global account with the best of both worlds—an international bird's-eye view of its business with the supplier, *and* local expertise in each country.

Conclusion

Ultimately, the supplier should seek to enhance returns to the global account's shareholders by helping the account increase revenues, reduce costs, and/or reduce investment. It may achieve these goals by delivering a strategic product to the global account in the right place at the right time. It may solve an operational issue or make it easier for the global account to do business. The supplier may offer value in terms of the inter-organizational relationship or it may use its global account program to deliver direct economic benefit. The key issue for GAMs is to take the time and energy to identify these value propositions.

It is one thing to deliver a discreet item of value to the global account, it is quite another to put in place a process that not only delivers value today, but also promises to deliver value in the future. We noted in Chapter 8 the role that customers may play in the global account planning process. By building in customer participation, you will improve the chances for delivering value to the global account. If you institutionalize this element of your planning process, executives at the global account will expect you to deliver value, and that value delivery will secure and enhance your position.

Delivering Value to the Firm

Just as the ultimate value the supplier delivers to the global account is improved returns for the global account's shareholders, so the ultimate corporate value from a global account program is improved shareholder value for the supplier's shareholders. As we noted in the previous section, it is often difficult to make the leap from firm actions and operational results to shareholder value.

In most large firms, the finance function has a major role in defining value and, typically, a major focus is on financial results in the short run. This poses somewhat of a problem for managing global accounts. A successful global account program delivers value today in the form of good short-term financial results. But, it should also create intangible value today that eventually contributes to the firm's bottom-line financial success tomorrow. Of course, though often no less important than hard financial results, intangible items are much harder to measure and track.

These issues are especially critical early in the life of a global account program, before it earns positive bottom-line financial results. We noted earlier that global account programs often face significant internal resistance. Unless value-based measures are agreed up front, it is all too easy for detractors to point out that good bottom-line profits have not yet been delivered.

We agree that increased sales and profits are good indicator variables for increased shareholder value. But, we also identify two types of intangible value to form three value categories. We organize discussion on the value of global account management to your firm as:

- Financial and competitive value
- Value in improvements in customer relationships
- Internal firm value.

Financial and competitive value

Frequently, the rationale for global account management is to secure financial and competitive advantage. Indeed, unless these advantages are secured, the program will not survive and the other types of value will be lost. In this sense, these values are necessary for maintaining the global account program.

Help cement the firm's business base

In Chapter 1, we asserted that, in this era of globalization and interdependence, firms with global ambitions must develop global account programs. If customers are developing global strategies, a global account program is an *ante*. It is quite simply the price of admission. An effective global account program ensures that global accounts are treated holistically, rather than in an uncoordinated manner by separate geographic- and/or product-based teams. Developing a seamless, effective, and efficient global account program is not easy, and few firms are doing it well today. As we go forward, the global account program will increasingly become a requirement for developing and maintaining ongoing relationships with global customers. Maintaining customer loyalty pays off big time for supplier profits. Increasing loyalty by just a few scale points can have an exponential benefit on the bottom line.

In the mid-1990s, Marsh Inc., an insurance brokerage risk consultancy firm, received requests to prepare global proposals from two of its major customers, Johnson & Johnson and Corning. Marsh successfully responded to these requests. It developed global proposals and, as a result, became the global provider of insurance brokerage and risk consultancy services for both firms. Had Marsh been unprepared, each customer would have awarded both its U.S. and international business one of Marsh's major competitors. Now, several years later, Marsh sees global reach and coordination as a significant entry barrier in addressing the *Fortune* 1000, and has established global practices and global profit centers throughout the firm. Marsh now aggressively sells its global capabilities as a competitive differentiator.

Improve firm profitability

Careful development of global accounts can lead to larger and less volatile, revenue and profit streams. For example, many customer firms are now installing global procurement programs. If the firm has done a good job of selecting global accounts, and becomes a preferred global supplier to one of these accounts, its business may increase as the global account rolls out its global procurement initiative more broadly. Also, supplier revenues increase as the global account expands into new geographic areas. Of course, such add-on business is typically less expensive to secure from an existing global account than from a new customer.

> For both IBM and Xerox, business with global customers has grown more rapidly than business with other customer segments. Furthermore, improved customer relationships, resulting from their global account programs, allowed both IBM and Xerox to engage in value-added service initiatives. These initiatives have had a highly positive impact on revenues and also profits.

Further, an effective approach to managing global accounts allows the supplier to eliminate wasteful programs, previously handled on a country-by-country basis. For example, it can streamline costly customer service activities so as to enhance and regularize its profit streams.

Improved competitive position

As your customers' global provider, your global account program should put your firm in a position to service the global account—*better, cheaper,* and *faster*. Further, enhanced understanding of the global account should allow the supplier to build efficiencies into the entire inter-organizational relationship. By understanding the global account's business in-depth, the supplier is better able to anticipate and address global account needs, and develop new and improved products and/or services. An effective supplier assists the global account both strategically and operationally, and lays the groundwork for increased business. If the supplier is doing a first-rate job, its global account program offers significant added value to its global account. By delivering the sorts of value discussed in the previous section, the supplier may secure a significant point of difference that helps distinguish it from competitors. The global account program may deliver critical differential advantage as competition becomes tougher, and the ability to differentiate by product becomes ever more difficult. For many firms, global customer feedback is very consistent regarding global coordination, consistency, and availability. We often hear, "If you can't do it, we will find someone who can." The global account's business experience with your firm worldwide is becoming the ultimate differentiating factor.

Increased switching costs for global accounts

In successful global account programs, suppliers and global accounts do not haggle about the last penny on each global contract. Rather, the two firms engage in longer-term, broader, mission-critical collaboration. By assisting the global account to achieve its objectives, the supplier becomes embedded in the global account's key processes. By becoming a strategic partner, the supplier raises a significant barrier against competitors. Should the global account contemplate changing suppliers, it faces a variety of financial, emotional, and practical switching costs. For example, Xerox's position with several Asian banks became very secure when those institutions began printing monthly customer statements on high speed, highlight color Xerox devices.

Global marketplace recognition as an enterprise-transformation leader

As a critical supplier to high-profile global accounts at the cutting edge of global procurement, the supplier gains high credibility among new global and/or globalizing customers. The ability and experience in treating existing global accounts in a truly global manner may offer significant risk-reduction value for these new potential customers. Because of its expertise, the supplier may be able to differentiate and stand out from its competitive set.

Reduce overall risk

We noted in the previous section that the risk reduction following from a customer's status *as* a global account is an important value *for* global accounts. The same is true for suppliers to global accounts. Increasingly, suppliers are forming partnerships with global accounts, even formal joint ventures. These entities reduce risk for both the supplier and the global account—they not only share potential rewards, but also share project costs and investments. As a secondary benefit, developing these relationships in one arena provides the global account with a vested interest in continuing the supplier relationship in other arenas.

> Because of rapidly increased business between the two companies, an alliance pattern developed between Schneider Electronic and IBM. IBM feels sufficiently confident with Schneider Electric's service domestically that it increasingly seeks to expand the relationship internationally.

Value in improvements in customer relationships

Over time, value from the inter-organizational relationship morphs into financial and competitive value.

Nobody fires a friend

If the supplier properly implements its global account program, it should be able to develop deep and enduring business and personal relationships among global account and supplier personnel. These deepening relationships should significantly increase global account loyalty to its supplier. For example, during the banking crisis in the early 1990s, Citibank's global customer franchise was loyal to the Bank, despite the increased level of counter-party risks.

Of course, we should not confuse customer loyalty with customer satisfaction. Any well-run global account program should enhance customer satisfaction. But, research has consistently shown that, prior to a shift in suppliers, 80 percent of customers switching vendors rated their primary vendor relationship as satisfactory. Quite simply, high levels of satisfaction may not be enough to retain your global accounts. You must continually strive for greater program effectiveness so as to propel global account satisfaction into global account loyalty.

A loyal customer envisions a long-term relationship with its supplier. It increases spending over time, and recommends the supplier to other firms. An effective global account program can encourage such behavior by providing the framework for developing strong business and personal relationships among supplier and global account. Said another way, it is easier to fire a nameless, faceless supplier than to fire a person. It is often very painful for customers to terminate a set of personal and business relationships. No one likes to write off the time and resources invested to develop these relationships. An effective global account program fosters these relationships and builds global account loyalty to its supplier.

An effective global account program provides the structure for the firm to increase its understanding of, and communication with, the global account. The GAM's personal attention and dedicated focus allows the supplier to gain an in-depth global account understanding that it cannot secure in any other fashion. An effective GAM truly understands the global account's decision-making processes, political landscape, key business issues, current- and long-term operational objectives, executive compensation drivers, and so forth.

> The Marsh GAM at Johnson & Johnson (J&J) described himself as practically a J&J employee He gained such a deep understanding of the J&J "DNA" that he was often asked to mediate disputes and handle difficult political situations within J&J.

Long-term planning

An effective global account program drives the relationship focus toward the strategic and longer-term—from short-term—account retention to building a joint future. If the supplier develops and fosters the sorts of relationships we have outlined, the global account is more likely to share its aspirations, fears and difficult issues with the supplier. When there is reciprocal sharing between supplier and global account, the stage is set for significant relationship enhancement and value for both.

Internal firm value

Finally, the global account program offers several types of internal value for the supplier. Some of these values directly involve the global account; others are more general benefits that provide value to the supplier as a whole.

Ensuring a consistent face to the customer

Because of the complexity of dealing with global accounts—across time zones, across countries, across cultures—and with multiple supplier/global account touch points, "keeping the supplier's story straight," can be a recurring problem. There is nothing worse in managing a supplier/customer relationship for the customer to receive contradictory supplier messages.

A critical value from the global account process is enhancing the probability that the supplier will treat the account consistently, across product divisions and geographies. The international alignment that is part and parcel of the global account process not only benefits current global accounts, but also aids the supplier's business development efforts.

> Citibank's "Compass" project is designed to train firm employees—across divisions and around the globe—to treat personnel at a given global account in a consistent manner on a worldwide basis. Further, Citibank developed a "marketing encyclopedia" enabling its offices around the globe to access history and other information about pitching new customers.

An effective enabler

Just as basketball superstar Michael Jordan used to improve the performance of his entire basketball team, so also, an effective global account program can enhance firm credibility and improve performance of the entire field sales organization. Consider, for example, a global contract won by the GAM that must also be sold at the local level. Because of the supplier's success at the global level with the first selling step, the local approval process should be quicker and less effortful. And local representatives can move on to their next opportunity sooner.

Further, the GAM may be able to raise local levels of contact for geographic-based representatives, get products onto an approved list and, if very successful, secure preferred or sole vendor status. Once again, the GAM's successes speed the sales cycle and cut costs. Finally, global contracting can achieve time and cost reduction, bypassing the seemingly endless legal-review process in every country and make contract renewal much less complicated.

Providing career opportunities

An effective global account program provides the opportunity for a new career and may increase firm morale, especially in customer-facing roles. Coming out of the recessionary period, sales force turnover is reaching new highs with its consequent negative implications for developing enduring customer relationships. Certainly, high account-manager turnover flies in the face of developing deep and lasting business and personal relationships with the firm's customers.

Making the job interesting and challenging enhances tenure in any position. Salesperson and account manager positions are no exception. A sure way to extend tenure in these positions is to develop a career path that offers an interesting and challenging progression in professional account management. Such a career path may place the GAM position at the apex as its most sophisticated and complex manifestation. In a well-developed global account program, the GAM has significant decision-making authority and bottom-line responsibility. This GAM position is incredibly challenging and allows the sales professional to use all of his skills and competencies on a daily basis. In a well-designed global account program, it can become a "to die for" appointment for a career-professional account manager.

> Historically, GAM turnover at Xerox has been very low and, despite Xerox's problems, morale has been correspondingly high. Indeed, the major cause of turnover has been retirement. Why? Because the position was so rewarding that none of the GAMs were willing to leave the position. Tough job, yes, but those with the right skills wanted to remain as GAMs.

The ripple effect

From where are tomorrow's leaders of major corporations increasingly sourced? Even for historically ethnocentric U.S. firms, some level of foreign experience is increasingly the norm. Indeed, some firms design career paths with expensive expatriot assignments to "season" managers. Others import high potential executives from foreign geographic regions.

An effective global account program provides unique value by educating supplier personnel about international business, at least in a practical every-day sense. An effective global account program can also help your firm "pull-together" internationally, and increase corporate morale.

> Schneider Electric reports that coordination among its different locations around the globe has a strong positive emotional impact. According to one executive, "it connects us to those kinds of (more remote) countries."

More effective organizational processes

The processes that you put in place to develop and manage your global accounts represent the pinnacle of the firm's account management capabilities. These global accounts are your largest and most challenging customers. Many processes, procedures, systems, and training are developed especially to support these global accounts, then modified based on firm experience.

These processes, methodologies, and key learning can be transferred from the global account arena to other parts of your organization. For example, they may eventually benefit the field sales organization and the firm's entire customer base. To illustrate, the supplier may use knowledge gained from handling global accounts in managing large national accounts with small international presence in just a few other countries. And GAMs can impart their wisdom to account managers whose customers are beginning to expand internationally.

Making the Value-Ad Visible

It is one thing to deliver value, it is quite another to communicate that value is being delivered. The supplier is responsible for ensuring that both the global customer and the firm understand the delivered value.

Value for the global account

The GAM must show executives at the global account the value that the global account program is delivering. Ideally, this value is quantified via such economic measures as total cost of ownership (TCO), but for some values, such as an early look at new technology or improved time-to-market, this may be difficult. In any event, it is imperative that the values that the firm delivers are made highly visible. Indeed, the firm should develop procedures for assembling and communicating these values regularly and systematically.

One approach is to require your GAMs to maintain a *Value-Ad Record*. The Value-Ad Record is a rolling 18–24 month list of the incremental value that your firm has delivered to the global account, validated by global account executives. Securing these data requires a very broad and deep set of internal customer contacts around the world to both identify and document incidents of value-added activities.

This sort of initiative is especially important for those accounts that employ supplier-assessment procedures, typically generated in the procurement function and focused on such issues as price and delivery. Ideally, of course, the supplier will influence the development of these instruments so they capture the wide variety of values that the firm delivers. But, if this is not possible, a thorough Value-Ad Record can function as an important additional source of information for the customer.

It is one thing to capture and document the variety of value that the firm delivers. It is quite another to make sure that the appropriate global account personnel clearly understand that value. Education is a critical function and this should occur in periodic reviews with the global account.

Further, this sort of information forms an important briefing document for any high-level meetings the PE may have with senior global account executives.

You should be very clear that it is one thing to deliver value, it is quite another for global account executives *to know that you are delivering value . . . and will continue to do so.* At some level, value already delivered is "water under the bridge." You build competitive barriers and increase switching costs on the expectations of future value. You must never forget that your global accounts are likely to be under the same sorts of competitive pressures as your firm, maybe tougher, and a "what-have-you-done-for-me-lately" attitude is oftentimes pervasive.

Value for the firm

The Executive Owner, backed by the Global Account Program Office, is responsible for ensuring that the global account program remains on the top management agenda. The economic value the program delivers must be assessed, and communicated internally on a regular basis. It is also important that people throughout the organization understand the importance of global accounts and act accordingly. "Branding" the program, and reinforcing the message via success stories and other means, is critical to embedding global accounts into organizational life.

There are two important levels of measurement. First, you need a measurement system to assess the performance of individual global accounts. Second, you need a measurement system for the global account program as a whole. Clearly, the foundation of program-level measurement should be the cumulative success of individual global accounts, but additional metrics may also be important. (The firm must also measure GAM performance—discussed in Chapter 7.) We discuss measurement at the global account level, and then move to discuss the global account program as a whole.

Firm performance at the global account

Measuring the firm's performance at an individual global account is not a simple matter. Typically, P&L statements run through individual countries and the firm must develop a "shadow system" for assessing firm performance at its global accounts (Chapter 9). Traditional measures are revenues, revenue growth, wallet share at the account, and other "bottom-line" profit-type performance indicators. In order to identify incremental value, the firm needs to separate out performance that is driven by the global account program, from performance that would have happened anyway. To do this, the firm should make some comparisons. For example:

- How does actual performance compare with planned performance?
- How does the firm's performance at the global account compare with other accounts—global and not global?
- How does this year's performance compare with performance in previous years?

Further, you should not wait until the end of the operating period (for example, year end) to secure your answers. You should employ a "steering-control" philosophy that enables you to make course corrections if global account performance is not up to par, and you are not securing planned results.

Notwithstanding the importance of these "output" metrics, there are other measurement considerations. A critical issue is, of course, that output metrics tend to focus on the short term. And, managing global accounts is, almost by definition, a long-term issue. If you focus solely on the short term, you run the danger of cutting corners, under-investing in your global accounts, and so damaging your future prospects.

We firmly believe that the measurement system should also include "input" and "intermediate" metrics. Essentially, input variables represent what the firm does to produce its results (the output variables). Candidate input variables include such metrics as quality and timeliness of the global account plan, effectiveness in managing the global account team, and use of the PE.

Intermediate variables sit between input variables and output variables. Intermediate variables require some action or set of actions by the global customer. They are not "outputs," but without intermediates, you will not secure the outputs you require. Candidate intermediate metrics include various pipeline measures, depth and breadth of supplier/global account executive relationships, and the extent to which the global account implements jointly agreed-upon actions.

Note that the input and intermediate variables have more of a long-term sense to them. Further, some variables, especially output variables, are quantitative, whereas input and intermediate variables tend to be more qualitative or subjective. In general, there is significant value in using the same set of metrics across all global accounts for comparison purposes. On the other hand, each global account represents a specific firm challenge, and some criteria should probably be customized to individual global accounts.

Let us be perfectly clear. We are suggesting different types of measure, but we are not suggesting a large number of measures. Twenty measures are probably too many; one measure is too few. The firm must make a thoughtful selection that balances the need to measure different things, but makes sure that measurement is manageable and understandable, and provides direction for future action.

A popular approach to combining input, intermediate, and output metrics, quantitative (hard) and qualitative (soft) metrics, and value-creating activities and financial measures is the Balanced Scorecard.[3] The basic thrust of the Balanced Scorecard is to tie strategy—the firm's approach to creating value—to operational goals. Strategies are translated into operational goals through four views—financial, customer, internal, and learning and growth. Candidate metrics in each of these categories are in Table 10.1.

Table 10.1   Candidate Variables for a Balanced Scorecard Approach to Measuring Firm Performance at the Global Account

Financial	Internal Business Process
• Year-on-year sales growth	• Quality of global account plan
• Customer profitability	• Timeliness of global account plan
• Shares of current customer wallets	• Quality of internal team relationships
• New wallets developed	• Response speed to customer
• Product mix	• Speed in responding to proposal requests

Customer	Learning and Growth
• Customer satisfaction	• Completing personal growth plan objectives
• Customer loyalty	• Implementing education plans for the global account team
• Quality of professional relationships	• Best practice exchange with fellow GAMs
• Quality of strategic alliance	
• Preferred supplier status	

[3] Robert Kaplan and David Norton, "The Balanced Scorecard," *Harvard Business Review*, (January–February 1992), pp. 71–77. For a more thorough and recent treatment, see also, Robert Kaplan and David Norton, *Converting Intangible Assets into Tangible Outcomes*, Boston: Harvard Business School Press, 2004.

Performance of the global account program

The Balanced Scorecard is an excellent way to measure the firm's performance at an individual global account. Performance on the scorecard paves the way for helping to decide where the GAM should place emphasis to improve that performance. But, over and above the performance at individual global accounts, the firm must be able to assess the performance of the global account program overall. For example, we should understand how the performance of global accounts compares with other groups of accounts? And, how the global accounts are performing this year compared to previous years.

Recall that our second critical success factor was all about securing top management commitment. If you secure this commitment, top management will certainly want to know if it is receiving an appropriate return for that commitment. Being able to measure the performance of your global account program is critically important.

The essential approach we suggest is similar to that for individual global accounts—the Balanced Scorecard. We identify the sorts of metrics you may use for measuring global account program performance (Table 10.2). As previously, the scorecard provides important data for improvement.

Table 10.2 Candidate Variables for a Balanced Scorecard Approach to Measuring the Global Account Program

Financial	Internal Business Process
• Year-on-year revenue and profit growth	• Percent of customers with global long-term contracts
• Sales expense as a percent of revenues	• Percent of customers with "solutions" contracts
	• Process improvements achieved through collaboration (for example, summary billing, product development)

Customer	Learning and Growth
• Customer satisfaction and loyalty	• Number of best-practices adopters
• Access to customer at the C-level—CIO, CEO, COO, and CFO	• Improved management practices

Cautions and Risks in Global Account Management[4]

Notwithstanding the significant potential of global account programs to deliver value to both global accounts and the firm, we must address some cautions. The supplier may encounter many risks and difficulties during development and implementation of a global account program. Our list is by no means exhaustive, and you will certainly encounter peculiarities and uncommon situations as you develop your own global program, and build your global account portfolio. Said another way, you will most certainly experience many hassles and problems—and we cannot pretend to know exactly what they will be. Nonetheless, the common difficulties we list below will give you some idea of what to expect. We divide the discussion into two areas—cautions and risks related to the global customer, and cautions and risks related to firm functioning.

Cautions and risks related to the global customer

Customers may try to drive prices down

As a general rule, customers prefer paying lower prices than higher prices. If the global account operates a decentralized procurement operation, separate buying entities do not have a good sense of the relative prices their firm pays for similar products around the world. Accordingly, global account status may sensitize the customer to this issue and lead it to seek lower prices. For example, the customer may wonder why the same product or service is priced differently depending on country of purchase. It may ask the supplier to reduce prices to the level of those in the "cheapest" country. Further, the global account may seek volume discounts based on global procurement. A successful global procurement initiative certainly benefits the customer, but it may also negatively affect the supplier's profitability. (Of course, the customer may rationalize purchases to a more standardized product line—the supplier secures scale economies, and both firms benefit.)

> Xerox sold a particular copying system around the world. In Brazil, where Xerox enjoyed upwards of 85 percent market share, prices to global accounts were 2.5 to 3 times higher than in the U.S. These global accounts worked up a local price based on U.S. prices, freight,

insurance, import duties, allowance for risk, and so forth. They did not believe these factors justified the 2.5 to 3 times multiple. They successfully applied heavy pressure on Xerox to reduce these prices.

Ted Dalrymple, AMP's global marketing VP makes this point succinctly: "Customers love a vendor's global-account-management system because as soon as a global account manager is designated, they see one person whom they can beat to death to get a lower price."[5]

You need to get it right the first time

We noted above the considerable value a global customer may earn from global account status. In general, once the customer has agreed to become a global account, it wants to see the value fairly quickly. Indeed, the customer may become impatient while global account program details are still being worked out. No matter how thorough are your preparations for the design and implementation of your global account program, some details will need "ironing-out" after program launch. This period is crucial, for the customer may feel that its local relationships were better before it entered your global account program. Suppliers must focus clearly on this risk and be very clear about expectations, including the timing of value delivery. Customers have only so much patience with your promises and may not be willing to wait for the program to improve. Our research shows that success at the first implementation attempt is crucial.

A Citibank executive observed that it seems to "have a maximum of two shots" to successfully introduce a client into Citibank's global account program. As a result, when Citibank proposes that a customer should join the program, Citibank executives go to great pains to engage in an honest discussion about the benefits the customer can expect to receive from program membership, and their timing.

Customers will push for a uniform service level

The global account may demand identical service levels across the globe, even though purchasing patterns differ. For example, a customer purchasing large quantities in North America but small quantities in Asia may, nonetheless, insist on receiving similar service and treatment in each area. This may be beneficial to the customer, but inefficient and costly for the supplier,

---

[5] Quoted in Das Narayandas, John Quelch and Gordon Swartz, "Prepare Your Company for Global Pricing," *Sloan Management Review*, (August 2000), pp. 61–70, at p. 69.

especially in the short run. For example, a HP executive put the issue succinctly: "You can't provide the same level of service worldwide for a company that's buying $80 million in Cincinnati, and one laser printer from a dealer in Thailand." Of course, *this is one of the fundamental purposes of a global account program—consistency of the customer's business experience worldwide.* It is the GAM's job to deal with this issue and to get his firm to come to grips with the trade-off between service comparability, and the expense of delivering that service.

There may be insufficient value for the global account

The supplier must carefully manage the global account's expectations for value delivery from the global account program. Firms that promise the moon from their global account programs, but cannot deliver, will certainly suffer from not meeting expectations. If the global account sees little benefit in the relationship, considerable dissatisfaction may ensue. Far better to under-promise and over–deliver, than to over-promise and under-deliver.

The customer's global procurement operation cannot make its decisions stick

It is one thing to conclude a global arrangement with a customer, it is quite another for the customer to keep its part of the bargain. For example, global procurement may be a corporate intitiative, but decentralized decision-making and measurement systems focused on individual geographic performance, may cause its rejection by the geographies. We saw this issue with Van Leer in Chapter 4. Naryandas, Quelch and Swartz report an example of a U.S. advertising agency that won a global contract to manage world-wide advertising for a *Fortune 100* firm. The agency accepted lower fees, and agreed not to represent any of the customer's non-U.S. competitors. In return, the agency anticipated higher volumes, especially in non-U.S. markets where it did little business with the customer. The agency later discovered that executives in the customer's non-U.S. markets had considerable autonomy—they essentially rejected the global contract. Eventually, all non-U.S. operations stopped using the agency, which was then far worse off than before signing the global contract.[6]

---

[6] Narayandas, Quelch and Swartz, *op. cit.*, pp. 61–62.

Changes and risks related to firm functioning

Change often causes difficulties

In Chapter 3, we briefly mentioned the need for a change management component to implement any successful global account program. A new program, by its nature, threatens the *status quo*, especially traditional ways of managing product lines and geographies—we gave several examples. The important issue is that you need to be sensitive to how people view their power positions in the firm, and how global account management changes may threaten them. In particular, global account management poses greater demands for data collection and transmission on locally based personnel. For example, global account management may require data that was not previously needed locally, or data that was developed but with less urgency.

Coordination is difficult to achieve

Several firms have told us that they made serious attempts to deploy an effective global account program. Regardless, it was very challenging to deliver a "single voice" to the customer, and to effectively coordinate among different divisions and geographies. It is not easy to create a seamless information flow within the firm, and to-and-from the global customer. Further, organizational decentralization can be a significant inhibitor to appropriate resource allocations for global accounts, and to developing account-wide pricing strategies.

> A 3M executive told us that sharing information about global customers across the firm was a major challenge. The diversified nature of the 3M's business and its line organization for managing global accounts did not support this effort.

Global account programs can be expensive

Implementation of a global account program can be very costly, especially initially. For example, one executive told us that his firm's global accounts required more application engineering and technical support than other accounts. Although firms develop different ways of budgeting global account programs, it is sometimes the case that the global account program costs more than the additional revenues it generates. This is a special problem when the cost of the global program is charged back to the geographies—serious resistance may develop. It may also be difficult to measure operational excellence, return on investment, and profitability from global accounts.

GAM (fully loaded)	$200,000
Dedicated global account analyst (fully loaded)	$150,000
Direct infrastructure costs per global account	$ 10,000
GAM travel/entertainment	$ 50,000
Global account team travel/planning meetings	$ 30,000
Office space/telephone	$ 30,000
Miscellaneous	$ 30,000
Total	$500,000

Clearly, the cost of a global account program depends upon many factors, not the least of which is the firm's compensation system. In addition, some *hard* infrastructure costs may be relatively low if the firm has a global IT platform, but will be much greater if they are specially built. The preceeding figures give a sense of global account program costs for a single global account:

Regional differences can persist

Global account management typically encounters resistance from the geographies when managing global accounts cuts across organizational lines. This is a particular problem in the early phases of GAM responsibility. When the GAM has been in place for 3–5 years, and learns to work the system, these difficulties may dissipate. We mentioned cultural differences as a critical challenge for participating in international business transactions. Coordination among sister international divisions may also lead to substantial friction.

A former Marsh Inc. GAM cited territorialism due to cultural differences as one of his most salient issues. Several European countries felt their input was not considered at headquarters, and they did not like "taking orders" from the U.S.

Outsourcing is increasingly more common

As discussed earlier, the supplier may choose, or the customer may require, that certain tasks be outsourced to local suppliers. When outsourcing occurs globally, the supplier has to coordinate considerably increased complexity. It has to standardize supply chains, product lines, and services among not only its own geographically based subsidiaries, but also among local firms to which it does the outsourcing.

An executive from Schneider Electric told us that global customers often require Schneider to partner with local suppliers. This vastly complicates communication and standardization of Schneider's products and services on a global scale.

International differences in contracting and legal systems create problems

In Chapter 1, we noted challenges involved in standardizing products and contracts internationally. Legal systems are different from country to country; this affects legal agreements and product standardization. The supplier may spend significant time and financial resources in building the infrastructure to deal with this issue.

There may be limitation of opportunities fallout

Successful global account programs increase interaction between supplier and customer on a global basis. One downside of closer relationships may be an insistence by the global account on producing a list of firms (typically its competitors) with which the supplier may *not* do business. Supplier firms would already have found this threatening domestically. When this situation occurs internationally, the supplier may feel too dependent on the customer and cut off from otherwise desirable opportunities.

The global account program is a short-term wonder

We have seen several cases where an enthusiastic executive was given significant resources and the go-ahead to develop a global account program. This program flourished but then, for one reason or another, it atrophied. In some cases, the program's protector moved on, or the program driver also moved on. New people assigned to global account roles did not have "the fire in their bellies"; other initiatives became more important, and responsibility and accountability for global customers returned to the geographic regional organization. Global accounts were less well served and, ultimately, the firm lost business. When this cycle occurs, it is a good bet that the global program was launched without a broad-based shared value of global account management within the executive management team.

The premise of our book is that managing global accounts is a critical organizational competence in this globalizing world. Done correctly, a solid global account program offers considerable value both to the firm and its global customers. But the firm should not run headstrong into a global account management program. The cautions we note are very real and must be considered along with the values as the firm embarks on its journey of managing global accounts.[7]

---

[7] For examples of firms that have embraced global account management, and had success using many of the principles that we address in this book, see the Strategic Account Management Association's (SAMA) performance award.

Key Messages

- For the global account program to deliver value to the firm, the firm must deliver value to the global account.

- The ultimate value for both the global account and the firm is improving shareholder value.

- Improvements in financial measures such as sales, costs, and investment performance are good surrogates for improving shareholder value, but they tend to be short-term in nature.

- Many important values from a global account program are intangible, but are no less important as they address future financial performance.

- You must develop appropriate metrics for measuring firm performance at individual global accounts and for the global account program overall.

- Global account management is no panacea. The firm contemplating global account management should consider several serious cautions.

CHAPTER 11

ALIGNING CRITICAL SUCCESS FACTORS IN MANAGING GLOBAL ACCOUNTS

PROLOGUE

George finding his way

George was frustrated with his efforts on global account management. He had worked out the hiring program, and education for global account managers was now in place. He had rebalanced the scope of his program to make it more manageable, and had reengineered account selection. The advice from **Jace** and **Constance** was very useful. Lately he had been focused on fixing some of the infrastructure issues.

George had contacted both **Jace** and **Constance** to try and get rebalanced. He explained to **Constance** that "things are always going wrong," and it seemed as if he had to constantly step in to refocus people on the goal. As she listened, **Constance** could feel her head nodding in agreement with what *George* was saying. It seemed that many things were "out of sync" with the Global Account Program.

George had a similar conversation with **Jace**. "How can I have accomplished so much change, yet some of the same problems recur?" **Jace** had seen this before, but had been a little selfish in holding back some of her insight. After all, *George* had not been paying for her advice; there is just so much you can give away. Feeling a little guilty, she decided to give *George* her not-so-secret secret.

"*George*, there is one aspect of your program you haven't spent much time thinking about—alignment!" *George* thought for a minute. He wasn't exactly sure what **Jace** meant. He had read several articles on strategic alignment and felt as though he had succeeded on that dimension. "But **Jace**," he said, "the company strategy now includes managing global accounts. I've made sure our executives understand our global account strategy and they support it fully. What am I missing?"

"*George*, alignment is more than thinking of strategy, executive support and things like infrastructure separately. It sounds as though you've done a good job with several of the key areas in managing global accounts, but have you really thought through how they all fit together and whether they support each other. Think of your spinal vertebrae—each supports the one above and they *work together so you can stand upright and move your body into different positions. Then there's the rest of the organization. It sounds as though you've done a good job on your senior management but the entire organization is not always in lockstep with the top—you know that as well as I do."*

Dimly, **George** *thought he could see what* **Jace** *meant. But after a few lame questions he realized he was getting out of his depth. "***Jace,*** I think I should engage you to work with me on this? I am not sure where I'll find the budget, but I can certainly use your help." Finally,* **Jace** *thought. Some billable hours! "***George,*** you're on. I'll send you a questionnaire to help me see where you are today, and we'll crack the alignment problem."*

George *wasn't sure what* **Jace** *had in mind, but he was sure he needed help to get his global account program to run more smoothly.*

In Chapters 3 through 10, we presented eight critical success factors for managing global accounts. These CSFs are:

CSF1 Establishing the scope—size and boundaries—of the global account program

CSF2 Securing senior management commitment

CSF3 Nominating and selecting the "right" global accounts

CSF4 Designing the line organization for managing global accounts

CSF5 Securing effective global account managers

CSF6 Developing effective global account plans

CSF7 Establishing the supporting organizational infrastructure

CSF8 Demonstrating the global account program's incremental value to the firm and to the global account.

In this chapter, we deal with issues of *alignment* that concern the eight critical success factors.

CSF9 Aligning critical success factors in managing global accounts

For each CSF, the firm must make a broad series of decisions. For example, for CSF1—establishing the scope of the global account program—at the very least, the firm must make decisions about the number of accounts that make up the program. For CSF5—securing effective global account managers—the firm must make a host of decisions involving recruiting, selecting, training and development, measuring performance and compensating, and retaining GAMs.

To develop and evolve an effective global account program requires that the firm make serious decisions for each of the CSFs. But there is more to it than that. Any decision that the firm makes cannot be independent of all the other decisions. The critical issue is alignment—making sure that the entire set of decisions about the global account program forms a coherent whole, and interfaces appropriately with other organizational dimensions. In particular, we focus on four areas where alignment is important:

- Alignment *within* each of CSFs individually—intra-CSF alignment
- Alignment *among* the various CSFs—inter-CSF alignment
- Alignment *between* the firm's global account program and the rest of the organization—holistic alignment
- Alignment *between* the firm's global account program and the firm's global customer base—cross-boundary alignment

We commence by discussing the non-compensatory nature of the eight CSFs.

Critical Success Factors Are Non-Compensatory

Many fields of business endeavor operate under a "compensatory" system. In a compensatory system, poor performance on one dimension can be made up for (compensated) by superior performance on other dimensions. For example, you may not like the color of the only available automobile in the showroom, but this negative assessment is compensated for by excellent gas mileage and superior acceleration, so you purchase the car anyway.

Managing global accounts does not work like that. You have to have "all your ducks in line." Excellent performance on seven CSFs will not compensate for poor performance on the other CSF. Select the "wrong" global accounts and you will fail, regardless of how well you do in securing top management commitment and putting in place effective GAMs. Similarly, if all else is well, but you cannot secure and retain high-performing GAMs—or if other elements are fine, but you have crappy infrastructure—you will also fail.

The implication of the non-compensatory nature of global account management is very clear. You cannot afford to ignore any of the CSFs—you must work on all of them simultaneously.

Alignment within critical success factors—Intra-CSF alignment

Intra-CSF alignment concerns the various decisions relating to an individual CSF. For each of the CSFs, these decisions must form a coherent whole. For example, for CSF5—securing effective global account managers—we noted earlier that the firm must make a host of decisions. As a simple example, suppose the firm recruits GAMs from a pool of its own salespeople, or district sales managers with little international experience. We may expect that an extensive training and development effort will be needed to make these recruits effective in the global arena. On the other hand, if the firm exclusively recruits seasoned GAMs from competitors, the degree and type of training required will likely be very different. The different recruiting pools will also probably require different compensation levels.

As another example, CSF6, developing effective global account plans, requires each GAM to develop a vision, mission, strategy—including objectives and action steps—and, secure resource commitments for their global accounts. Each of these items must be completely aligned with each other. For example, it makes no sense to develop an elaborate vision, mission, strategy, and action steps, if resources are not forthcoming for implementation.

Alignment among critical success factors—Inter-CSF alignment

Although intra-CSF alignment for each CSF is very important, a more complex alignment challenge concerns multiple CSFs. When the firm achieves good inter-CSF alignment, each CSF complements the others to support the overall vision of the global account program. By contrast, if even a single CSF is misaligned with the others, an otherwise potentially successful program may be crippled. We like to use the metaphor of alignment/misalignment of even a single spinal vertebra.

Consider, for example, just two CSFs—CSF1: establishing the scope of the global account program, and CSF2: securing senior management commitment. Suppose the firm decides on a full-blown entry into global account management with a large number of global accounts. Senior management commitment to a large program is very important—if separate individuals were not put in the roles of executive sponsor, executive owner, executive steering committee members, and PE, the program would be seriously weakened. By contrast, a small global account program would not need each of these roles to be filled with a separate person.

Or, consider three CSFs—CSF1: establishing the scope of the global account program, CSF3: nominating and selecting the "right" global accounts, and CSF5: securing effective GAMs. Suppose, for example, that the firm decides on a narrow scope of just a few global accounts, but its nominating and selecting process identifies customers that together are responsible for a large share of the firm's revenues. Indeed, the loss of any one of these accounts would represent a major blow to the firm and even threaten its continued operations. These decisions on CSF1 and CSF3 have major implications for CSF5—the entire array of decisions concerning recruiting, selecting, training and development, measuring, and compensating GAMs. The challenge the firm faces in dealing with these few critical accounts is not a situation for novice GAMs transferred in from a domestic sales force. Rather, appropriate candidates would be seasoned executives who can travel easily in senior management circles at the account.

This type of alignment emphasizes that the design of any single CSF is critically dependent on the design of all of the others.

Alignment between the global account program and the rest of the organization—Holistic alignment

Holistic alignment is independent of the degree of intra-CSF alignment and inter-CSF alignment. The focus is on the relationship between the global account program and the rest of the organization. Holistic alignment is based on a shared vision of the global strategy, and agreement with program objectives, operating principles, and design implementation across the firm. Holistic alignment is reflected in globally focused managerial behavior captured in the procedures/processes in all functions, groups and countries. Measurements, rewards, recognition, and internal communications must have a complementary effect, rather than one that is contradictory.

Nothing is more damaging to the success of the global account program than mixed messages from management about expected local behavior in the field. Especially damaging are policies that make it difficult to "do the right thing" for the account, and/or reward and recognition schemes that encourage behavior that is inconsistent with effective relationship management.

In one global account program that we otherwise judged as relatively well designed, we found the following set of circumstances:

- GAMs were not allowed to travel internationally.
- Global team members were denied permission to attend global account planning sessions.

- Finance staff harassed GAMs over cell-phone use.
- Local country representatives did not cooperate with GAMs on account strategy.
- GAMs had extreme difficulty securing accurate account activity data from individual countries.
- Local country management resisted paying GAMs for "foreign" activity.
- Countries assigned their best people to favorite local accounts rather than to the local operations of global accounts.
- Countries refused to "offer" the global contract price to local offices of the global account.

As a result:

- Customers were frustrated by the supplier's inability to deliver a consistent global experience to its subsidiaries. Ultimately, the supplier's share of the global account's business started to decline.

Two types of misalignment with the rest of the organization may lead to the problems noted above—*design misalignment* and *execution misalignment*.

Design misalignment

Design misalignment occurs because of insufficient concern with the rest of the organization in developing the global account program. Sometimes executives get the religion that customers are the firm's core assets, and that global customers are critically important for the firm's survival and growth. It is then very easy to become evangelical about a global account program, and pay insufficient attention to those areas in which the global account program interfaces with the rest of the organization.

In the example noted above, the first three items—international travel, attending planning meetings, and cell phone use—all relate to the budgeting process. The problem was a misalignment between the firm's budget process and the global account program. In this case, GAMs and their team members did not have budgetary authority over their activities.

Execution misalignment

Execution misalignment concerns the day-to-day actions of firm employees that frustrate the global account management process. For example, suppose GAMs need local account data, but the relevant personnel are too busy with other activities and do not respond as requested. Also, local management does not assign its best people to global accounts. These are not matters of design but, rather, internal cultural issues. Other parts of the organization have simply not bought into global account management as a critical issue for the firm as a whole.

We cannot overemphasize the importance of aligning the global account program with the rest of the organization. Key executives in global account management must work consistently at this alignment. We do not mean to scare you, but a few more examples of misalignment help make the point.

To facilitate revenue roll-up for individual global accounts, the Global Account Program Office asked for a global account code for all transactions. The European administrative head refused to direct smaller countries to add this code. He claimed these countries could not manage the extra workload without incurring unbudgeted overtime costs. The GAMs were annoyed and frustrated by their perception of lack of local cooperation. Some GAMs were sufficiently upset that they resigned and joined other global firms.

Other GAMs continued to track customer revenues using a time-consuming inefficient paper-based process. Several global accounts insisted on receiving spending data globally, and were dissatisfied with the GAMs' inability to provide accurate and timely data. They believed the supplier was not treating their requests seriously, and was not really committed to meeting their requirements.

The consequences of the European administrative head's decision were dramatically disproportionate. What appeared to be a minor process misalignment in several smaller countries led to GAM resignations. Further, important customers were developing closer relationships with alternative suppliers, and raising the prospect that the firm could lose business.

If we assume the coding requirement was well understood in the original planning for the global account program, then this local unwillingness to provide designed support is a clear example of *execution* misalignment. Perhaps the cause was a senior management failure to establish a shared value of program support across geographies. On the other hand, if the planners had not identified the global tracking requirement, then the failure was a *design* misalignment. Indeed, thorough planning should have exposed local country workload concerns up front and forced a resolution in advance.

Of course, design, and execution misalignment interact, and many specific problems in managing global accounts have elements of both. We cannot emphasize enough that either type of misalignment can be deadly for managing global accounts.

Some additional examples of holistic misalignment are:

Marketing has proposed a new compensation plan for GAMs—20 percent salary, 60 percent installation commission paid monthly, and a 20 percent quarterly bonus (5 percent for achieving each quarter's objective). The Global Account Program Office is furious because of the potential negative impact on GAM's behavior—specifically, the plan seems designed to drive a short-term focus. What is marketing thinking? The pay-plan design is heavily weighted on monthly sales results; yet, the GAM role is designed for relationship building, partnership development, and solutions implementation?

U.S. Sales Operations has developed an expense-planning model for travel, telephone and customer entertainment that would be applied to all U.S.-based account mangers—both NAMs and GAMs. The goal is to keep the planning process simple and consistent. This model may be administratively simple for U.S. Sales Operations, but a problem for the global account program whose account managers have very different requirements than their domestic counterparts.

The implications of holistic misalignment are highly significant and far-reaching. We see many firms with otherwise well-designed global account programs, having significant misalignment. We believe that there are several reasons for the low incidence of good holistic alignment. Each of these reasons suggests actions for the firm.

Insufficient knowledge/understanding about alignment

Quite simply, within the firm, there may not be a deep understanding of the importance of holistic alignment. Alignment issues may not yet have arisen in new programs and/or the consequences of nonalignment have not been recognized. These situations can occur if the Global Account Program Office is ineffective, and no single individual or group has taken the time to understand the potential problems.

Lack of senior management willingness to "take a stand"

This reason is much more serious. Alignment issues have risen to the level of concern by senior managers, but they are not prepared to act. Of course, putting in place a well-designed global account program, with high levels of intra-CSF alignment and inter-CSF alignment is difficult enough. To secure good holistic alignment requires even greater effort, compromise, cooperation, and allegiance for the greater corporate good. In-grained culture, internal politics, and geographical parochial interests are often strong dynamics working against proper alignment. Senior managers may commit to the global account program in terms of dollars and human resources, but to support the global program in the face of entrenched interests is "the extra mile" they may not be prepared to travel.

Conflict with current line organization and/or the corporate culture

Global account programs often get in holistic alignment trouble when the firm is highly decentralized and local managers are highly empowered. Decentralization has the virtue of pushing P&L responsibility deep into the organization, but is a severe impediment in gaining cross-organizational cooperation. Of course, a clearly stated global account program vision, a well-defined mission and objectives, and a clear and consistent direction from the top, all help secure holistic alignment. Nonetheless, this can be difficult to achieve in a highly decentralized firm.

It may seem as though we are beating holistic alignment to death, maybe so. But our collective experience shows that analysis of troubled global account programs typically reveals holistic misalignment as a root cause.

Alignment *between* the firm's global account program and the firm's global customer base—Cross-boundary alignment

Thus far in this chapter we have discussed the non-compensatory nature of CSFs, and three types of alignment—intra-CSF alignment, inter-CSF alignment, and holistic alignment. But there is only one underlying reason to worry about these types of alignment, and that is to make sure that the firm's global account program is fully aligned with the global environment in which it operates.

If good work has been done with each individual CSF, and the appropriate decisions made to secure the various types of alignment already discussed, then the firm should have good cross-boundary alignment. The problem, of course, is that the firm's own strategy evolves, environmental pressures change, and the needs of the global customer base are moving targets. What may be the appropriate design for a global account program at one point in time may not be appropriate for another.

The danger, is that global program executives get so caught up in day-to-day application of the eight CSFs and the previously discussed three types of alignment that they do not keep on top of these more broad-scale changes. And, whereas global program executives have varying degrees of control over global account program design and related alignment issues, they may be less involved in the firm's evolving strategy and related environmental implications.

As a result, cross-boundary alignment represents the highest "degree of difficulty." A well-designed global account program has built-in mechanisms to monitor the firm's strategy evolution, and changes occurring in the global environment. Many economic, technological, and competitive changes may lead to evolving the global account program. For example, technological change may allow new forms of communication with global accounts, or competitive benchmarking may show superiority in one area of global account management that the firm must at least match, and maybe exceed. Similar forces also affect your global customers, but in different ways, further requiring continual global program updating to maintain cross-boundary alignment.

Securing cross-boundary alignment is a continuing challenge but, ultimately, the most important form of alignment. Though difficult to achieve, making sure your global account program is aligned with your firm's evolving strategy, with the evolving global environment, and in particular with the demands of global customers is the pot of gold at the end of the rainbow—forever desirable, and forever beyond our reach, but well worth striving to secure.

Success is Yours to Manage

As we have discussed throughout this book, for most readers, managing global accounts is a very different arena from any that you may have managed, or participated in, during your business careers. Whatever your role in the process, managing global accounts is extremely difficult, and requires the full mobilization of both your personal and company resources. Hopefully, your personal resources are up to the job—if not, lean on your HR department to put in place, or otherwise make available, the appropriate development opportunities.

Company resources are another matter. As global competition increases, you will only succeed with a complete firm effort. From the CEO to the brand managers; from the CFO to the pricers and expeditors; and from those managing the supply chain to those holding the purse strings—each must play his or her part in delivering their best efforts in the goal of securing and retaining global customers. We like to think that we have provided you with a road map to help achieve your objectives. Certainly, if you work conscientiously on the eight CSFs, and the alignment issues we discuss in this chapter, we believe that, at a minimum, you will raise your chances of success.

Good luck and see you in an airport somewhere!

Key Messages

- The CSFs for managing global accounts are noncompensatory—poor performance on one cannot be compensated for by superior performance on others.

- Alignment is a critical concept in global account management—there are four key types of alignment for executing a successful program.

  - Alignment *within* each CSF individually—intra-CSF alignment

  - Alignment *among* the various CSFs—inter-CSF alignment

  - Alignment *between* the firm's global account program and the rest of the organization—holistic alignment

  - Alignment *between* the firm's global account program and the firm's global customer base—cross-boundary alignment.

Returning from Europe

Headed back to New York from a European consulting engagement, **Jace** settled happily into her business-class seat. She had just put in place a global account planning process for a major German client. Now she turned her mind to the friends she had made several weeks earlier, and who continued to tap her expertise in managing global accounts.

Todd was a very enthusiastic global account manager. But **Todd** was having so little luck in getting decent senior management commitment, he was even pursuing **Constance** for a potential global account manager position. **Constance** seemed totally sold on the global account management concept. She was the boss and could move ahead if she were truly convinced. But **Constance** still seemed hesitant to make the full commitment. Then there was **George**: his problem was less a matter of company commitment, than of making things happen. With **George** she would finally get some billable time. Friends or not, **Jace** was still a consultant and she needed to be paid for her counsel.

Jace thought she had been able to help them all, even though it may have been a small contribution. But now she had a carefully thought out and tested set of nine critical success factors for managing global accounts. She believed that with the eight individual factors and alignment, she had a blueprint for the global account management problems that **Todd, George** and **Constance** were facing.

Jace pulled the table from the seat and grabbed her laptop. Now all I have to do is turn the nine critical success factors into a "road-map-type document" that "puts it all together" for them. Of course, I shall have to take account of their different circumstances as I put the emails together. It felt good to be able to set each of her friends on a path that should make them more successful in dealing with their own global account program issues.

Returning from Europe

Headed back to New York from a European consulting engagement, **Jace** settled happily into her business-class seat. She had just put in place a global account planning process for a major German client. Now she turned her mind to the friends she had made several weeks earlier, and who continued to tap her expertise in managing global accounts.

Todd was a very enthusiastic global account manager. But **Todd** was having so little luck in getting decent senior management commitment, he was even pursuing **Constance** for a potential global account manager position. **Constance** seemed totally sold on the global account management concept. She was the boss and could move ahead if she were truly convinced. But **Constance** still seemed hesitant to make the full commitment. Then there was **George**: his problem was less a matter of company commitment, than of making things happen. With **George** she would finally get some billable time. Friends or not, **Jace** was still a consultant and she needed to be paid for her counsel.

Jace thought she had been able to help them all, even though it may have been a small contribution. But now she had a carefully thought out and tested set of nine critical success factors for managing global accounts. She believed that with the eight individual factors and alignment, she had a blueprint for the global account management problems that **Todd**, **George** and **Constance** were facing.

Jace pulled the table from the seat and grabbed her laptop. Now all I have to do is turn the nine critical success factors into a "road-map-type document" that "puts it all together" for them. Of course, I shall have to take account of their different circumstances as I put the emails together. It felt good to be able to set each of her friends on a path that should make them more successful in dealing with their own global account program issues.

INDEX

About the Book

Increasingly firms are realizing that customers are their critical assets. Further, a subset of customers can be designated as strategic customers (accounts)—those that really matter for the firm's future. Finally, many of these customers operate around the world—they are truly global customers. In this book, we take the strong position that to manage these global strategic customers, the firm needs a program designed specifically for them. This book is about developing and maintaining a global account program.

In this book, we explain why senior executives in companies large and small are realizing that their future health, indeed their very survival, depends on success with major global customers, both current and potential. Strategic (or key) account management has become a critical area of focus for successful corporations domestically; however, many firms have failed to realize that global strategic customers are the key to future firm success. Suppliers wishing to truly satisfy the needs of these critical global assets must address them in a global manner.

The authors argue that successful global account management is not simply country-based strategic account management ratcheted up a notch. Just as doing business globally is qualitatively different from operating in a national context, successful global account management is qualitatively different from managing strategic national accounts. Drawing on their extensive collective experiences, the authors elaborate the nine critical success factors for designing and executing a world-class global account management program.

About the Authors

NOEL CAPON is the R.C. Kopf Professor of International Marketing and past Chair of the Marketing Division at the Graduate School of Business, Columbia University. He is also author of the highly acclaimed book *Key Account Management and Planning* (The Free Press, 2001), and director of senior-executive Strategic Account Management Programs at Columbia Business School and the Global Account Manager Certification Program (GCP) offered jointly by Columbia and St. Gallen University, Switzerland.

DAVE POTTER had a 35-year career at Xerox, a company known for significant managerial innovation. After holding a variety of domestic sales management and quality officer positions, he filled numerous Asian posts, including director of marketing, China South Pacific, general manager, South East Asia, and vice president of marketing, Fuji Xerox Asia Pacific. From 1995 to 2002, he was the director of marketing, global account management.

FRED SCHINDLER had a similar 33-year career with IBM during which he consulted with IBM account teams and customers to improve global account management. For seven years, Fred was program executive for IBM's Global Customer Management program, encompassing its top 150 global clients. He consulted with multinational client teams and with team leaders of various IBM infrastructure groups—the international special bids group, relationship management process owners, services support groups, and brand divisions.

About WESSEX

Wessex publishes college and graduate level textbooks at significantly reduced prices compared to traditional publications. Wessex textbooks are also available for reading online at even lower prices. For information on *Managing Marketing in the 21st Century* and *The Virgin Marketer*, see www.mm21c.com. For information on *Fundamentals of International Business*, see www.fib21c.com.

Wessex also publishes trade books like *Managing Global Accounts*, see www.wessex21c.com.

You can find out more about Wessex and Dr. Capon's other activities at www.axcesscapon.com.

About the typeface

This book was set in 10.5 point size and Bembo font. Bembo was created in 1496 by Pietro Bembo of Italy. This typeface is known for its quiet presence and graceful stability.

Library of Congress Cataloging-in-Publication Data

Capon, Noel.
  Managing global accounts : nine critical factors for a world-class program / Noel Capon, Dave Potter, Fred Schindler.
      p.   cm.
  Includes bibliographical references and index.
      ISBN 978-0-979744-3-4 (alk. paper)
  1. Customer relations—Management.   2. Sales management.
3. International business enterprises—Management.   I. Potter, Dave.
II. Schindler, Fred.   III. Title.
HF5415.5.C365 2006
658.8'4—dc22

                                                            2005027960

CPSIA information can be obtained at www.ICGtesting.com
Printed in the USA
BVOW010532020312

284265BV00007B/1/P

9 780979 734434